Condensing the Cold War

Condensing the Cold War

Reader's Digest and American Identity

Joanne P. Sharp

University of Minnesota Press
Minneapolis   London

Copyright 2000 by the Regents of the University of Minnesota

Published by the University of Minnesota Press
111 Third Avenue South, Suite 290
Minneapolis, MN 55401-2520
http://www.upress.umn.edu

Library of Congress Cataloging-in-Publication Data

Sharp, Joanne P.
    Condensing the Cold War : Reader's digest and American identity /
Joanne P. Sharp
        p. cm.
    ISBN 0-8166-3415-7 (alk. paper)—ISBN 0-8166-3416-5 (pbk. : alk.
paper)
    1. Reader's digest. 2. Cold War—Press coverage—United States. I.
Title.
    PN 4900.R3   s53   2001
    051—dc21

                                            00-009523

Printed in the United States of America on acid-free paper

The University of Minnesota is an equal-opportunity educator and employer.

11 10 09 08 07 06 05 04 03 02 01 00   10 9 8 7 6 5 4 3 2 1

Contents

Acknowledgments

It was no more than a passing comment, really: "Why don't you look at *Reader's Digest*?" asked John Western. This book started out as a term paper too many years ago. When I first looked at the *Digest*, I saw it simply as *an* example of American popular culture and believed that any other media source would do in its place. As I got to know the magazine and understand its place in American society, however, I realized that its role in the construction of the country's national identity is truly unique. Not only has the *Digest* charted and interpreted the changing state of global affairs, it has done so from a position of moral guardian, guiding America and its people on what the magazine saw as their historic mission. And so, as he often reminds me, John Western is due my first debt of gratitude.

Over the course of my education, I have had the privilege of being taught by and working with a number of stimulating, generous, and talented people. A (very) long overdue thanks must go to Kenneth Maclean, my school geography teacher, whose enthusiasm for the subject and commitment to teaching was inspiring. At Syracuse University, when I was undertaking postgraduate work, I was lucky enough to have met Jim and Nancy Duncan, who were a constant inspiration and great friends. The postgraduate community in the Department of Geography was always a source of support (and, more importantly, diversion), and I would especially like to thank Lorraine Dowler, Tim Conway, Shannon Des Roches (as she was then), Luis Lujan, and Jim Pickett. John Agnew, my adviser, deserves the most thanks for encouraging me and having faith in this project even on the occasions when my faith had deserted me.

I have also benefited from invaluable conversations and debates with colleagues and friends in various universities and would especially like to thank Linda Alcoff, Beverley Allen, David Atkinson, Klaus Dodds, Tom Klak, Gearóid Ó Tuathail, Michael Shapiro, and James Sidaway. Particular thanks must go to Simon Dalby, who has read this work more times than is humane and who battled the December weather in upstate New York to attend my exam. I am indebted to Carrie Mullen at Minnesota for her encouragement of this project at various stages of its development. Thanks must also go to my colleagues at Glasgow University—in particular John Briggs, Ronan Paddison, Chris Philo, and Paul Routledge—whose support and sense of humor have got me through the last stages of writing this book.

Finally, I would like to thank Ann and Graham Sharp, who have always supported me in my work, however bizarre it has often seemed to them.

Introduction

Although some inhabited places are further north on the map and
actually as cold, Russia's lumbering heritage of isolation and
backwardness makes it more frozen. Russia remains psychologically
the most northern of nations.[1]

The Soviet Union has announced—through its invasion of Afghanistan—
that it is conducting a classic war for geopolitical domination. One of the
most important lessons of Afghanistan is that *we have led the Russians
into irresistible temptation.* Our ostentatious unwillingness to contest
Soviet expansionism in place after place, *our* repeated failures to take any
action in one crisis after another, have led the Soviets to conclude that
they could pursue their own desires without fear of reprisal.[2]

However much the Soviet leaders fear our weapons, they fear the truth
even more.[3]

The Russians do not grab merely real estate. They also grab people.
And *this is where you come in.* . . . No-one is too small or insignificant,
too young or too old, to be shackled and regimented or pauperized and
destroyed. . . . The communist masterplot . . . is focused on everyone,
everywhere. It proceeds step by step and region by region. By its all
encompassing timetable *sooner or later it has to reach you.*[4]

Reader's Digest might offer the single most important voice in the creation of popular geopolitics in America in the twentieth century.[5] The
magazine offers a unique insight into the workings of American political
culture. Since 1922 it has been reflecting upon the state of world affairs
for its readership and explaining both America's and the reader's role and

responsibility in the unfolding of these events. The *Digest*'s geographical imagination links the individual reader to the destiny of the United States, and to the operations of foreign powers, most significantly of course those of the Soviet Union, the Cold War enemy whose character the *Digest* is often credited with helping to create. The magazine constructs a series of geographies, as the opening quotations indicate. First are those based in the importance of geography itself, here represented by an environmental determinism that produces the Russian character based on a timeless quality of this part of the world. The second quotation is representative of the *Digest*'s global geography of power relations, in which any weakness or liberal action on the part of the United States and its allies would inevitably lead to Soviet expansion. In this scenario there is no third way. Only one country—either the United States *or* the USSR—can ever benefit from any situation: the other must always lose out. The third quotation emphasizes the power of words that have been granted the authority of "truth." This underscores the significance of linguistics to the Cold War. For the *Digest*, it was not always what happened that was significant, but how it was described and explained, essentially who had the power of "the truth." And finally, and most importantly, the *Digest* produces a geography that links together the processes and events occurring around the world with the *Digest* reader. This final geography explains to the reader both global politics and his or her location within this global system. It illustrates why readers should care about global politics and what relevance distant events might have in their lives. Inevitably, the *Digest* explains why vigilance and action are required of individual readers in order that any threat to the United States can be stopped before it takes hold and challenges them and their families directly.

The *Digest* offers other geographies of the world and America's place in it, but none strays too far from the model outlined here and characterized by these quotations. Through articles on a diverse range of topics, *Reader's Digest* can be seen to create an imagined geography of the world and America's place within it—even when it is not apparently offering a geopolitical explanation. As Martin Lewis and Karen Wigen have suggested, "Every global consideration of human affairs deploys a metageography, whether acknowledged or not."[6] And yet, as they continue, this underlying geographical model is rarely acknowledged. In the case of *Reader's Digest*, as well as offering clearly political articles that explain international relations and threats to peace, the magazine provides another geographical context for the operations of political discourse in its descriptions of American and Soviet life. Ethnographic articles detail how unlike Americans Russians are, or how different life in the USSR is from life back home in the United States. Russians' music is different, their food is different, their sense of humor is different ... even their sex life is different.[7] Through the constant creation of this ultimately *different* place on the pages of the *Digest*, a picture of a corresponding place— "America"—is created for the magazine's readers. This is what makes the *Digest* such a vital source for understanding American political culture over the course of the twentieth century. The magazine explains American identity through this unequivocal geography of "their" place and "our" place. The difference between "us" and "them" is reified through this geography and so given a natural character. Although other media have undertaken elements of this form of identity, none has been so consistent or influential as the *Digest*, and none has so effectively contextualized its geographies within the morality of the nation's historic destiny.

In this book I seek to examine the changing ways in which *Reader's Digest* has explained America and its relation to the world and, as a result, the sense of American identity that the magazine has created. Central to this story is the depiction of the Soviet Union from the early stages of the communist state through the extremes of the Cold War to its apparent end in the early 1990s.

The *Digest*'s representation of the USSR during the Cold War fits neatly into conceptualizations of identity and difference promoted by recent theoretical work in "critical geopolitics" and international relations theory. A good deal of theoretical reflection has gone into considering the necessity of an Other, or an alter ego, to the operation of national or state identity, to conclude that identity functions as much (or more) through what it excludes as through what it includes.[8] It is through the construction of an imagined geography of national identity that a sense of belonging is achieved. Nations are imagined to be composed of a homogeneous community whose members share common characteristics and, most importantly, differ in a significant sense from those existing beyond the bounds of the nation.[9] It has been noted that if all nations are imagined, then the United States is "the imagined community *par excellence*." More than in any other nation, national identity in the United States has been organized around the impetus of the "articulation of danger, the specification of difference and the figuration of Otherness."[10] Over the course of post–World War II politics, much of this imagining was achieved through the production of the Cold War moral geopolitical model of good and evil. Here the "imagined community" of American citizens had a common goal, one required of them because of their historical role and Manifest Destiny. Just as Americans had triumphed over the wilderness of the continent during the frontier experience, so the continuing narration of American destiny necessitated triumph over other threats. A central threat to the continued unfolding of American destiny has of course been the specter of global communism, a new articulation of barbarism set to test the resolve and dynamism of the American ideas of freedom and democracy.

The Cold War offered a clearly inscribed battleground over which American citizens could triumph, as could the values seen as identifying the American national character. David Campbell has gone so far as to suggest that instead of being inherently threatening to American identity, the USSR, the "Evil Empire," rendered American identity secure.[11] The Soviet threat was necessary to maintenance of U.S. identity. The USSR offered a mirroring conceptual space to that occupied by America; into this space were projected negative characteristics against which a positive image of American character could be reflected.

The USSR has represented all that America is not in the political culture of the Cold War. *Condensing the Cold War* aims to examine how this binary geography emerged, through looking at the pre–Cold War period, at how such an extreme form of imagined geography could be maintained through the Cold War itself, and at how the form of political culture represented by the *Digest* has come to terms with the end of the Cold War and the binary geography that it helped to produce.

Reading Popular Geographies

On the whole, both traditional forms of geopolitics and international relations scholarship and more recent critical works have focused predominantly on the statements of political elites, specifically state leaders and their advisers. Popular culture has been seen to have little bearing on international politics. Once we accept the importance of the geographical imagination to the construction of political identity and the operation of politics more generally, however, the cultural context of elite discourses must be understood. It is here that "metacultural" values are re-produced. These inherited values stand as "common sense" in relationship to the rest of the world and point to the importance of the established cultural norms through which both political elites and their constituents are socialized. In the introduction to his influential cultural analysis of the figure of "John Wayne," Garry Wills says he was often asked:

> Why *him*? When I began this project three years ago, that was the question most often asked when anyone learned of it. I had received no such queries when I said I was writing about Richard Nixon or Ronald Reagan. They, after all, held political office, formed political policy, and depended upon a political electorate. People cast *votes* for them. They just bought *tickets* for John Wayne's movies. Yet it is a very narrow definition of politics that would deny John Wayne political importance. The proof of that is Richard Nixon's appeal to Wayne's movie *Chisum* when he wanted to explain his own views on law and order. Nixon had *policies*, but beneath those positions were the *values* Wayne exemplified.[12]

Nixon could claim to be restoring law and order in American society by reference to Wayne's performance in *Chisum* without having to explain the importance of this cultural reference. Instead he could assume the existence of a set of stories about America that his audience had learned through popular culture. Various media exemplify these foundational myths and stories.[13] Wills's study refers to the genre of Western films and stories, most prominently the figure of Wayne. The values that the films extol and Wayne personifies are so powerful and work so perniciously because dominant forms of political theorizing, in the academy but also in wider American political culture, assume that these are "just" movies and work only in the realm of entertainment. As stories, they are seen as apolitical entertainment. Yet the values that Wayne epitomized have celebrated, reinforced, strengthened, and in many ways made possible the decisions and actions of statesmen and women. So Nixon can refer to *Chisum* and the values of the Western, and a majority of the populace will know his reference (however subconsciously or tenuously) and under-stand its origin in relation to an imagined geography of America.

Similarly, *Reader's Digest* provides a uniquely important source in understanding the formation of a popular American geographical imag-ination, and more specifically the geopolitics of the Cold War, from the magazine's first issue in 1922 through its continued publication through-out the twentieth century. The importance of the *Digest* as a cultural force—a distinct voice within American society—can be established both statistically and anecdotally.

From its humble beginnings, *Reader's Digest* soon became the highest-circulation general-interest magazine in the United States; it now reaches more than 16 million readers a month. From 1938 onward, foreign editions were launched; more than 27 million copies are now bought around the world each month and the *Digest* is available in seventeen languages. Other ventures followed, including the phenomenally successful Condensed Book Club, general books, and records and cassettes. The *Digest* is a cultural production that cannot be ignored given the wide reception of its message in America and across the world; it is an important and trusted source of information, advice, and knowledge for many people.

In addition to being prominent as a producer of American popular culture, *Reader's Digest* is also held up elsewhere in popular culture as an icon of conservative, small-town Americanness. President Reagan quoted the magazine as a source of reliable advice and apparently saved a box of useful articles for reference. The *Digest* has also been referenced in cultural productions as diverse as Fellini's *Juliet of the Spirits* and Matt Groening's television cartoon *The Simpsons*.[14] It is usually depicted as a trusted and established institution of Americanness, celebrating the possibilities of the American Dream and extolling the optimism of that view of life.

Reader's Digest offers an important point of inquiry in any attempt to understand the changing political climate in the United States. Most obviously, the *Digest* has the highest circulation of any magazine in the United States with the exception of the weekly *TV Guide*, and a remarkably high subscription renewal rate of around 70 percent, suggesting significant reader loyalty. Since over 16 million copies are sold each month in America, the *Digest* is a fairly significant presence in the day-to-day representation of identity and purpose to American people in a simple numerical sense. What makes this of greater significance in the reproduction of a sense of identity is that *Reader's Digest* presents itself as guardian of American values. The *Digest* does not simply describe events but always offers a moral to the story. Furthermore, because it juxtaposes articles about global affairs with pieces on issues of personal importance to the individual reader, the *Digest* articulates personal and moral concerns with global and national issues. An analysis of the *Digest* can help to present an image of how political issues can be made to resonate with individuals who have little or no direct relationship to them. *Reader's Digest* offers insight into the way in which politics works in America; into how individuals are drawn into political issues and gain an identity from their perceived location within these images of American society. *Reader's Digest* constructs models of how the world works, of what America could and should do as a major player in this international political geography, and of what the individual American could and should do to help this national mission.

My intention is not to compare the *Reader's Digest* view of the Soviet Union and other threats to America to other, more scholarly or apparently more "accurate" accounts.[15] Nor is this an attempt to produce a revisionist history of the USSR in order to suggest that American commentators have been foolish to react to a phantasmagoric threat. I am not rewriting a relativistic history of the USSR. I am not suggesting that there was never any material threat to America, nor that the USSR was innocent of aggressive or repressive actions.

Instead, I want to examine how this influential cultural production's changing representations of the communist threat to America produced a particular image of Americanness for its readers, and how readers were drawn into the story to become complicit subjects of this political identity. This will involve an examination of how anticommunism became, in George Kennan's words, a form of "mass hysteria" in a country where communists had never achieved more than half of a percent of popular support.[16]

Reader's Digest could not view the USSR independently of "symbolic politics," a politics that seeks emotional satisfaction rather than material reward.[17] Although the editor of the magazine would see the *Digest* as simply reporting the facts, and cultural critics might see it as simply manipulating the facts, in actuality the process is much more complex. I believe that the editors of the *Digest* were trying to understand the Soviet Union, what its relationship with America might be, and what individual Americans needed to know about it. But they could not understand the Soviets outside the discursive structures of symbolic politics, structures that came to position the USSR as totalitarianism and America as freedom in a binary that allowed no gray areas. Through these discursive lenses, any vision of the USSR was redolent with meaning that derived from American domestic concerns.

As a result, this book is not about the Soviet Union, or the empirical details of any other threat to the United States, in any but a tangential sense. Instead, it is a book about America and the changing roles that one component of American hegemonic culture saw for the country and its citizens. The aim of *Condensing the Cold War* is to understand how representations of this Evil Empire simultaneously created roles for America and for American citizens. There is always a choice of words and phrases that can be adopted when describing a place or people. If one is to take seriously questions about the creativity of the process of representation, then the world is not simply rendered mimetically upon the page but is recreated based on intertextual references and languages. The languages used to create the USSR—languages that have become commonsensical and unproblematic—need to be understood. The politics of the choice of words and terms needs to be laid bare in order to denaturalize the connections that have been made and to understand the implications for the formation of a model of good citizenship for its readers.

In order to achieve this, it is necessary to examine an overlooked aspect of the political process. Rather than focus on the formal arena of state and international politics, it is essential to consider the mundane, everyday, often subconscious rituals that instill and reinforce political identity. It is through various repeated practices, such as reading the *Digest*, that individuals are drawn into hegemonic culture as subjects of its constituent discourses. This means that certain values are accepted as natural or "commonsense" and thus uncomplicated. These values can then be drawn upon by political leaders (either consciously or less manipulatively) in explaining a political situation and trying to generate public support.

It is important to understand how people are drawn into political beliefs and spurred into action of any sort. *Condensing the Cold War* attempts to answer this question by examining the *Reader's Digest* representation of the world through three discernible but entangled scales: its understanding of international politics, the role of America in this arena, and the role of the individual in American society. In the convergence of these three "layers" of narration of the nation, the identity and concerns of individuals are written into those of America and its role in international life. Here readers attain an understanding of their (and America's) place within changing global geographies. It is through such narration that national political culture is reproduced, reinforced, and, on occasion, challenged on a day-to-day basis.

Reader's Digest and American Identity

Chapter 1 offers an analysis of the role of the media in general in the reproduction of American culture and identity, and, more specifically, the role of *Reader's Digest*. This analysis seeks to combat the tendency of arguments to see American culture as an unproblematic whole. *Reader's Digest* needs to be placed within the dynamic processes of hegemonic culture formation and understood in historical context. Of special importance was the rise of popular magazines as a significant force in American political culture in the early years of the twentieth century.

It is also necessary to place the *Digest* into a wider theoretical context relating to the interrelations of representation, imagined geographies, and identity. Chapter 2 explains the central role of language and description to the operation of global politics. The ways in which geopolitical arguments are put forward not only have implications for the ways in which people understand international relations but also are central to the ways in which national identities are formed. After exploring these themes, I will turn more directly to the *Digest* to explain how the structure of articles, the repetition of themes, and forms of reader address work to create the reader's place within the geographical orders the magazine is writing.

The body of the book, however, is a detailed reading of the *Digest* over distinct periods of its publication. Chapter 3 examines the first twenty-four years of the *Digest*, namely, the period preceding the beginning of the Cold War. I have chosen to begin the study at this point rather than at the more conventional starting point of the beginning of the Cold War for one very important reason. In this initial period, hegemonic American culture, here represented by the *Digest*, was unsure of the role that America and the Soviet Union, as the emerging hegemons, would play in world affairs. The impact and implications of the Russian Revolution had yet to be assessed fully by American culture. The ambiguities and ambivalences of the period are well represented in *Reader's Digest*. By looking at the period between 1922 and 1945, we can discern competing descriptions of the USSR and its relationship to the United States before the logic of Cold War rhetoric emerged to dominate the other potential interpretations of the geopolitical situation.

Hence, I will trace the competing discourses that constructed the "imagined geography" of Soviet-American relations at this point. This will be paralleled by analyses of *Reader's Digest* articles about America's role in world society and individuals' role in American domestic society, in order to explore both the changing relationships between the perception of America and the Soviet Union and the manner in which the imagined geographies of this relationship were presented to the American population as being significant. In the intersection between these "levels" of the *Digest's* narration, it is possible to see the ways in which global and national events are scripted to be of direct relevance to the lives of individual readers. This period clearly indicates the process by which the Cold War binary opposition between the Soviet Union and the United States arose in American popular culture.

The emergence of the Cold War is the subject of chapter 4. In this most virulent period of Cold War conflict, *Reader's Digest* shifted its textual strategy to employ naturalizing metaphors to grant credibility to dramatic claims about Soviet evilness. By adopting a number of textual and narrative strategies, the *Digest* naturalized the opposition between the United States and the USSR. The magazine made this conflict seem inevitable by using discourses of destiny, "dis-ease," and perversity.

Chapter 5 looks at the changes in Cold War rhetoric that emerged from the *Digest's* reaction to the geopolitics of détente. In the period of relaxation of superpower tensions that followed the American-Soviet talks in the early 1960s and public awareness of the Sino-Soviet split, *Reader's Digest* created a sense of internal danger in addition to touting the external danger lurking in the guise of Soviet communism. Rather than seeing this as a time to ease Cold War tensions, the magazine understood détente as a period in which heightened vigilance was required. According to the *Digest,* there was an urgent need to "arm for peace." The *Digest's* expectations for the outcome of moves to détente or peaceful coexistence are best analyzed using Albert Hirschman's three concepts of "the rhetoric of reaction": jeopardy, futility, and perversity.[18]

Chapter 6 offers a study of the heating up of the Cold War between 1979 and 1985. Because of years of coverage, *Reader's Digest* could rely upon the reader's cognizance of the Soviet menace. During this "Second Cold War," the magazine's demonization of the USSR and communist systems had become "common sense," so that extreme forms of "Othering" the USSR could be enunciated without any need for explanation of the difference.

Although I divide the Cold War into the three conventional divisions—the initial period of Cold War, détente, and the "Second Cold

War"—I want to stress continuities rather than changes in attitude over this period. This suggests a different history than do traditional accounts. The *Digest* did not sense a de-escalation during détente. On the contrary, the magazine thought that détente simply meant to the Soviets the continuation of war by other means and so required *greater* preparedness on the part of Americans.

In the last chapter to analyze the content of the magazine, I examine the *Reader's Digest* construction of world geography with the decline of the Soviet Union. In the post–Cold War period, not only has the "moral void" of the Soviet Other, against which the magazine defined American identity and mission, fallen apart but also—perhaps as a result—America's global moral leadership of the "free world" has declined. Containment of the USSR simultaneously contained "America": it disciplined the myriad possible characterizations of "America" into a coherent moral agent—with a clear sense of mission and inevitable destiny—that provided power of authority to those who upheld and espoused these characterizations. Now these "containers" of American identity are leaking. *Reader's Digest* believes that America is no longer internationally respected as a moral leader, and perhaps even more significantly that the American people too seem to have abandoned this historic role. The loss of America's high ground in the wake of a new moral geopolitics means that the moral authority of *Reader's Digest*, as supporter of the old geopolitics, is also under renewed challenge. The *Digest* has written its way into a particular history and identity of America. With the decay of the moral geopolitics of the old order, *Reader's Digest*, like the America it supports, is struggling to redefine its role. At the end of the Cold War, the *Digest* was faced with a fluidity that presented its territorial-based geopolitics with a conundrum: with the end of the Evil Empire, there was no geopolitical mirror against which it could present an image of America. If, as various theorists have argued, an Other is required for any construction of identity, then at the close of Cold War geopolitics, *Reader's Digest* should shift critical attention to alternative Others, both foreign and domestic, in its creation of a model of post–Cold War national identity. The magazine, however, sensed a new danger in this period: this time a threat from within in the shape of those who had given up on the American Dream. To the *Digest*, this was the most dangerous threat of all.

CHAPTER ONE

Consumption, Discipline, and Democracy: The "New Magazines" and *Reader's Digest*

Reader's Digest was first published in 1922 at the end of a period of social, cultural, and economic change in the United States that heralded the rise of consumerism now regarded as central to U.S. culture. This chapter will place *Reader's Digest* in the context of this trend in American culture by describing the changes occurring in American media at the turn of the century. It is also necessary to examine the cultural shifts through which the new magazines emerged, affecting the relationship between journalist and reader, influencing even the reading process itself.[1] This has implications for the way the *Digest* has been read and the effects of this changed relationship on the creation of political subjectivity. I will conclude this chapter with a discussion of the specific textual and editorial strategies of the *Digest* and their intended effects on the magazine's readership.

The Emergence of Mass Media-tion

The early decades of the twentieth century witnessed an important transformation of the media leading to the rise of mass media. The initial transformation occurred in the production of magazines.[2] The intellectual literary and political magazines that had dominated periodic journalism at the end of the nineteenth century went into decline at the turn of the century. In their place arose a new type of publication, aimed at the growing middle classes and written for middlebrow rather than intellectual tastes, whose audiences encompassed the entire country rather than specific geographical regions of it. None of these were isolated characteristics but instead each represented and perpetuated more general trends in American culture at the time.

The rise of the new media was inseparable from the rising power of the middle class and the values both extolled by and facilitating the emergence of this class. Most important was a belief in democratic society within which prestige and distinction could increasingly be found through consumption—whether of goods or of knowledge—in the "democracy" of the free marketplace. Popular magazines were geared economically toward the American middle class and both embodied and reproduced the consumerist beliefs of this social group. In short, these magazines helped to perpetuate middle-class subjects as consumer-citizens.

The previously dominant form of journalism, produced within the intellectual climate of Victorian "genteel" culture, had not necessarily excluded mass readership intentionally, but the costs of production meant that in fact the majority of the population was priced out of readership. In the late nineteenth century, technological developments made printing faster and more efficient. This, in addition to the widespread introduction of advertising, allowed cover prices to be lowered significantly, opening up the potential readership of these magazines to a much larger portion of the American population.[3] Improvements in the railroad network facilitated the national reach of the magazines, while the Postal Act of 1885 lowered second-class rates from three cents to one, again allowing for wider circulation in both geographical and sociological terms.[4]

These new economies of production were appropriate to the rhetoric of the new magazines, which held that knowledge should not be a preserve of the rich. Rejecting the intellectual elitism of the nineteenth-century productions, mass-production magazines saw their role as informative and educational, though in such a way as to be accessible to all. The magazines espoused an ideology of democratic access to information that aimed at cutting through the class boundaries established by elitist Victorian intellectual publications. The new magazines also intended to go beyond partisan party politics, expecting their readers to discard local for national allegiance and favoring policies geared toward producing good government rather than blindly following a political party. Their frequent exposés of political corruption earned them the name "muckrakers," so that, for the first time, "a *national* medium of mass communications, the popular magazine, became a major political force, making news as well as reporting it."[5]

The national reach of the new magazines was significant because at the time they were the only medium that reached this audience on a regular basis. The national constituency was reinforced by the magazines' claims not to represent a particular interest group, political party, or subculture, but rather the community of "Americans." Thus, Matthew Schneirov claims that when a story appeared in one of the popular magazines, "this in fact already conferred on it a kind of substantiality, acceptability, or weightiness. Popular magazines, more than any other medium seemed to represent 'America' itself."[6] In other words, popular magazines fed into the initial development of America as a coherent national identity for citizens across the United States. The geographical imaginations of American people were drawn together in the magazines through the juxtaposition of concerns and issues from around the country on the pages of periodicals and newspapers.[7] The magazines positioned readers through identifications that aimed to transcend local and partisan political beliefs and values for those of the state, "America." They enabled the media-tion of American identity throughout society by encouraging readers to "identify themselves as citizen-consumers or citizen-taxpayers rather than in terms of community-based ethnic or job identities." Three primary subject positions or social identities available to the readers of popular magazines at the turn of the century have been identified: the reader as a spectator and consumer, as a client of professional expertise, and as a member of a "public."[8] These identities positioned mass communication as an important force in the secular modernization of American society.

The new magazines projected a vision of American society within which politics was based upon the involvement of all Americans in their government. Although direct participation in the political process was impractical for all but a minority, the national scope of the magazines at the turn of the century offered the possibility of disseminating reasonably up-to-the-minute information and opinion to all citizens. The magazines facilitated the construction of cultural communities linked not by shared interaction but by shared information.[9] Magazines provided the information that individuals required to become true citizens of this community and to participate fully in running it—in other words, to make informed and reasoned choices in voting.

The new magazines' democratization of knowledge was inseparable from the commodification of knowledge. It has been argued that *Time* magazine, for example, commodified current affairs. Knowledge of current events was compartmentalized, ordered, disciplined, if you will, into discrete sections, which facilitated simple comprehension and rapid consumption (it could be read in an hour).[10] The interwar period also represented the rise of the "outline" from populizers of knowledge. Most prominent were H. G. Wells's *Outline of History*, H. W. Van Loon's *Story of Mankind*, and Will Durant's *The Story of Philosophy*. These outlines promised consumers a way to become familiar with important aspects of culture while maintaining a unified perspective on the development of culture, society, and knowledge. Haldeman Julius's summaries of literature known as "Little Blue Books" earned him the title "the Henry Ford of publishing." These pamphlet-like publications were abridged from the original to omit the "duller" parts and were produced to be both manageable and disposable.[11]

This new popular culture was of great sociological importance in that it repositioned audiences into passive recipients of culture. Christopher Wilson suggests that the nature of the act of reading itself changed around the end of the nineteenth century. He argues that contemplative intellectualism, the model of consumption typical of nineteenth-century magazines, offered the reader direct access to literature. This was replaced by the popular consumption of a realistic, informational, and, perhaps most significantly, *interpreted* product. The "raw materials"—facts and context—were preprocessed for the reader; rather than having to work out their own position from the material provided by articles, readers were presented with a ready-made resolution of conflicting information. The reading process, Wilson concludes, was skillfully managed so as to produce in the passive reader the illusion of reading as political activity. The (re)production of passivity in the reading process was facilitated as follows. Rather than "being called upon to offer insights into the world's workings, the reader was first awed by its complexity and then counseled by 'experts' ostensibly closer to the action." Experts told readers what events meant and how they *ought* to react to them. Instead of "promoting participation, the magazines elevated 'seeing.'"[12]

I believe that this might represent a written version of the voyeurism that Laura Mulvey has described as operating in films. Mulvey explained how the "spectator is forced to identify with the look of the camera, to see as it sees."[13] The reorganized reading process described by Wilson replicates this visualization so that magazine readers became spectators of political life; they were placed into a voyeuristic relationship with it and given an angle on events as seen through the eyes of experts. Readers were thus positioned so as to be complicit with, rather than critical of and distanced from, conclusions drawn by the "experts."

The expertise promoted by the new magazines was of a very specific nature. As I have indicated, the editors of new magazines were critical of established figures of authority, and especially of those who claimed expertise by reference to their connection with intellectual institutions. The critical-intellectual expertise of the genteel publications was superseded by more scientific (especially technical) and managerial experts through which the magazines presented a positive/practical knowledge system.[14] The authority given to experts represented the "alter ego" of the educational drive of the new magazines. Many cultural critics have observed that the prominence of expertise has led modern society toward new forms of discipline. As Schneirov suggested, if "the captain of industry was the cultural hero for the dream of abundance, the engineer and the manager were the cultural heroes for the dream of control."[15] The languages of management and engineering were expanded into other social realms indicating naturalization of the desirability of self-control and self-discipline in all aspects of personal and professional life.

Contradicting their democratizing ideals, the magazines' advocacy of the importance of staying "informed" by experts only served to highlight the gap between the reader's apparent ignorance and the power of those "in the know." Over the course of the twentieth century there was a rise in the number of journals and other forms of mass media-tion of political life. I do not think that this is merely a coincidence. These magazines acted as mediators in the political process, drawing their readers into political debate, insisting on the importance of readers' staying informed about the political process and as a result conveying a sense of engagement with the political sphere. Fredric Jameson has argued that this is indeed the role of the mass media: to arouse fantasies and desires within structures that can diffuse them.[16] Although historians generally have seen the new mass-circulation magazines as part of a revolt against genteel tradition and "a refreshing turn toward 'progressive' politics and 'realistic' literature," Wilson makes the point that "in the name of democracy the new magazines further undermined the political and cultural autonomy of their audience."[17] Readers were expected to consult magazines regularly for assistance in understanding the complexity of their world.

Another way to understand the operation of the new magazines is to locate them within the emergence of "therapeutic culture." Richard Fox and T. J. Jackson Lears suggest that a key shift in American cultural values at the time was tied in with "the shift from Protestant salvation in the next world to therapeutic self-realization in this one."[18] Therapeutic culture was premised upon the goals of self-understanding and self-realization.

The promotion of therapeutic discourses was a key instance of the disciplining of American society through expertise, as described here: therapeutic culture represented new techniques of social control as it involved surveillance of the self.[19] Discourses of therapeutic culture enabled the regeneration of bodies and minds for work, but of equal significance was the fact that they also directed the attention of consumers away from *social* sources of their dissatisfaction.[20] This deflected attention away from the need for collective action and toward more introspective, individualistic solutions. More than any other element of the new magazines, this aspect of their value system typified the movement toward individualism that has come to characterize mainstream American political culture.

Undoubtedly the "new magazines" were part of society-wide changes in American culture at the turn of the century, but how are we to understand their specific role in the subsequent development of twentieth-century American culture? The new magazines can in fact be seen as both an outcome and an agent of the cultural changes occurring in America in the last decades of the nineteenth century and the first decades of the twentieth. They contributed to ideological domination not because of any conspiracy but because of their "gatekeeping" function. As Schneirov states, the "need for magazine editors to hold on to large audiences for advertisers required that only those ideas and feelings that worked within 'invisible hegemonic limits' could be admitted into the 'arena of the discussible.'"[21]

The magazines and their editors were products of the same set of discourses that they in turn helped to reproduce. Following Michel Foucault, I understand the effects of discourses to be a disciplining of all possible representations and thoughts into an "arena of the discussible." Editors and journalists were not always able to transcend these discourses in order to manipulate them for the public as some "culture industry"–

informed critics might suggest.[22] Lears goes as far as to state that advertisers and editors were "often as confused and ambivalent as the audience they addressed."[23]

Of course, these cultural changes were not without their critics. Writers whose authority depended upon the intellectual distinction of the genteel cultural system were wary of the new magazines, fearing both their commodification of culture and their proclaimed educational role. Writing in 1900, for example, Samuel McChord Crothers, a former minister, saw the contemporary trend toward commodification as a move that would have deleterious effects upon reading and knowledge: "the modern reader 'goes to a book just as he goes to a department store.'"[24] In part, this kind of criticism was a response to the use of advertising by new magazines. In line with their view of the emancipatory potential of the market, the new editors regarded advertisements as sources of information, which not incidentally also provided a means to lower the price of the publication. Proponents of intellectual culture were more distrustful, fearing a breakdown of the relationship between editor and readers if this were more overtly mediated by the market:

> By the late nineteenth century, when revenues came primarily from advertising, readers would be packaged as commodities and essentially sold back to the advertisers. But the genteel editor could still see his readers as personal friends, roughly sharing the same tastes and level of education.[25]

Intellectual reaction to the new magazines cannot be tied solely to their use of advertising, however. The new magazines were institutions of "middlebrow" cultural production, the aspect of culture most disdained by intellectual commentators. Middlebrow represented to Virginia Woolf neither proper art (highbrow) nor real life (lowbrow), but a commercialized hybrid of the two. The notion of "brows" originated in the "science" of craniology and refers directly to beliefs of cultural development: lowbrows were less intellectually developed and more natural than highbrow intellectuals who were insulated from everyday life by their culture. Highbrow writers were sure of their own intellectual superiority but had a romantic attachment to lowbrows whose natural behavior and closeness to reality (unmediated by cultural convention or reflection) provided the raw materials for highbrow cultural productions. Middlebrow culture, however, threatened the art-life distinction that Woolf and others held dear, through its claims to educate the masses. Addressing an (imaginary?) lowbrow audience, Woolf asked, "How dare the middle-brows teach *you* how to read—Shakespeare for instance? All you have to do is read him."[26]

It was the middlebrow's claim of self-improvement that appeared to worry authors such as Woolf. Middlebrow represented a transgression of the binary intellectual structure of highbrow/lowbrow. Structurally not unlike Homi Bhabha's colonial hybrid, middlebrow culture represented a challenge to the political-cultural power of the relationship between colonizer/highbrow and colonized/lowbrow.[27] The culture of middlebrows represented a dynamism stemming from their desire for self-improvement not available in the more passive notion of recreation central to the lowbrow mass cultures. More specifically, Schneirov sees popular magazines as a hybrid of high-quality magazines' emphasis on cultural uplift, independent newspapers' tradition of political education, and sensational newspapers' focus on personality and human interest.[28]

Reader's Digest, established in 1922, at the tail end of most of the changes described here embodied both the spirit and the letter of many of these newly emerging cultural values.

The Official Story of *Reader's Digest*

> He [DeWitt Wallace] was a quiet man, who said little publicly. He spoke instead through Reader's Digest, which became the world's largest international magazine and the most-read publication in the history of journalism. In its pages he told more stories, brought more information—and laughter—to more readers than perhaps any other man who has lived.[29]

The official story of the establishment and rise to success of *Reader's Digest* is the epitome of the standards and values espoused by the magazine in the narrative of its articles. The official story recounts the American Dream of an industry outsider (Wallace) making good in the face of conventional wisdom (established publishing houses) and other apparent barriers to success (relatively humble beginnings).

The Wallace family was an intellectual one: DeWitt's father was a scholar of Greek and a college president, and an older brother, Benjamin, was Minnesota's first Rhodes scholar. Wallace twice enrolled in college— first at Macalester and then at Berkeley—but in both cases he failed to complete his degree. He had a great interest in reading magazines and began to note the pertinent points of memorable articles on small cards. When he was convalescing at a U.S. Army hospital following an injury at the Meuse-Argonne offensive in 1918, Wallace began to develop the "art of condensing" articles because it struck him that this might serve as a basis for a general-interest digest.[30]

After failing to interest any of the established magazine publishers in his idea of a digest, Wallace realized that he could bypass these organizations by mailing his magazine directly to readers. True to the narrative necessities of the poor-boy-makes-good tale of the American Dream, Wallace managed to scrape together enough money for a first print run. He married Lila Bell Acheson in 1921, and the two of them produced the first issue in their home in Pleasantville, New York. The first issue of the *Digest* was prepared for February 1922, with a final lot of five thousand copies. The official history of the magazine narrates its origins in dramatic terms:

> Will the Little Magazine. . . . appeal to readers? For years professionals in the business have been saying no. So now with the help of his new bride and a couple thousand dollars, much of it borrowed, the amateur from the sticks is going to win it on his own.[31]

In tune with developments in magazine publishing over the past few decades, Wallace realized that change and timeliness were of central interest, though he felt that people were flooded with news and speculation. Thus:

> Not a few harried readers found themselves so carried along by a tide of information that they could not distinguish between what was meaningless and those facts that could be fitted into a larger pattern. . . .
> A magazine—half-way between newspaper and book—offered time to discern the significant, to develop an underlying theme, while still dealing with the fresh and new.[32]

The magazine would be aimed at people like Wallace himself—not intellectuals, but everyday folk "hungry" for knowledge:

> Self-improvement was the key. Success could be achieved through learning. But learning was no longer book-bound and abstract. It was down-to-earth, practical.[33]

Wallace realized that knowledge could be made available for those like himself who did not have the time, money, or inclination for leisurely contemplation of abstract knowledge (the service that he saw universities providing). Instead, in the *Digest* (The Little "Pocket University")[34] he offered the bare essentials with which individuals could stay informed, keep up with changes in society, and thus understand new developments. The content of *Reader's Digest* has remained more or less the same for more than seventy years (see figure 1). Each issue has articles of a topical nature—current affairs, foreign policy, geopolitics—explained in terms of their historical and national significance and related to problems of government inefficiency and corruption, and American cultural standards and values. Also ubiquitous are human-interest stories of bravery in the face of danger, selflessness in the face of hardship, and perseverance in the face of hopelessness, plus lighter pieces: humor, travel writing, and fictional stories.

With an attitude similar to that held by the editors of the "genteel" Victorian journals, many family friends regarded Wallace's move into moneymaking business as overly materialistic. For Wallace, however, "material progress was far from a threat. Rather it promised a new age, a time of fulfillment when everybody would have enough of everything."[35] In later life, the Wallaces were true to their word, donating money to charities and the arts in a "regal" style.[36]

Reader's Digest soon became the highest-circulation general-interest magazine in the United States, today reaching more than 16 million readers each month. From 1938 onward, foreign editions were launched; more

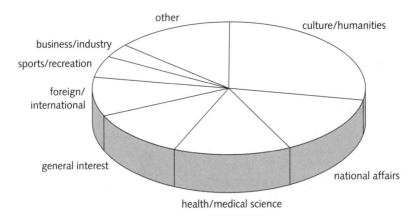

Figure 1. Analysis of *Reader's Digest* editorial content, 1990.

SOURCE: *Hall's Magazine Report 1990*, cited in "Quality Does Matter: 1990 Editorial Classifications," *Reader's Digest.*

than 27 million copies are now bought around the world each month, and the *Digest* is available in seventeen languages. Other ventures followed, including the phenomenally successful Condensed Book Club, general books, and records and cassettes. Various attempts at branching into television have met with much less success.

In 1973 the Wallaces retired, both aged eighty-three. By this time, DeWitt had established a formidable formula for the magazine, which has continued more or less regardless of individual editors in chief. DeWitt Wallace died in 1981, Lila three years later.

A Critical Engagement with the Official History of *Reader's Digest*

In many ways, *Reader's Digest* represents an intensified version of some of the social and cultural changes discussed in the first section of this chapter. The rise of DeWitt Wallace and the magazine he dominated until the mid-1970s represented the social and cultural dynamics and characteristics the magazine subsequently took as axiomatic of "America." Two of the main themes that underpinned *Reader's Digest*'s discursive base ties directly into the emergence of the new types of publications outlined here. First, Wallace believed that much journalism was unnecessarily verbose. As a guide for the modern consumer, only the facts or the essence of the text were required. He spent hours perfecting the art of condensing articles from their original length to a minimum without losing the essential message of the text—"trimming away the noncommercial ornamentation," to use John Trebbel and Mary Ellen Zucherman's somewhat cynical phrase.[37] Wallace disregarded the artistic merit of the convergence of content and form in seeking to produce an "efficient" product for his readership. Second, Wallace wanted to provide a wider audience for articles that he considered to be of political, social, or moral importance but were hidden away in specialized magazines. At first each issue of *Reader's Digest* was entirely composed of articles condensed from other sources so that the message of these important essays could gain greater influence.

Although the *Digest* has been characterized as a Midwestern publication, it in fact unites the country in its scope both in the audience it addresses (the American public) and its actual readership.[38] In tune with the general trend of the new magazines at the turn of the century, *Reader's Digest* spoke to its readers as American citizens. Its demarcation of specifically American concerns, the American state's role in world society, and the citizen's role in American society has helped mold a sense of national cohesion among its readers.

Reader's Digest claimed to be of particular use to those wishing to stay informed because it represented itself as a commonsensical, unbiased summary of the most important journalism. The *Digest* sorted through the range of magazines, journals, and newspapers available to the reader, separated the factual sheep from the ideological goats, and consequently claimed to provide a comprehensive guide to the world as it really was. The editors set out their own appraisal of the magazine's contribution in a tenth-year editorial in May 1931:

> Through it all the effect of the *Reader's Digest* has been to reflect not the immediate material facts but the meaning and trends, seen in perspective ... in other words ... [it is] devoted to current literature *of more than current interest.* That there was widespread demand for such a publication is indicated by its steady growth. Supported by this good will among readers, our own major effort remains editorial. Without advertising, with no editorial bias, replacing no other medium of expression *but supplementing all,* our single aim is to be impartial in the selection of articles of lasting interest, to offer subscribers the most stimulating variety of entertaining reading, and to serve as a monthly guide to the riches of current literature in general.[39]

The magazine, presented in straightforward terms, relied upon a commonsensical form of knowledge that most closely represented the practical, useful, and uncritical knowledge systems exemplified by the new magazines. Since the first issue, within its general interpretative schema of common sense, the *Digest* has compartmentalized not only the news but all elements of life.[40] On one level, common sense as utilized by the *Digest* represents an archetype of capitalist production: as the magazine's name suggests, it presents a predigested interpretative schema.[41] This manufactured product (interpreted knowledge) presents itself as self-evident, unquestionably true, and therefore requiring no further interpretation, just acceptance and use. Any elements of a situation that could complicate the demarcation of right and wrong are disciplined to binary simplicity in the rhetorical structure of common sense. By forcing people, situations, changes, and so on into catagories of right/wrong, true/false, fact/fiction, the magazine cuts any ambiguities out of its accounts. Common sense adopts a realist textual strategy structured around prodigious use of facts, the rhetoric of objectivity, and description so that any opposing views of a situation are rendered false, ideological, or fictitious. This textual strategy imposes an identity and a role for the reader that are again structurally similar to that produced in Durant's outlines, which

> implicitly conceded that the "busy reader," in Durant's words, had neither the time nor the need for more depth; it further assumed that Durant's function involved operating within those constraints by dispensing with anything debatable or obscure.[42]

"Experts" present maps of the territory of truth to *Digest* readers. As with the new magazines more generally, this expertise is based on practical experience rather than intellectual ability. *Reader's Digest* has produced a taxonomy of expertise in its labeling of authors. A large majority of the magazine's writers are described as having some legitimate *experiential* knowledge or *practical* institutional affiliation that makes their articles worthy of inclusion.[43] In addition, some articles and views gain authority because they are written by or about great people. The attractions of such articles lies in what Leo Lowenthal has called "pseudoindividualism," the opportunity to overcome anonymity by identifying with people who stand out from the crowd.[44] Exceptions to this celebration of the institutions of experience and fame are articles about average individuals who have triumphed in the face of adversity not in spite of their averageness, but *because* of it.[45] The implication of these latter articles is that individuals who are *just like the reader* were able to take on challenges—and succeed.

Reader's Digest should not be viewed, however, as a faceless cog in the modern leviathan of the culture industry.[46] The "politicized" readership that I have just described has to be understood in relation to the culture of consumption that emerged in the United States in the early twentieth century in a more complex manner. The production and subsequent fulfillment of the desire for knowledge is not unlike the production and fulfillment of desires for commodities, axiomatic of capitalistic reproduction. The knowledge offered by *Reader's Digest* can be regarded as a commodity in that it was offered as something with which readers could improve their own capital: their wisdom. The desire for self-improvement produced by the magazines left the consumer continually seeking up-to-date information with which to "stay informed." It is not surprising that Henry Ford was one of DeWitt Wallace's heroes. As John Heidenry noted, Ford "put an automobile within reach of the average family. Ostensibly

[Wallace] was the first to provide the public with an even more precious and hitherto inaccessible gift—an education."[47] It was an act very much in line with the philosophy of the magazine: Wallace and the *Digest* democratized access to knowledge. In tune with his view of democracy as equality of access to opportunity, the *Digest* equalized access to knowledge, so that intellectual differences would be merely the result of different talents and motivations.

As with the general trends of the cultural changes in America at the turn of the century, however, it is important to study the apparent *Reader's Digest* democratization of knowledge for its further consequences. Wallace's intent to democratize knowledge so as to provide equality of opportunity in fact also produced the opposite effect. At the same time that the *Digest*'s basis in common sense appeared to equalize social standing, it reinforced the status quo: the status of those who already had knowledge—the *Digest*'s experts—was reinforced. The *Digest* presented itself as providing the kind of knowledge that would allow its readers to make commonsense decisions when they were faced with new and conflicting information; readers must continue to consult the magazine to ensure that they had access to a balanced presentation of the issues of the day. In order to fulfill their desire for a sense of political mastery, or at least competence, people were to become dependent upon publications such as *Reader's Digest* for understanding of the political sphere. There is a clear tension between *Reader's Digest*'s desire to provide individuals with the capacity to make sense of conflicting information presented to them by experts and the magazine's goal of maintaining high circulation by establishing itself as an expert on the meaning of current events.

In one sense, "staying informed" *is* the role of the good citizen in the media-ted political world of *Reader's Digest*. In a democracy, a good citizen must understand current events so as to be capable of voting wisely and rationally.[48] Such is the *Digest*'s belief in this notion that over time it has sponsored advertisements featuring famous political figures underlining the importance of an informed citizenship to the preservation of democracy. For example, a June 1960 advertisement quoted President Dwight D. Eisenhower saying, "Our magazines are a leading force for moral and cultural growth in our country, and one of the surest guarantees of an informed public" (figure 2). "Informed citizens are the guardian and spirit of democracy," Eisenhower added. Two years later, in a similar advertisement, John F. Kennedy cited John Adams's claim that

"Liberty cannot be preserved without a general knowledge among the people." These advertisements demonstrate the *Digest*'s belief in its own importance in the reproduction of informed, educated citizens, the cornerstone of the American political system.

From time to time, the *Digest*'s belief in its singular importance to the American citizen was reinforced to the reader: prominent figures have been quoted on the inside back cover proclaiming the *Digest*'s vital role in American society, or its global and even cosmic significance. For example, on its thirtieth birthday, in 1952, the *Digest* was described by one such figure as "essential to an informed, alert citizenry in a democratic society" and "as American as the flag."[49] In June 1950, excerpts of letters from "enslaved Poland" were published, including one that claimed that "we are hungry for facts and you feed us" (and of course this predigested sustenance was not hard to swallow!). Finally, in May 1956, the secretary general of the Organization of American States put the magazine's role into a most grandiose perspective: "It is not too much to say that The *Reader's Digest* points the way to the return of the conscience of man as the center of gravity of the universe."

At times the *Digest* provided its readers with a more direct method of entering the political process. In the February 1969 issue, for instance, Wallace launched a "Fly this Flag Proudly" campaign, inserting flag decals into the 18 million copies of the magazine (figure 3). A follow-up survey indicated that 78 percent of readers had detached the decal, and half of them had put it to use.[50] A few years earlier, an article on how Brazil had resisted communist takeover was deemed to contain such "vital, useful information for every nation menaced by communist subversion" that readers were encouraged to send it—and free reprints of it—to friends in foreign countries, or to put it into "the hands of concerned people [whom readers] may meet" on vacation.[51] The *Digest* even offered advice on how to mail copies to others.[52] In most issues, the editors offer readers the opportunity to purchase (at low cost) additional copies of articles they consider to be particularly timely or important. Some especially important articles are offered free of charge.

Wallace established a production-line approach to construction of the *Digest*. In effect, editors learned by trial and error. A chosen article moves its way along "murderer's row" from the most junior editor to the editor in chief; each person rewrites the version passed on to him or her.[53] There are no written guidelines for new employees, who learn by reading what

Figure 2. *Reader's Digest* advertisement explaining the importance of magazines to democracy (June 1960, pp. 234–35).

"INFORMED CITIZENS ARE THE GUARDIAN AND SPIRIT OF DEMOCRACY"

—President Dwight D. Eisenhower

"For more than a century, our magazines have spoken out on domestic and international matters—sometimes from a highly individualistic view; often with broad vision. It is inevitable that none of us will always agree with, or like, all that magazines have to say. But over the years, magazines have provided new ideas, brought fresh insight into old problems, shed light on new ones, and have served to inspire and advance our understanding and knowledge on many subjects—from the arts to finance, from government to science, from the individual to the world scene. Our magazines are a leading force for moral and cultural growth in our country, and one of our surest guarantees of an informed public."

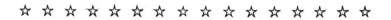

THIS MESSAGE IS PRESENTED BY

Reader's Digest ON BEHALF OF MAGAZINES

...A LEADING FORCE FOR MORAL AND CULTURAL GROWTH

How to Show This Flag

There is a trend in this country toward widespread and patriotic display of the American flag. It is a trend which deserves the utmost encouragement from all of us.

The replica of the flag which is affixed to this page has been designed so that it can be impressed on a pane of glass—on a corner of a car window, for example. Follow these instructions for displaying the flag:

1. Remove entire unit—including flag and its waxed-paper backing—from this magazine.

2. If you wish to use the flag on your car, safety experts recommend that you place it on a side window toward the rear of the car, so as not to obstruct vision. (Be sure to clean any dirt from the inside window surface.)

3. Next, peel any corner of the flag away from the waxed-paper backing, being careful to keep the flag flat so that the pressure-sensitive adhesive will not stick to itself. *This adhesive needs no water.* Position the flag carefully, and press it firmly against the inside of the car window. (If you do not use this flag on your car, you may wish to affix it to the inside of any window in your home or office.)

The editors hope that all of our readers will want to display these flags. We are making quantities available —at cost plus handling—to other institutions and firms.

Address Reprint Editor, The Reader's Digest, Pleasantville, N.Y. 10570.

Would You Like More Flags? Prices postpaid to one address.

2	$	.25
12		1.00
25		1.50
100		4.50
500		18.00
1000		32.00
Add'l 1000s		30.00

Figure 3. Wallace's flag campaign in *Reader's Digest* (February 1969, pp. 104–5).

Fly This Flag– Proudly

It has given heart and hope and strength to Americans ever since this nation was born.

It has flown in times of trouble and in times of triumph as a symbol of America's unquenchable ideals, ever since those ideals were first proclaimed.

It flies today as a sign that Americans, proud of their country's stirring heritage, are determined to carry the American dream forward.

When we fly the flag each day, we salute the blessings we enjoy in this great country.

—We affirm our belief that only as each one of us gives strength to America can America give strength to us.

—We express our support of the American credo: one nation indivisible, with liberty and justice for all.

Let us fly this flag proudly, to show that we know what a privilege it is to be an American.

is sent along the editorial hierarchy.[54] Wallace provided few guidelines to his editors beyond the *Digest*'s "Three Commandments":

> *Is it quotable?* Is it something that the reader will *remember*, ponder and discuss?
> *Is it applicable?* Does it come within the framework of most people's interests and conversation? Does it touch the individual's own concerns?
> *Is it of lasting interest?* Will it still be of interest a year or two from now?[55]

Wallace conceived the booklet form in order to produce a publication that would be regarded as having some "lasting interest" but was portable so that the consumer could read an article a day, perhaps when traveling to or from work. This was achieved via an editorial strategy based upon the "art of condensation."[56] Many articles have been cut by more than 75 percent of their original length.[57] The *Digest* contained condensed articles that could be read quickly, without the effort required for the full-length versions.

Beyond its prefabricated scheme of knowledge production, *Reader's Digest* can be understood as a Fordist institution in yet another sense. In his *Prison Notebooks*, Antonio Gramsci noted the attempts of Fordist companies not only to influence the mode of production of their workers but also to have an impact on periods of recreation. "It is worth drawing attention," Gramsci states, "to the way in which industrialists (Ford in particular) have been concerned with the sexual affairs of their employees and with their family arrangements in general."[58] Lila and DeWitt Wallace, especially in later years, were also intent on controlling the familial values and actions of their staff, extending their moral discourse from the pages of *Reader's Digest* into the lives of the magazine's employees.[59]

A major difference between *Reader's Digest* and others of the "new magazines" was that the *Digest* did not accept advertising until well into the 1950s. From the outset, the magazine had depended overwhelmingly on subscriptions. Wallace chose to publish the *Digest* without the support of ad revenue not because he disliked advertising, but because he had a good economic reason to resist it. *Reader's Digest* paid source publications little for reprinting rights, and once it began to develop a large market, Wallace did not want its circulation to be known, as advertisers would demand. Wallace believed that if his competition were to see the *Digest*'s profitability, they would raise reprinting rates, refuse to allow the *Digest* to reprint their articles, or launch competing digests. It was not until the *Digest* faced decline after World War II that Wallace allowed advertising (but banned alcohol and tobacco ads). By this point, the magazine had established sufficient prominence that its circulation did not surprise anyone, and it could attract good articles itself.[60]

Wallace dominated the editorial process until his retirement in the mid-1970s. Under his editorship, the *Digest* always returned a healthy profit (his estate was two and a half times that left by *Time* magazine founder Henry Luce).[61] But it was not profit for its own sake that motivated Wallace. Instead, caught up in the mythos of Manifest Destiny and national exceptionalism characteristic of his prose, he wanted the *Digest*'s success to be recorded by influence, by the number of people who read it and subscribed to its values. Many of the foreign editions launched during his ownership operated at a loss, but Wallace felt they provided other benefits. The first foreign-language version, in Spanish, for sale in Latin America, was launched in 1938 with support from the Roosevelt administration's Division of Cultural Relations. The Italian version was initiated as a direct response to the expected success of the Popular Front of Communists and Socialists in Italy's 1948 national elections.[62]

These activities prompted many claims that the *Digest* was propaganda and had connections to the CIA.[63] Although there are no formal connections between the *Digest* and government propaganda, there are plenty of examples of informal collaboration, from the American government's supplying the magazine with rationed paper for the British edition during World War II to editor in chief Hobart Lewis's friendship with Richard Nixon. This does not mean that the *Digest* can be dismissed as propaganda. For example, there is considerable evidence of tensions within the editorial structure: some staff obviously proposed an agenda that was directly influenced by CIA policy, while for others this was perhaps a more innocent coincidence of viewpoints; still others opposed these linkages. The magazine would always have a "house liberal," although it has been suggested that views opposed to the dominant position did not usually get much latitude.[64] Nevertheless, *Reader's Digest* should not be regarded simply as a covert arm of American government. The magazine has often been highly critical of government administrations, Republican as well as Democratic. Most (in)famous are the *Digest*'s desire to reduce government, and its frequent exposés of corruption in Washington and in government institutions around the country. This critical stance is not limited to domestic politics but often extends into the arena of foreign policy.

After Wallace's death in 1981, the *Digest*'s policy changed. *Reader's Digest* shares were split between voting and nonvoting stock. Wallace bequeathed voting shares to two charitable trusts, although in the year 2000 this will have been reduced to 50 percent of voting stock to fall in line with tax law.[65] Wallace warned company executives against excessive profits, but since the magazine is run as a business, the ethos underwriting the business side of Wallace's empire has been undermined. Unprofitable sidelines and foreign editions have been closed down, staff numbers reduced by 20 percent, and some of Wallace's paternalistic measures, such as a free bus to work for his New York employees, have been terminated in an effort to maximize returns to investors.[66] In 1986 CEO George Grune chose to drop the base rate of 17.75 million subscribers to 16.25 million by eliminating the high cost of mailing to "marginal" subscribers (those who need to be repeatedly reminded to renew their subscriptions). Profitability soared as a result of this very un-Wallace-like maneuver.[67] Still, profit margins at the *Digest* are thought to be narrower than the 10 percent earned by many successful media companies,[68] and at this point profit is linked to the marketing power of the reader database rather than sales from the magazine itself.

Reader's Digest rose to become a significant presence in American society and has been prominent for several decades despite the rise and fall of other magazines during this period. The majority of the new mass-circulation magazines have faced financial problems, even bankruptcy—*The Saturday Evening Post, Munsey's, McClure's*—but *Reader's Digest* has weathered the cultural and social changes that sunk its competitors.

While it is undoubtedly necessary to question the romantic visions of nineteenth-century magazine production and reading patterns in reviews such as Christopher Wilson's, it is nevertheless still possible to acknowledge that in the early decades of the twentieth century, magazines as institutions underwent a shift in role in the production and reproduction of information and opinion. The danger of viewing *Reader's Digest* as merely one of many examples of this turn-of-the-century magazine boom is that the histories of media production have tended to portray the readership of the magazine as a helpless mass of victims subject to the control of a faceless and homogeneous culture industry. This victimization of "the masses" has led to the undermining of popular culture by academics. Ariel Dorfman's evocation of the *Digest* as a conservative political plot hidden behind tales of trivial individuals read by "other equally trivial being[s]" is indicative of a cynical academic arrogance that supposes "the masses" to be entirely malleable, empty vessels to be filled with meaning shaped by the media, but open to the possibility of conversion to the radical position advocated by the critic.[69] Dorfman flattens out the sociology of knowledge production into a battle for the minds of the masses fought out between good intellectuals and the bad media. By interpreting and articulating the "best interests" of nonintellectuals, Dorfman effectively silences their agency.

Instead, I think it is more appropriate to see *Reader's Digest* as a production of its times as well as understand its role in creating its times. The *Digest* is not an innocent voice of the people, but neither are its editors beings who transcend the discursive domain within which they are situated. As one commentator has noted, Wallace, along with MGM director Louis B. Mayer and *Time* founder Henry Luce, "perhaps inadvertently, are particularly responsible for the American self-image. Trying to reflect it, they also helped create it."[70]

The *Reader's Digest* mailing address, in Pleasantville, New York, conjures up an image of idyllic small-town American life. Surely, if Pleasantville had not actually existed, *Reader's Digest* would have had to invent it.

In fact, once it became successful and its readership started to grow, the *Digest* moved out of Pleasantville but retained its mailing address there because of the traditional American associations the town's name carries. Now, the town is hardly emblematic of small-town America, but is dominated by the *Digest's* massive post office. Pleasantville, it would seem, is as much a fantasy of the *Digest's* American identity as the Kremlin is of its Other.

CHAPTER TWO

Reading the *Digest* Writing the World

Recent critical work in political geography, international relations, and political science has underscored the importance of taking seriously the ways in which we write and speak about the world and its workings. Such work acknowledges the fact that writing and describing are inherently creative processes. Language is metaphorical and, as a result, description is achieved by deferral to other concepts. Language is not then transparent or innocent, but is part of the process of world-making, since the choice of referents—the ideas and narratives that are quoted in order to make sense of a situation—will affect the meaning of any resultant explanation. Gearóid Ó Tuathail has suggested that for political geographies and geopolitics, the term geo-graphy is useful in emphasizing the creative nature of a geographical description:[1] there is not simply a geographical order "out there" awaiting description. Instead, through the descriptions of the world and global politics in the speeches of political elites, in media coverage and school textbooks, orders are made and remade in the aim of producing the meaning of events. A central part of this process is the construction of boundaries to produce global maps. Such boundaries also define inside and outside: a cartography of "us" and "them." Descriptions of geography therefore also have implications for the creation of identity.

In this chapter I will examine the importance of understanding the construction of geographies through the language used in *Reader's Digest*. After examining arguments for the importance of language in geopolitics, I will consider how the writing of geopolitical relations affects the construction of national identity at a general level to provide some context for my analysis of *Reader's Digest*. Before looking at the content of *Digest* articles (the focus of the next five chapters), I will examine the *content of the form* of the articles.[2] This involves understanding the structure of the articles and the various textual techniques used to make the magazine's argument credible, thus drawing the reader in to become subject of the political discourses there encoded.

The Language of Geopolitics

Recent critical approaches to geopolitics seek to make the operation of commonsense assumptions about the objectivity of geographical information unworkable. Analysis of the language used in international relations texts reveals the use of geographical concepts as apparently innocent, apolitical, and timeless explanations of the necessity to invade, to send aid, to sever ties, and so on. Language is not unproblematic, somehow *simply* describing what is there. Language is metaphorical, explaining through reference to other, known concepts. There is always a choice of words and metaphors. The type of terms used—the conceptual links made—affects meaning. There is, as a consequence, a politics of language.

Recognition of the power of language in the writing of international relations is not as nonconflictual as my description might suggest. Among those who accept the power of language to constitute international relations, there is a difference in the strength of influence they grant it. On the one hand are those who believe that language reflects reality but that it is not intimately linked to specific objects or processes. In this case, there might be, for example, a time lag between events and changes in interpretative structures to take account of this: individuals might be working on an earlier model of global geopolitics (for example, Margaret Thatcher's insistence that Britain was an imperial power in the mid-1980s was working on an earlier global order).[3] But others would want to see more causality given to language, rather than simply following "reality." At the extreme is the French thinker Jean Baudrillard, who dismisses any distinction between reality and representations of it within his concept of the "hyperreal." This flattening of signifier and signified to a superficial play of images led him to claim that the 1991 Gulf War did not happen except as a spectacle of violence on the television screens of CNN-viewing millions around the globe.[4] He claimed that public opinion was so entirely manipulated as a result of its total dependence on the media for information and opinion that "it completely loses touch with any knowledge of real world issues and events."[5] Political discourse, however, is not the entirety of political culture.

Instead, it is more useful to adopt a position that lies somewhere between that which regards language to be lagging behind reality and that which sees language as entirely constitutive of reality. This position regards geopolitical discourse as providing a series of scripts for those operating within the international realm. First, this approach acknowledges the narrative and tropic construction of language, recognizing that "all language … is ineradicably metaphorical, working by tropes and figures; it is a mistake to believe that any language is literally literal."[6] Second, viewing geopolitics as a set of scripts allows for the intervention of significant figures and institutions, saving analysis from the potential chaos of discourse, through an understanding of the "rules, codes and procedures" that "assert a particular understanding through the construction of knowledge within these rules, codes and practices."[7] This approach sees a tacking back and forth between the discursive construction of the world and the effects of the materialization of discursive constructions, insisting upon the ultimate materiality of the descriptions without any requirement for some naive access to unmediated "reality."

The ways in which *Reader's Digest* writes the world and America's place in it help to create a place in this geography for the reader. Uncovering this geography lies at the heart of *Condensing the Cold War*. The implicit geography of discussions of international relations has been left unexamined despite the interrogation of other aspects of the construction of political discourse. Martin Lewis and Karen Wigen insist that "laypersons and scholars alike have uncritically accepted a series of convenient but stultifying geographical myths, based on unwarranted simplifications of global spatial patterns." These are not simple mistakes but instruments of global power that frame the way everyone from casual observers to state leaders approach the world and its political workings.[8] These "metageographical" concepts are reproduced uncritically in the media, in schools, and in the statements of state and other political leaders. They are central to the workings of hegemonic culture, and as a result influence identity formation.

Geopolitics and Identity

From psychoanalysis has developed the idea that identity is not simply about the characteristics and boundaries of the Self, but is rather about the difference of that Self from what is Other. There is no single identity, but always one defined in distinction from another. Thus, in order to enforce a coherent sense of Self, the Other has to be described and demarcated. For example, "man" is what he is by virtue of ceaselessly shutting out what has been defined as his opposite, by defining himself as opposite to it. "Woman" is therefore not just Other in the sense of being something beyond his "ken," "but an other intimately related to him as the image of what he is not and therefore as an essential reminder of what he is."[9]

This understanding of identification has influenced the study of international relations and critical approaches to geography and geopolitics. It suggests that national identity is not formed simply by the essence of what lies within, but, more importantly, by what lies beyond the state boundary. State boundaries do not simply mark one a priori identity from a different one, but are actively constitutive of these identities. In one sense, the essence of identity is not somewhere deep within the territory—at its "heart"—but is constantly being re-created at its boundaries to mark off the identity of that territory from what it is not, from what lies beyond the boundary. "At the origin of every nation" states Geoffrey Bennington, "we find a story of the nation's origin."[10] Bennington is suggesting that it is the daily, mundane repetition of signs and symbols of national identity that naturalize and depoliticize it as a form of identification. The drawing of boundaries to construct a coherent identity of national Selfhood from international Otherness is key to understanding the process of international politics.

This process of "geo-graphing," or writing spaces, is central to the practice of statecraft and formalized in the form of geopolitics. In a traditional sense, geography is simply the terrain upon which the rules of international politics are played out, exerting influence only through the timeless rules of geography. Geography means that certain spaces are either easier or harder to defend and that distance has effects on politics; proximity leads to political influence, and topography to security or vulnerability.[11] Space and spatial relations, however, cannot be seen as so transparent.

Ironically, geopolitical arguments are, in one significant sense, profoundly ageographical. Rather than being concerned with understanding geographical process, geopolitics reduces spaces and places to concepts or ideology. Space is reified into units that tautologically display evidence of the characteristics that are used to define the spaces in the first place: the "Orient" *is* exoticism, the USSR *is* communism, Iran *is* fundamentalism, and so on.

The very act of mapping can be seen to construct identities—such as international and domestic—rather than these identities' preceding the border drawing. This means that foreign policy "shifts *from* a concern of relations *between* states which takes places across ahistorical, frozen and pre-given boundaries, *to* a concern with *the establishment of the boundaries* that constitute, at one and the same time, the 'state' and 'the international system.'" These boundaries are the "result of domesticating the self through the transfer of differences within society to the inscription of differences between societies."[12] It follows that the constant articulation of some form of external danger to national integrity in the praxis of foreign policy is not a threat to a state's identity or existence but is a condition of its existence:

> Thus the contract theory of the state relates directly to the creation of Otherness and the political creation of the identification of the Self in terms of the state in whose territory one exists.... Security is thus about the spatial exclusion of Otherness.[13]

Furthermore, the view that boundaries mark difference rather than play an active part in creating it assumes that national identity precedes statehood. Yet much work on nationalism has shown that in the vast majority of cases, nationhood has most often followed from the construction of states and in all cases has been reinforced and refined by the institutions of statehood. Thus, nations should be regarded as a kind of "invented tradition" or "imagined community." Although this is true to varying degrees in all states, it is especially the case in America, for, as David Campbell has opined, "if all states are 'imagined communities,' devoid of ontological being apart from the many and varied practices which constitute their reality, then America is the imagined community *par excellence*."[14] The very nature of America was created in the minds of Europeans before the establishment of any sense of coherent American identity. Frederick Dolan argues that en route to the New World, John Winthrop had already constructed images of American exceptionalism in "A modell of Christian charity."[15] Alternative images (and materialities) of history and society on the North American continent were violently erased as this model of American national character and destiny emerged.

Many have pointed to the operation of identity described here as being central to the U.S. political culture during the Cold War. Anxieties over conditions in America were projected into the Other space of the USSR. The positioning of Otherness as a creation established to define the Self—the mad to define the sane, to cite one of Michel Foucault's examples—is not to suggest that there are no conditions of madness, nor in this case that there are no differences in the way in which different countries are governed. Instead, the implications point toward the way in which we understand and define what "madness" and "difference" are, and the conditions these definitions subsequently produce. In the case of dominant discourses defining America in the twentieth century, especially between the early 1950s and the late 1980s, the primary alter ego (defined through all the discursive practices mentioned here) was communism, territorially manifested by the Soviet Union. But this geopolitical-ideological alterity, like madness, does not have a stable definition: depending on the project or event in question, the American alter ego could be limited to the geographical extent of the Soviet Union or only a particular strata of the Soviet ruling class, or it could be extended to all those anywhere who fall victim to its "perverse logic" (communist or socialist ideology), including, most terrifying of all, those whose corrupting influence had got inside America itself.

The construction of Otherness, and particularly the sense of danger that alterity presents, has implications for the practice of domestic affairs in addition to foreign policy. Thus Simon Dalby suggests that geopolitics is "about stifling domestic dissent; the presence of external threats provides the justification for limiting political activity within the bounds of the state."[16] The construction of Otherness simultaneously presents a normative image of identity, here an image of an idealized American society.

In many ways, however, the literature that critically analyzes the national grounding of geopolitical discourse itself reinforces neorealism's privileging of the prime agency of the territorial national-state unit: the nation-state is taken as a more or less single voice that constructs a national "us" in contradistinction to a foreign "them." As Robert Cox has remarked, neorealist theory in the United States "has treated civil society as a constraint upon the state and a limitation imposed by particular interests upon *raison d'état*, which is conceived of, and defined as, independent of civil society."[17] Geopolitics is most usually presented as a form of "high politics." Simon Dalby explains:

This supposedly autonomous realm of *raison d'état* is now staffed by national security managers, supposedly expert in the art of co-ordinating diplomacy, covert action, intelligence and military preparation.... Arguments from the Oliver Norths of this world inform us that this sphere of human activity is both beyond the comprehension of most Western publics and far too important for democratic oversight.[18]

Geopolitics thus posits a separation of the sphere of international politics from a sphere of domesticity and the politics of day-to-day life. This division perpetuates privilege by implying that international politics is beyond the ability of most people, and thus should be left to experts.

Gearóid Ó Tuathail reinforces this point by separating "geopolitics"— the act of implementing foreign policy—from "geo-politics," the political creation or inscription of space.[19] The latter is a constant process, operating throughout society in everyday political discussion, in media reports, and in education. However, the division of activities—the power-political from the everyday—somehow renders geopolitics beyond the everyday, as if geopolitical figures were able to operate free of cultural context. The "moment of geopolitics" is not fixed, but is diffused through society in the constant re-creation of images and understandings of the world and how it works. The rhetoric of international political discourse is evidently not simply for the ears of other elite members: it is part of a national and international culture that is mediated and negotiated in a number of national institutional locations. I believe that it is important to expose the concealed workings of the state in the construction of international politics to be revealed. Such an analysis is in tune with Richard Ashley's appeal for a "geopolitical perspective on the field of geopolitics."[20]

A concept that links the discourses of foreign Otherness with national political process is hegemony. For Antonio Gramsci, it is in the concept of hegemony "that those exigencies which are national in character are knotted together."[21] Hegemony represents an "unstable equilibrium between the classes,"[22] a complex set of dominances that together form the norms regulating social reproduction. Gramsci understood social norms and rules of behavior to be reproduced by and through the actions of every person, but not equally; positions within the institutions constituting the hegemonic blocks are more empowered to affect normalizing standards. These institutions, which range from formal institutions of government to less formal (but no less powerful or textualized) institutions such as the family, ensure the spontaneous consent of the majority of the members of a society to the actions of its dominant classes. This is because hegemony is constructed not only through political ideologies but also, more immediately, through detailed scripting of some of the most ordinary and mundane aspects of everyday life.[23] Gramsci's concept of hegemony posits a significant place for popular culture in any attempt to understand the workings of society because of the very everydayness and apparently nonconflictual nature of such productions. Any political analysis of the operation of dominance must take full account of the role of institutions of popular culture in the complex milieu that ensures the reproduction of cultural (and thus political) norms.

In her refusal to focus primary attention upon the role of elite members of the state in her discussions of international relations, Cynthia Enloe has similarly exposed the political nature of processes operating in the supposedly nonstate (private) sphere.[24] Enloe's concern is to expose the silencing of the gendered discursive practices upon which international relations depends. She suggests that "ignoring women on the landscape of international politics perpetuates the notion that certain power relations are merely a matter of taste and culture."[25] It is imperative, therefore, to study the institutional structure through which norms of power and knowledge are produced in such a way that the illusion of a division between political and "nonpolitical" spheres is enacted. Put somewhat differently, an analysis of the ideologies and discursive practices that reproduce the political sphere "which fails to include an analysis of the corresponding institutional mechanisms is liable to be no more than a contribution to the efficacy of those ideologies"[26] and of discursive practices, in this case, those that separate the public and political from the private.

In practice, I believe that following the logic of hegemony entails studying the institutions of knowledge production and the exchange of meaning and legitimation that flows between such institutions. Returning to the question at hand here, the manner in which hegemonic American culture incorporates events occurring in the designated international sphere provides an important insight into changing conceptions of identity and difference. The ever more powerful mediascapes of contemporary global capitalism mean that any division between "high" cultures of statecraft and "low" or "middlebrow" cultures of the media and popular culture is becoming ever more tenuous. The circulation of images in the media and the almost total mediation of any but the most local political activity have lead to the ever increasing importance of the media in our (Western) everyday understandings and conceptualizations of global geopolitics. This can be seen in the types of references made by international relations texts. Increasingly, intertextual references are made not to the great tomes of traditional geopolitical reasoning, but to texts of popular culture. As James DerDerian has suggested:

> We are witnessing changes in our international, intertextual, inter*human* relations, in which objective reality is displaced by textuality (Dan Quayle cites Tom Clancy to defend anti-satellite weapons),... representation blurs into simulation (Hollywood, and Mr. Smith, goes to Washington), imperialism gives way to the Empire of Signs (the spectacle of Grenada, the fantasy of Star Wars serve to deny imperial decline).[27]

Furthermore, DerDerian argues that through intertextuality, "we can see how the American popular literature of international intrigue shares and privileges a narrative of the truthsayers of the security state: beyond our borders the world is alien, complex, practically incoherent—an enigma but one which can be unraveled by the expert story-teller."[28]

Firsthand experience is not dependent upon physical presence. Few hear much politics directly from the politicians who supposedly make policy and set agendas. Instead, events are reproduced in the media, and to attract attention they are made into spectacles, so that political reporting "continuously constructs and reconstructs social problems, crises, enemies, and leaders" as spectacles of media entertainment.[29] This has lead to the "creation, transmission, and adoption of political fantasies as realistic views of what takes place."[30] More often than not, the media takes the initiative, and political figures "increasingly find themselves responding to rather than initiating public issues."[31] Political issues and events are linked to media-friendly individuals, the major actors who most competently deliver the scripts of geopolitical reasoning to the public and to other players. To a greater and greater extent, the public is being asked to select between actors rather than policies or ideologies. Ronald Reagan, "the Movie President," typified this political persona in that it is thought that he spent one-third of the working hours of his time in office answering "fan mail."[32]

Thus, the media do not simply reflect current events but also help to create them. In addition, they are central to the grouping of individuals into "publics" through which people identify themselves and their role within society. There are in fact three major formal institutions responsible for the creation of publics in the United States: the government, education, and the media. John Hartley uses the term "public-ity"[33] to refer to the creation of publics because it evokes not only the creation of knowledge but also the audience or readership's self-identification within this knowledge in a manner not dissimilar to Louis Althusser's concept of the interpellation of subjectivity through discourse. By accepting or using media information, individuals become subjects of it, learning their place in relationship to the issues, processes, events, and actors that they are hearing or reading about. Each of the three institutions of public-ity have different roles and influences within contemporary U.S. society.

The role and power of government have certainly received significant attention in analyses of American political culture. Whereas the government undoubtedly plays a significant role in the scripting of American political and cultural life, narrow reliance on this institution as conveyor of knowledge or as articulator of U.S. identity is simplistic. To paraphrase Gearóid Ó Tuathail and John Agnew's words, the president, as the personification of the U.S. government, is chief *bricoleur* in the construction of history, present and future,[34] but this does not give him a full range of power. He cannot *invent* aspects of political culture. Instead he has the power to select, combine, and juxtapose already existent elements of national mythos; it is his role to form coherence from the identities resulting from American national experience. As I suggested in the introduction, political elites must draw upon metacultural concepts already in existence within society. These concepts emerge more diffusely than reliance on the centrality of government would suggest.

Another important source of knowledge and a sense of U.S. history and identity is of course education. George Kennan was clear in his belief in the necessity of ensuring that "our public is educated."[35] The events unfolding in the middle of the twentieth century were too significant to be judged by an ill-educated populace. However, in a paper on U.S. foreign policy after the Cold War, Michael Vlahos states:

> More than any other modern societies, America relies, even depends
> on myth to cement its confidence in current policies. Americans are
> profoundly ahistorical; we do not share a coherent sense of our history in

formal academic terms. Popular culture, not an educational system, shapes our common sense of history.[36]

Frances FitzGerald's study of American school history textbooks would seem to underscore the relatively weak influence of this knowledge.[37] Despite the near universal reach that school texts achieve in American culture, FitzGerald found little long-term impact. First, reception of the texts' information was limited to a general sense of history in adult memory rather than anything more specific. Although a bold understanding of American mythohistory was achieved, few details were retained. Second, especially in recent decades, the history and identity produced by these texts is regional and so does not promote the forging of a national sense of destiny. Finally, the content of the texts and the identification they produce have changed markedly over time depending upon domestic concerns and political struggles.[38]

The final institution of public-ity is the media. The media are less formal institutions than government or education, yet in many ways are more powerful. Despite the growth of surveillance in the modern state system,[39] it is perhaps the media that have the closest picture of the makeup of society. The media have the most complex taxonomic picture of citizenship, formed around consumption cleavages, a picture constructed through heavy investment in research. The media also play an important role in constructing national identity. As Benedict Anderson has highlighted, it is the ritualistic, everyday element of consuming the media that constantly replicates a sense of belonging to a national "imagined community."[40] This sense of belonging to a finite group of people who share values, aspirations, and, in the most general sense, a genealogy, confers upon the reader-consumer membership in the nation.

A number of commentators have argued that the media play a particularly important role within American society. Media theorist Armand Mattelart believes that

> few countries asked as much as the United States of their apparatuses of mass communication, not so much because the media there had attained a more advanced degree of technological development than in most other industrialized countries, but rather because the media had, throughout the whole period [the first half of the twentieth century], become the very cornerstone of a project of national integration.[41]

As I have mentioned, *Reader's Digest* and the emergence of the new magazines more generally were key to the formation of a specifically American popular identity at the beginning of the twentieth century.

A result of this focus on the importance of popular sources of description in the formation of political identities has been the study of "popular geopolitics," which has examined the relationship of state elite geopolitics to popular conceptualizations of the working of the world. Popular geopolitics advances critical approaches to geopolitics in a number of ways. First, overconcentration on the understanding of elites tends to collapse the sociology of knowledge production into the internal dynamics of the geopolitical text. Geopolitical knowledge does not simply "trickle down" from elite texts to popular ones, nor are elite texts produced only to be read by other elites. The specific intertextual nature of much geopolitics (referring to tropes that structure spy narratives and sports commentary, for example) is evidently not solely employed for other political elites; it represents a vehicle for meaning transfer to the populace. For example, Michael Shapiro has suggested that American leaders have taken advantage of the widely held interpretative value of sports analogies. The "sportization" of explanations of international conflict permeated government discourse to such a degree that during a bombing campaign in Vietnam, President Nixon adopted the code name "quarterback" and used terms such as "end run" and "play selection" in foreign policy.[42] This explained not only the condition of conflict, but also why those hearing about it should accept the interpretation that Nixon offered: it provided a taken-for-granted cultural referent that the majority of his American audience would accept.

This would suggest that there is not a distinct division between elite and popular: elite texts are intended for popular consumption, and members of a distinctively elite institutional locale contribute to and consume popular media. The place of government-supported missions in narratives of American identity and destiny are an important consideration. David Campbell suggests that, as a consequence, "we should no longer regard those who occupy the secretive domains of the national security bureaucracy as being outside of the cultural parameters of the state in whose name they operate."[43]

Second, because texts produced by those not directly implicated in the power and knowledge of statecraft do not always present their arguments as political statements—and, I would contest, are certainly read with less suspicion of motive than the text of a politician—the political encoding of such texts is more subtle and thus more easily reproduced. Certainly the rhetoric of the American state is one that insists on the importance of popular participation and on ensuring that the government never goes out of the reach of the population.

But even to those who are not willing to accept the actuality of popular participation in government, the way in which people receive and accept dominant values is significant. Such analyses help to explain why people accept what they are told, and why it is that individuals can hold apparently contradictory beliefs without failure of their belief systems. Reading *Reader's Digest* articles in an exercise such as this book seeks to follow can unearth apparently unbelievable stories and questionable information. The pronouncements of right-wing politicians such as Jesse Helms and Newt Gingrich might seem equally incongruous to those of a more liberal persuasion. Only when we understand the context of these pronouncements can we account for the predominance and longevity of such political beliefs.

Reader's Digest can be considered to be a creator of public-ity. In the magazine, global issues and events and apparently "universal" considerations are articulated with matters of more immediate relevance to the day-to-day lives of individuals; side by side are issues of personal concern and international importance. More than any other single media source, the magazine, in its specific articulation of these themes, provides individuals with a particular understanding of the political system and their position within it. *Reader's Digest* helps to formulate a role for the reader; it suggests what the reader is capable of achieving.

Reading the *Digest*

An important aspect of the *Digest*'s explanation of global geographies is the manner in which the articles are put together to seem not only truthful but also essential to readers' understanding of ongoing events. The magazine uses a number of techniques to achieve this effect.

The *Reader's Digest* worldview is presented in objective language. Many of the stories are personal, about individuals surviving trying ordeals or surmounting incredible odds, but are rendered in factual language. This converges with the magazine's claim to authority derived from practical knowledge and experience rather than painstaking research or intellectual contemplation. The *Digest* produces a naive empiricism that rests upon acceptance of the "disciplined" eye being able to discern the true order of things in the world. Such language suggests to the reader that "if you were there, you would see it the same way."

The sense of "objectivity" in the text is achieved in two ways. The first is through the use of factual language. In his analysis of the *Digest*, Samuel Schreiner states that in a typical issue, forty-three hundred facts are checked.[44] This prodigious use of "facts" in the text adds to the "reality effect" of first-person reporting and underscores the veracity of the *Digest*'s perspective on world events. In addition, the fact-filled style conjures up reality through a richness of detail that both aestheticizes and sanitizes contentious issues and deflects attention away from deep or critical understanding.

Second, the *Reader's Digest* format reinforces the notion of objectivity. As a digest, the magazine "creates the illusion that the editors were diligently culling the cream of the current magazine crop without regard for political content."[45] There is, however, a bias toward certain sources, especially in more recent years; radical magazines such as *Mother Jones* and, with the exception of its first two decades of publication, the *Nation*, are not to be found within the covers of the *Digest*. The magazine draws upon a relatively wide range of journalism to give the impression that "both sides" of an issue are given coverage. This appearance of total coverage, however, makes invisible the political position of the *Digest* and in so doing subtly reinforces its ideological stance. According to John Heidenry, issues supported by the *Digest* are given substantial, factual, and authoritative coverage and convincing polemics. Opposing arguments are presented in much less plausible terms. Furthermore, conservative magazines are condensed to produce articles on weighty political topics; liberal magazines are used for less consequential matters.[46] Given the appearance of balance in reporting of most issues, then, the magazine's singular position on communism from the late 1940s onward—when only critical articles were published—would have appeared "natural": if the rhetoric of the magazine was known to be "impartial," its position on communism was less likely to be read as a political one, the implication being that there simply could not be a positive side to the communist system.

A more contentious practice helped to further secure the appearance of universal coverage. This was the practice of "preprinting" or planting

articles. As the Depression deepened in the early 1930s and other magazines were forced out of business, Wallace found it increasingly difficult
to find suitable articles for condensation. Preprinting was an ideal solution: *Reader's Digest* sponsored an article to be written for another magazine, then paid the magazine for first rights to condense it. The *Digest*
could promote the type of articles it required while maintaining its image
as a review of the best of the press, and thus appeared to be broadly
representative rather than politically biased. Preprinting benefited other
magazines in that they received free articles for which they were then paid
by the *Digest*. As the *Digest* gained more influence, however, its power in
defining the nature of journalism across the board began to worry other
editors. In the 1940s some magazines, including the *New Yorker*, began to
withdraw from this scheme. It was not until the mid-1970s, however, that
a number of public exposés of this practice convinced editor in chief
Edward Thompson to abandon planting altogether.[47]

Going beyond the Simple Facts

Perhaps one reason for the continued hold *Reader's Digest* maintains
on the imagination of the American populace has to do with the fact that
the magazine does not *simply* report the facts of what is going on at any
given time. Instead, the details of a situation are contextualized within
both what could be called "the lessons of history" and an overtly moralistic language: there is always a moral to the story in *Digest* articles. Most
clearly, it places events into the historical context of the unfolding narrative of the American Dream and Manifest Destiny. Such "historical"
vision reinforces the verity of the *Digest*'s interpretation: here is an opinion apparently devoid of the effects of changes in intellectual fashion, but
one that is based on an understanding of the long-term historical view.
Weight and importance are added to the *Digest*'s view.

Of course, the lessons of history do not simply allow one to see what is
happening in "historical context"; they also allow for some degree of prediction. This is a key concept within geopolitical practice and thought. As
Gearóid Ó Tuathail has explained, part of the "science" of geopolitics has
traditionally been a predictive power.[48] Geopolitics posits that geography
holds the key to the development of historical powers: the "geographical
pivot of history," to use Halford Mackinder's rather grandiose terminology.[49] The laws of geography (including the strategic positioning of continents and resources, distribution of population, and so on) facilitated

the conquest of one power by another. According to geopoliticians, these laws do not change; they are the immutable foundational truths upon which the history of the world has been built. Future political conquest and power struggles could thus be predicted, and geography, again to quote the "father" of geopolitics, Mackinder, became an essential "aid to state-craft."

Reader's Digest eagerly adopted the role of geopolitical prophet (see figure 4). It (in)famously took a front seat in the initial stages of the Cold War, predicting the Soviet Union's threat to America and warning that action would have to be taken to prevent the otherwise inevitable Soviet world domination.

Paul Boyer has suggested that in fact prophecy belief is central to U.S. culture, in that it unites religious and secular views and provides

> a way of ordering experience. It gives a grand, overarching shape to history, and thus ultimate meaning to the lives of individuals caught up in history's stream.[50]

Boyer's study examines the ways in which biblical meaning and prophecy have permeated contemporary American culture, despite a high level of ignorance of the actual words of the Bible. The "atomic age" provided renewed vigor for biblical arguments, which offer the specter of Armageddon. *Reader's Digest*, in its geopolitics of the Cold War, falls directly in line with the prophesying that Boyer discusses, especially in its merger of apparently scientific and objective references to geography and the dramatic, moralistic biblical references. Indeed, Boyer argues that the Cold War cannot be understood outside of an awareness of the religious context within which it unfolded. He suggests that in the mid-1980s, one-forth of Americans viewed the U.S.-Soviet conflict in theological terms, and more than half of them endorsed President Reagan's "Evil Empire" terminology.[51]

Thus, in addition to the *Reader's Digest* justification for its interpretation of events from the direction of American history, it had the added power of implicit theological meaning. Although biblical and theological references were not used directly in geopolitical articles, the presence and language were there nonetheless. The fire and brimstone of the millennialist genre was more obvious in articles concerned with American culture than in those describing the Soviet Union, but parallels ran throughout all articles: a moral is powerfully present in the vast majority of tales. From

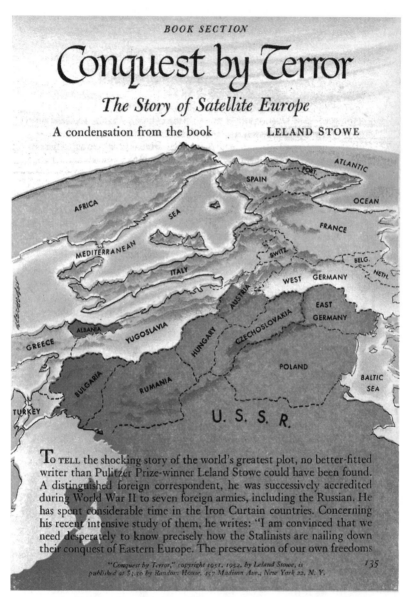

Conquest by Terror

The Story of Satellite Europe

A condensation from the book   LELAND STOWE

To TELL the shocking story of the world's greatest plot, no better-fitted writer than Pulitzer Prize-winner Leland Stowe could have been found. A distinguished foreign correspondent, he was successively accredited during World War II to seven foreign armies, including the Russian. He has spent considerable time in the Iron Curtain countries. Concerning his recent intensive study of them, he writes: "I am convinced that we need desperately to know precisely how the Stalinists are nailing down their conquest of Eastern Europe. The preservation of our own freedoms

135

Figure 4. Map of the Soviet invasion of Eastern Europe, as depicted for the title page of a condensed version of the book *Conquest by Terror*. The "Soviet-style" view of the map maximizes the impression of Soviet power.

the beginning, in the early 1920s, the *Digest* was concerned that America might be in decline, presenting an image of a once virtuous society fast succumbing to Satan through "loose morals" and, later, drugs, AIDS, and homosexuality. The magazine often worried that although the United States was virtuous in its fight against communism overseas, its growing materialism was leading to serious problems at home.

At a basic level, the *Digest* structured its explanations of America and the world by reference (direct or indirect) to a metageography of American mission, destiny, and responsibility. Geopolitics are not enacted only when descriptions of location and spatial relations are called upon directly. Geopolitical analysis is important even when geography is not overtly invoked, as any pronouncement of international relations calls upon descriptions of places and relationships between places. As a result, it is important to look at some of the more mundane aspects of the magazine's articles.

The Structure of Articles

Despite the changing editorship of the *Digest*, the structure of the magazine has remained constant. Through his initial dominance, Wallace established a formula, proven so successful that it has remained virtually untouched ever since. This formula can be seen to be composed of three main ingredients: common sense, individualism, and optimism.

Common Sense

Common sense, as Andrew Ross has observed, is a powerful discursive practice:

> It works to incorporate and rearticulate the most uncommonly uncritical ideas and perceptions as part of its explanatory presentation of the values that survive—the values that endure—in a world whose volatility is depicted as politically hostile to the stability of all values.[52]

Common sense appeals through the obviousness of its claims; it makes the world seem simple and manageable through a silencing of complexity, of problems that do not produce "right or wrong" or "true or false" conclusions. In effect, the elements that tend to complicate argumentation are disciplined into binary simplicity through the discursive practice of commonsensical reasoning. Everything foreign or intellectually challenging can be reduced to the well known, the always already understood.

Thus, common sense is what Roland Barthes has termed a "mythology." Mythology deals with political phenomena, but

> its function is to talk about them, simply, it purifies them, it makes
> them innocent, it gives them a natural, external justification, it gives them
> a clarity which is not that of an explanation but that of a statement of
> fact.[53]

One of the attractions of common sense is its apparently democratic nature—it is a common form of wisdom, a natural sensibility rather than something that is learned through years of bookish education. This may appear to contradict the *Digest*'s use of authorities, but the type of expertise the magazine calls upon is very specific. Experts are recognized by the *Digest* because they have traveled to or resided in a foreign country, or have served in a particular government, military, or commercial position. This conceptualization regards authority as deriving from experience rather than learning. *Reader's Digest* experts claim to see things as their readers would, and they communicate this through tropes of presence. They gain their knowledge through a positivistic rite of passage, collecting information through experience. Thus the average reader can understand what is being reported. The authors present themselves as being sufficiently experienced to place their observations of events in a broader context. Informed wisdom through experience thus represents the highest pinnacle of commonsensical knowledge.

One of the main articulations of common sense in *Reader's Digest* is the "discourse of the natural," the key organizing structure for all articles concerned with alternative political, cultural, social, or economic systems. Indeed, I suspect that this discourse underlies the great majority of *Digest* articles. Since common sense requires a binary system of right and wrong logic rather than a more nuanced reflection on a whole spectrum of positions, the discourse of the natural is structured around the opposing poles of natural and unnatural. Any actual or proposed societal change is interpreted by the *Digest* as either a natural progression of human society, or, conversely, a change that would force humanity into an unnatural system.

Although *Reader's Digest* articles do on occasion call up the discourse of the natural directly by invoking tropes of nature or perversion, use of this discourse is not always so mechanic. Instead, different languages have been used to characterize the USSR and communism within the context of contemporary domestic concerns. For example, the magazine implicitly regards progress as a natural state for civilized human society. Other tropes of time such as degeneration or timelessness are used to introduce the impression of an unnatural society. For the *Digest*, aesthetics and morality also hold the high ground in the binary of nature so that descriptions of "ugly" people and landscapes and "immoral" behavior also call up the unnatural. Taken to an extreme, tropes of inhumanity (usually in the guise of sexual perversion or, more rarely, cannibalism) or inexplicability (irrationality or actions beyond reason) strip what is being described of any recognizable trait of (human) nature.

The discourse of the natural can encompass contradictions. For example, within the general framework of Cold War representations of the USSR, the Soviet system could be described as natural (a natural reaction to czarism, a natural move away from the texts of Marx) or unnatural (an unnatural restriction of freedom or individualism, an unnatural repression of monogamous heterosexual relations). What is significant is this constant use of a natural-unnatural division to make sense of changes, to let readers know, in essence, whether changes and developments are right or wrong.

Individualism

Individualism is a prominent *Reader's Digest* discourse that operates at two levels. First, the *Digest*'s construction of American society is based on an overt belief in the existence of individual agency. The equality of opportunity offered by American democracy, states the *Digest*, means that the differences between people in contemporary society are due principally to different talents and the uses to which they are put. Although this theme runs through all articles, it is most evident in the many pieces on individuals who triumph over adversity and in articles concerned with self-improvement. This implicit rejection of structural causality helps to explain the *Digest*'s infamous abhorrence of communism and socialism, which posit interdependence and the existence of structural barriers to the exercise of individual agency. In turn, this supposes the necessity of government support and therefore presents a fundamental challenge to individualism.

Second, paralleling this but in a less obvious manner, is the *Digest*'s compartmentalizing of knowledge. By dividing knowledge into discrete individual topics, the *Digest* silences any notion that there may be underlying systemic causes of phenomena. As I have mentioned, *Reader's Digest* is intended to be more than simply a journal supplying information on the most recent events and current affairs. This is illustrated in its catchphrase "An article a day—of enduring significance in condensed, permanent booklet form." Challenges to American moral values or political action are presented within a broad historical context as significant events that threaten the American way of life. There are no hidden structural barriers to individual success in the *Digest's* universe.[54] All those who have succeeded have in common the application of common sense and hard work; failures are linked to poor advice, lack of will, or laziness.

The wonderful irony in the magazine's antistructuralism is that underlying the various anecdotes—the seamless flow of triumphant individuals and the numerous challenges to the American way—is a fundamental structural unity carefully constructed over many decades. Through this repetition of enemies and heroes, images of America and its alter egos, the American identity promoted by the *Digest* is reinforced.

Optimism

Although its own structure is unchanging, the *Digest* promotes a notion of improvement; the magazine offers a "good read" that suggests that while everything may not be right with the world, there is nevertheless always something that can be done to make things right.[55] Articles are unceasingly positive and optimistic; pessimism and critique are rejected as destructive forces. In fact, *Reader's Digest* presents a remarkable belief in the power of positive thinking. Even as it constructs a sense of danger in its production of political life, the *Digest* shows that there is a way to avoid it—no matter how apocalyptic the future might appear to be, there is always something that can be done to prevent disaster, so long as action is taken immediately. Anecdotes from American history often are used to illustrate the positive potential of action. For example, in 1946, an author evoked the spirit of pioneering Americans to call people to action in the present:

> It can be taken as certain that, as the full implications of the Soviet system come to be better understood by the American people, it will revive in them the spirit which led their forebears to pledge their lives, their fortunes and their sacred honor to secure their personal freedoms.[56]

Readers and Authors

A number of characterizations are implicit in the magazine's address of its readers. There is an assumption of the citizen as a consumer with attendant rights; as an individual with agency; as an American; and, more often than not, as a white male head of a family, despite occasional articles that address women and ethnic minorities directly. In the next five chapters, I present an analysis of *Reader's Digest* content between 1922 and 1994. There are of course issues of interpretation linked to this presentation of my own readings of the *Digest* as the dominant ones of the majority of the readership throughout this seventy-two-year period. Although I acknowledge the theory of situated knowledges—which proposes that there is no singular reading of a text, but that each reader will engage differently with it depending upon experience, political outlook, education, and a multitude of other positionings—I would not want to take this position to an extreme. For just as there can be no single interpretation of a text, it is also impossible to have an infinite number of different interpretations. From this perspective, laws of language, accepted norms of interpretation, agreed upon facts of history and geography, and so on are necessary for communication. These enact closure on possible meanings. Put somewhat differently, there are not as many *different* interpretations as there are readers because there is no such thing as the truly *individual* reader. As a result of socialization through different social institutions, each individual is interpellated as a subject of a number of different reading communities. Each reading may be unique, but only in a trivial sense as it relates to the issue addressed here.

Although it is possible to suggest that every reading could *theoretically* produce an entirely unique text—and so each reader would take on the authorship function—this is actually never the case. The limitation on actual readings of a text stems from the production of discourses facilitated by institutional structures. Authors often gain authority from credentials (association with institutions recognized as being producers of knowledge for instance). Furthermore, authors are placed in the world just as readers are. Neither authors nor readers are able to think or communicate independently of socially accepted positions or beliefs; quite simply, none of them can "speak themselves" as if the self were entirely independent of social forces constructing others. Michel Foucault explains the importance of the recognition of author-ity:

The author's name serves to characterize a certain mode of being of discourse: the fact that the discourse has the author's name, that one can say 'this was written by so-and-so' or 'so-and-so is its author,' shows that this discourse is no ordinary, everyday speech that merely comes and goes, nor something that is immediately consumable. On the contrary, it is speech that must be received in a certain mode and that, in a given culture, must receive a certain status. . . . The name seems always to be present, marking off the edges of the text, revealing, or at least character-izing its mode of being.[57]

Foucault's definition of authorship can be brought to bear on this study in two ways. First, *Reader's Digest* employs writers who are recognized as being authorities on particular topics, either because they are famous or because the *Digest* attributes to them expertise based on experience. In both cases, recognition of authority places the author closer to the truth than the reader and thereby enhances the realism of the author's account. Second, and more significantly, the *Digest* itself can be considered an author. *Reader's Digest* has become a household name that for many peo-ple signifies an American cultural icon with the authority to define the most important elements of the culture. Record collections, book selec-tions, and videos are almost guaranteed success if they have endorsement from the *Digest*.

Study of individual *Digest* authors and their roles in American gov-ernment and society would be interesting, but is not necessary to my project. Evidently, the selection of individual authors for reprinting in the *Reader's Digest* is significant—not just anyone is chosen. Beyond the initial years when the magazine was trying to find a niche and reputation, however, it is not the *individual* credentials of the contributors that is important. What is important is that the editors chose these authors because of their expertise: *Reader's Digest* as an author can choose the right kind of voices and opinions to present to the American people. It is this general authority that is of lasting significance to the magazine's presence in American political culture. As the *Digest* has become suc-cessful and a significant presence within American culture, its choice of individuals to speak as authorities has influenced the political map by granting status to those chosen to speak.

The institution of author acts to contain the hermeneutics of recep-tion; the author's name points to a particular set of discourses and nar-ratives, drawing conclusions via a number of claims of authority. It determines a probable interpretation of the text if the reader is cognizant of the author's usual point of view and especially if, over time, the reader has grown accustomed to accepting the author's arguments. This expectation or acceptance of the author's position acts as what Wolfgang Iser has described as an external element in the hermeneutics of reading, an intertextual position outside the text being read that contextualizes new knowledge. "The gaps of indeterminacy can be filled in by referring the text to external, verifiable factors," claims Iser, "in such a way that it appears to be nothing more than a mirror reflection of these factors."[58]

Reader's Digest typifies this property of author-ity better than almost any other magazine in America, or indeed the world. In addition to having an audience that in many ways *does* reflect a large portion of American society (see the appendix), the *Digest* has the most loyal readership of all magazines. Its subscription renewal rate currently stands at around 70 percent, which is remarkable given the vast choice of magazines and other media available in the United States. Of the readership, 94.5 percent is direct subscription—not from newsstand sales—and 5 million new subscribers are added each year. *Digest* research in 1991 revealed that in the selected period, 68 percent read four out of four issues. The *Digest* has one of the highest "time spent reading" averages of popular magazines at eighty-six minutes, and "loyal readers" who read four out of four issues.[59] In addition, over half the readers state that they read the magazine cover to cover,[60] which again is unusual. This suggests a familiarity with, and general acceptance of, the arguments put forward by the magazine.

Further strengthening this relationship with its readers, the *Digest*, like *National Geographic* as described by Catherine Lutz and Jane Collins,

> is often a gift, usually from a family member. As such it comes to stand for that relationship in many peoples' minds—for family memories and personal continuity.[61]

Combined with its nearly eighty years of publication, this makes the magazine a significant presence in American culture.

There are two implications of the *Digest*'s audience. First, the reader loyalty suggests that a considerable proportion of readers probably adhere to the magazine's views.[62] Second, the readership figures are available because the *Digest* has conducted reader surveys after publication of every issue since 1969, making it the first magazine to compile reader databases. The accumulated database of reader surveys has been described as the "lifeblood" of all *Digest* enterprises as it allows for complex marketing schemes.[63] The database is now the most lucrative aspect of the *Reader's Digest* enterprise (the magazine itself accounts for only 28 percent of sales).[64] Editors are therefore aware of the articles that are popular and those that are not.[65] Some articles and some types of articles have been unpopular and so have been discontinued. This second point has significant ramifications for reception.

It would be simplistic to talk of readership surveys and their editorial aftereffects as being examples of the power of individual choice, and to assume that the media simply provide what their readers truly want and reproduce the world as readers already see it. Desire and demand cannot be innocently detached from production: individuals' desires are not the result of processes entirely internal to themselves. And yet, the *Digest*'s use of readership surveys does point toward a more complex process than that offered by theorists of mass communication such as Theodor Adorno, Max Horkheimer, and Ariel Dorfman, who insist that what people want is simplistically determined by forces of media production. There are of course myriad forms of mediation of the political word— radical, liberal, and conservative—so that desires and motivations cannot be so easily read off individual media.

The parameters for acceptance of articles by those who have generally come to agree with the precepts of the *Digest* are set by the "implied reader" constructed through the articles' discursive and narrative structures. The implied reader is a transcendental model that makes possible the description of the intended meanings in a text.[66] Uncovering this model requires a deep level of interpretation of the "content of the form" of articles.[67]

Iser has theorized the structures of literary texts for the manner in which they position the reader, arguing that the very fact that a text tells the reader something new forces it to provide the reader a standpoint from which to interpret it:

> Since the world of the text is bound to have variable degrees of
> unfamiliarity for its possible readers (if the work is to have any 'novelty'
> for them), they must be placed in a position which enables them to
> actualize this view.... The text must therefore *bring about* a standpoint
> from which the reader will be able to view things that would never have
> come into focus as long as his own habitual dispositions were determin-
> ing his orientation.[68]

The implied reader can be defined as the subjectivity created through the interpellative-ideological workings of the text. The function of ideology, states Ernesto Laclau following Althusser, is to interpellate (constitute) individuals as subjects of power/knowledge regimes; individuals are transformed into subjects in that "they live in the relation with their real conditions of existence as if they themselves were the *autonomous principle* of determination of that relation."[69]

The implied reader is constructed in the *Digest* through three rhetorical strategies that position readers in such a way as to establish a dominant reading practice. I term these strategies unmediated addresses to the reader, tales of individual triumph, and, finally, repetition.

Unmediated Address

A significant number of *Reader's Digest* articles contain direct appeals to the reader. Titles include "I" and "you," often in reference to what should be done. This is the most direct form of the interpellation of subjects.[70] The articles take on the apparent form of a two-way conversation of which the reader is a part. Rhetorical questions pepper the text and are especially common in subtitles, where they establish an active relationship between the reader and the topic. For example, an article on communist successes suggested to the reader that "If you believe that they were inevitable . . . *then you are already a Marxist.*" Another suggested that readers needed to "Face up to the blunt fact that you are now engaged in a real war." Some articles offered authentic voices: "I speak for the silent" and "Why I became an American."[71] Others form communities of readership: "we" or "Americans" versus "they." This I suspect has an effect similar to that of the readership communities Benedict Anderson describes as being so pivotal to the creation of the nation.[72] *Reader's Digest* scripts national concerns and goals; it therefore unites its reading community in national identification by explicitly addressing readers as Americans, consciously incorporating each reader into the imagined community of the United States.[73] In both cases, the community is of good citizens. The notion of citizenship presented by the *Digest* is reinforced in individual readers by positioning them within a larger community. The "appropriate" beliefs and behaviors for this group are articulated by the *Digest*. Readers are led to understand what is important with titles and subtitles like "All thoughtful people in the United States are worried about how to halt the spread of Cuban type revolution through

Latin America," "Are we worthy of our destiny?" and "We must face the facts about Russia."[74]

This process need not seem to be an *explicitly* nationalist one. Addressing readers as Americans with common identities, goals, hopes, and dreams is commonsensical or nonpolitical, what Michael Billig would term a "banal nationalism" in which images of American nationalism are continually reproduced in a completely unspectacular fashion. This does not mean that such banal forms of identification are unimportant: as a result of this everydayness and unquestioned nationalism, implicit feelings come to the fore when active nationalist support is required—at the extreme, in the face of war.[75]

Tales of Individual Triumph

Few *Reader's Digest* articles are purely programmatic. Most are substantiated by anecdote; they are illustrated with an example of someone who has struggled and succeeded. In connection with the construction of the good-citizen reader I described earlier, the individual in the anecdote is portrayed as a member of a group of citizens *just like the reader.* The suggestion is that all the reader would have to do, if he or she were faced with the same problem, is to take the same action. This rhetorical "proof" of solution positions the reader to accept the *Digest's* conclusions.

Reader's Digest renders the world and politics in such a way as to link success or failure to individuals' characteristics. These characters have become positive and negative role models, showing readers that the only way to cope successfully with a situation is to model their actions on those of successful others described in the magazine.

Repetition

The rhetorical structures of unmediated address and tales of individual triumph are reinforced by a third metarhetoric, repetition. The appearance of diversity of human experience in the magazine is merely superficial:

> Underneath the monthly anecdotal variation lies a profound structural unity. Each 'selected' piece cannot help but repeat the same language, procedure, technique and ideology as all other pieces. The same flag, climate and geology are cyclically reiterated on all apparently independent islands.[76]

If we accept the poststructural argument that the constitution of identity occurs not through a "founding act but rather a regulated pattern
or repetition,"[77] then the structural similarity of *Digest* articles has the
potential to serve to identify readers with the position carved out for
them. Richard Ohmann stated that by the beginning of the twentieth
century, monthly magazines represented the major form of repeated
national cultural experience for the American population.[78] Obviously,
magazines now have to compete with other forms of mass cultural ritual
(especially television), yet the loyalty of *Digest* readers suggests that the
magazine's role in the reconstitution of this version of American identity is still significant. For repetition to play a role in the reconstitution
of identity, however, the symbols and images that are repeated must be
accepted by the consumer; if they are not, repetition can actually undermine or challenge identity rather than enforce it. The unusually high
Reader's Digest subscription renewal rate marks it as a fairly constant
and generally accepted institutional presence in the reproduction of
American culture.

Subtitles play an especially important role in directing the reader
toward the *Digest*'s preferred reading of an article; illustrations further
reinforce the message of the title (see figure 5).[79] The title suggests the subject; the subtitle indicates why the reader should care about it. In some
cases, the subtitle is a quotation from another expert who acknowledges
the importance or truthfulness of the text that follows. Subtitles pro-
claim the article to be of vital importance ("Every American should read
these momentous disclosures," "The shocking proof...," "An article of
exceptional importance"), reinforce authority ("A distinguished historian reminds us...," "No army officer I know will question this"), and
enhance the truthfulness of what is to come ("A firsthand story," "The
facts," "An authentic report from eyewitness sources").

In the remainder of the book, I examine the content and form of
Reader's Digest articles in order to understand the role of this institution in the sociology of knowledge production in mainstream American
society.[81] This understanding has to be achieved at two levels. At the most
immediate level is the message the *Digest* produces in bringing together
the political and personal, world events and individual concerns. At a
deeper structural level lie the textual and rhetorical strategies the magazine mobilizes in order to convey this message.

Figure 5. Two *Reader's Digest* images underline the perception of Soviet power reported in the accompanying article (June 1955, p. 129; August 1956, p. 52).

Reader's Digest thus represents a site of knowledge production—in Anthony Giddens's structurationist terminology, an institutional locale[82] —a moment of fixity in the reproduction of politics where the concerns of individuals are actively articulated with global and national issues. Theorizing the media in this fashion can begin to allow a comprehension of how political issues can be made to resonate with individuals who have little or no direct material relationship to such issues. Readers become members of a group that they are confident is going through the same ritualistic identity affirmation as they are undergoing.

I have chosen to start before the Cold War to demonstrate how the *Digest*'s imagined geography of world politics came about. At this point, the USSR had not been established as America's Other, as it was to become during the Cold War. The "natural" association between communism and various discourses of alterity had not been made and alternative world orders were offered.

THE DEMIGOD
THAT WAS STALIN

By Robert Littell

So JOSEPH VISSARIONOVICH STALIN, praised in his day by Soviet press and politician as the "Wise Teacher and Father," the "Beloved of All Mankind," has become only three years after his death a bungler and a murderer. The "Hope, Light and Conscience of the World," whom hundreds of millions had been taught to revere as the "Glory of All Who Are Born With an Honest Heart," turns out, after reappraisal by his former partners, to have been vain, ignorant, cowardly, cruel, suspicious, malign, despotic, demented, monstrous.

Few outside Soviet Russia have realized to what superhuman, godlike heights Stalin had been raised by the very accomplices who are tearing him down today. The Stalin myth was the kind of obscene toadstool that can only flourish in the total darkness of a dictatorship.

His image was, of course, everywhere. There was one factory in Russia which turned out

CHAPTER THREE

Ambivalent Geography:
Writing World Orders, 1922 to 1945

Socialism is no longer in the realm of theory, no longer only a philosophy and a hope; whether for good or evil, it is an actuality.[1]

Reader's Digest was first published during a period in which the world order was in flux, especially as viewed from an American point of view. The United States had emerged from isolationism to enter World War I, and at the close of the second decade of the century, it was beginning to look like the inheritor of Britain's hegemonic role. Adding to this sense of global change was the impact of the Russian Revolution. With suggestions that revolution might spread across Europe, American commentators were unsure what the new Soviet state might offer. This anxiety was piqued by insecurity over the nature of emerging American society and the potential for the country to enjoy world leadership.

While these changes were restructuring the world system, American society was feeling the cultural impact of the processes of nationalization and consumption described in chapter 2. The middle class was rising to cultural hegemony, and this was reflected in the *Digest* by discussions of the country's rising patterns of consumption and the cultural implications of this new lifestyle. Along with the period's sense of prosperity came new anxieties: about the value of a culture based on consumption and materialism rather than "higher" ideals, and fear of loss of individual autonomy with the rise of assembly-line production and the growth of large business and labor, what Alan Trachtenberg has called the "incorporation of America."[2] These anxieties, as much as the actual changes occurring in the Soviet Union, affected the manner in which the new state was explained to *Digest* readers.

Although *Reader's Digest* in the 1920s was not presented with a blank map of world politics upon which to impose its own conceptual cartography, this period of instability did offer greater potential for speculation than did later years. The magazine, initially true to its role as a digest, reflected the tensions in American society, particularly those structured around the isolationism-interventionism debate, those between procommunism and anticommunism, and those focusing on the dangers of to imperialism if the United States rose to world leadership. The period from 1922 to 1945 thus offers a unique opportunity to understand how the new international presence of socialism was incorporated into the *Digest*'s sense of American identity, and how the *Digest*'s representation of the USSR became consolidated during the Cold War.

As this chapter's opening quotation suggests, the expansion of socialism and communism from the pages of Karl Marx into actual state practice in the Soviet Union presented America as the emerging global hegemon with a conundrum: the taken-for-granted model of capitalistic social and economic development faced competition. The unknown nature of the Soviet Union gave this new international power a threatening quality. Further, in contrast to the American Depression, tales of Soviet development reinforced perceptions of the dynamism of socialist social change. Although there were a number of "red scares" in America after World War I, they never came to much, and before the Depression, the middle class was comfortably well off. The threatened expansion of communism through Europe failed to materialize. It was not unusual for *Digest* articles to suggest that the ethics of citizenship in the USSR were compatible with those that it assumed underwrote American society. Yet many other articles in this period dwelt on the problem of America's coming to terms with this alternative project as the postwar world order came into focus and the United States and the USSR entered into serious conflict in their ascent to superpower status.

In short, the years following World War I constituted a key period in which *Reader's Digest* found itself explaining both America's changing world role and the part its individual readers as citizens should play in advancing American society. The *Digest* attempted to orient domestic society to the changing international sphere and at the same time to render the international in domestic terms for its readers. The magazine permeated its narration of American national identity with its under-standing of the character of world politics, simultaneously construct-ing the international through the mold of American national character. This brought home to its audience the significance of changes occurring around the globe.

In my examination of this first period of the *Digest*'s publication his-tory, I will consider in this chapter the intersection of the international, the national, and the personal.[3] First, I will examine the *Reader's Digest* portrayal of the Soviet Union, communism, and socialism between the magazine's initial issue in 1922 and the end of World War II.[4] Second, I will turn my attention to articles dealing with America's role in the world system and the historical reasons it presented as lying behind the coun-try's power and influence. Third, I will offer a discussion of the *Digest*'s vision of the American character. This section explores the magazine's presentation of the role of good American citizens and the dangers to the country of significant numbers of people deviating from these values. The chapter concludes with a reflection on the interconnections and interdependencies of these themes.

The Soviet Union, Communism, and Socialism

Socialism and communism were not entirely new concepts for Americans in the aftermath of World War I, yet the government of the newly formed Soviet Union obviously presented commentators with an "unknown" factor in world affairs. During the years following the end of the war, it appeared possible that other European countries would follow the Soviets' lead. This suggested that the Russian Revolution might not have been a unique event: societies more democratic than czarist Russia might follow in the Bolsheviks' revolutionary footsteps. Of more immediate concern, "red scares" broke out across the United States, though these potential threats to international and domestic order had diminished by the beginning of the 1920s, when *Reader's Digest* was established. Opin-ion was divided on whether the October Revolution was having positive or negative effects on the Soviet populace, and on what type of presence the Soviet Union represented. Drawing its articles from a wide variety of sources and perspectives, *Reader's Digest* initially was ambivalent toward this new international political presence.

During the 1930s, however, their country's evident economic vulnera-bility shook Americans' confidence in the strength of the economy and social institutions. *Reader's Digest* interpretations of the USSR became more wary, especially those by President Coolidge and others who saw the Depression as a product of foreign origins. Moreover, the strength and ideology of the Soviet state seemed to have the potential to have effects outside the USSR. Most worrying to the *Digest* was the threat that the rise of communist political practice might influence social relations *within* the United States itself. The magazine saw this most clearly in the labor movement, and in the ideological turn initiated by President Roosevelt's New Deal. The initial balance in the *Digest*'s descriptions of the Soviet Union began to reorient toward suspicion and hostility. Significantly, however, never during this early period did the Soviet Union become a fully developed alter ego separated from America as its conceptual Other; more lines of commonality than differences were still being described in articles about the USSR. With the outbreak of World War II, America and the Soviet Union were quite feasibly reconstructed as allies. At this point, the *Digest*'s coverage of the USSR became predominantly positive. This period lasted through the war; at its close, the representational tide turned again, this time decisively in the direction of the Manichaean world of the Cold War that I will describe in the following chapter. I will now explain *Reader's Digest*'s narration of the Soviet Union and communism between 1922 and 1945 more or less chronologically.

First Geographies

Articles published within the first decade or so of this initial period range from wholehearted support and even advocacy of the Soviet system to outright condemnation of it. The first two *Reader's Digest* articles on the Soviet Union, written in 1922, concentrated on the stark differences between prerevolutionary Russia and America to present the socialist revolution as a very *natural* response to the czarist aristocracy.[5] Both of these articles were structured around a natural-unnatural binary, and around a sense of the inevitability of human society's moving toward what is natural. The invocation of the "discourse of nature" in these first two articles was achieved through a number of contradictory tropes.

First, the articles suggested that, in fact, the Bolsheviks' actions were not fundamentally different from other human behavior. They insisted that all "human effort has been guided by trial and error, so today we find that the Bolsheviks, except for their desire for world revolution, are rapidly approaching other nations of Europe in their efforts."

Second, drawing upon centuries of Western representation of the significance of the Eurasian landmass, the articles claimed that the social environment of the Russian heartland made change all but impossible: it "was inevitable that [the Bolsheviks] should gradually apply the same autocratic methods that the Tsar had used." The article suggested that it was difficult for the Soviets to escape their "natural" draw toward autocracy, a characteristic that had typified Russian society under the czars.

Finally, these initial articles presented the communist system as the inevitable outcome of the conditions imposed by the czarist autocracy. They naturalized the Russian Revolution completely, saying that the Russians were "as much the victims of their social environment as is a chemical compound the result of the elements of which it is composed."[6] William Pietz has suggested that such representations of Soviet politics rendered the Bolshevik regime as nothing more than "traditional Oriental despotism plus modern police technology."[7] Orientalism is, of course, important as a long-standing conceptual apparatus through which first Europeans, then Westerners more generally, could understand the rest of the world.[8] Drawing upon this storehouse of familiar descriptions and metaphors presented great explanatory power. The parallels between the *Digest*'s description of the Soviet Union and Orientalist images became most clear once the Cold War became firmly established. The first two articles indicate the complexity and ambivalence of representations of the new Soviet country for this voice of American culture. The Russian Revolution was simultaneously shaped by the character of all human effort, the characteristics native to the Eurasian heartland, and the conditions established by czarist rulers. The result was the "natural" outcome of each of these processes and conditions, despite their apparent internal contradictions.

Subsequent *Digest* articles can also be seen to rely upon the discourse of nature either to applaud or to condemn the Russian Revolution and its longer-term implications. With the exception of the years 1922 to 1924 (when expansion of communism and socialism far into Europe looked quite probable to *Digest* writers)[9] and 1938 to 1941 (when a long-term alliance between communism and Nazism threatened) the former, positive position could be found in the majority of articles. *Reader's Digest* concentrated more on improvements in the lives of average Russians, the positive attitude of the Russian people to their government, and the honesty and equity of the new country than on critiques of the new system or fears of its consequences.

The issue of the spread of socialism or communism into other countries was handled differently from the positive and negative views of the new Soviet state. Those who welcomed the changes in the USSR thought that if further socialist revolutions were to occur, they would emerge "naturally" and spontaneously in countries that wished to replicate Soviet economic and social successes. Such articles tended to reinforce parallels between the United States and the USSR. This was *not* because the majority of people writing from this position believed in the necessity of a socialist revolution in the United States; on the contrary, most were sure that American values and morals—namely, equality and freedom—were very much akin to those advocated by the Bolsheviks. This implied that a Soviet-style revolution was simply not necessary in the United States. The *Digest* suggested that the hierarchy and class tension that caused the Russian Revolution were alien to the United States where "every worker [is] a capitalist."[10] As I will discuss later in this chapter, many articles of the time concentrated on the common interests of capital and labor in the United States, as if to weaken the power of revolutionary language. The *Digest*'s reappropriation of the terms was an attempt to demonstrate that in the United States there was not a great difference between the interests of capital and labor, even if these identities made sense elsewhere. This represented an apparently paradoxical rhetorical move for a country that was thought to be progressive: in America, conservatism was proposed as the alternative route to the results that required revolutionary change in Russia.

Another tactic used by pieces sympathetic to the new communist society was to highlight the differences between Soviet ideals and reality. *Reader's Digest* authors were of course aware of the negative connotations of the terms *socialist* and *communist* in American society and accordingly explained that the goals set by the Bolsheviks were unobtainable in real life.[11] Socialism and communism, argued the *Digest*, could not in reality move beyond the idealistic pages of the likes of Karl Marx. Charges of utopianism appeared in a few titles.[12] Other articles, however, sought to demonstrate that the USSR had deviated from the dogmatic letter of its laws.[13] In other words, despite the high-handed revolutionary rhetoric, in the day-to-day practice of politics, the Soviet Union was seen as very similar to America rather than as a radical departure from it. Russian communism was not presented as being incomprehensible to the *Digest*'s readers; the system had been domesticated for them by the magazine's editors. Although supportive of the USSR, this argument simultaneously challenged the Soviet way as a privileged social order, making it only one among many compatible states. This argument undermined attempts to offer socialism as an alternative to the American way.

At the same time, some *Reader's Digest* articles went even further in their praise of the new socialist state. In the early 1930s, two articles praised the openness and inspirational style of Soviet media, one comparing the *Evening Moscow* favorably to the *New York Daily News*.[14] Responding to criticisms of Soviet society, another *Digest* piece stated that "we are not called upon, nor are we morally in a position to interfere in Russia's internal life, or to pass judgment upon the acts of her rulers."[15]

This positive attitude toward the Soviet Union reached its zenith in articles on the popular origin of the revolution and continuing mass support for it, and an article that insisted on the necessity of American allegiance with the USSR to fight off potential aggressors. This latter piece went so far as to claim Russia as a vital geopolitical defense and physical protector of the United States:

> The strength of Russia under any kind of Government is a threat to all the physically possible enemies of the United States. Nothing could be more stupid than for the United States to make the way hard for the Russian government. Russia cannot by any conceivable possibility strike the US and it will always be a threat to a nation seriously opposing us.[16]

In an interview with Stalin, *Digest* regular Eugene Lyons attempted to counter dominant American characterizations of the ruler by focusing on his dedication and hard work. According to this article, recent changes in the USSR—including getting rid of Trotsky and other revolutionary figures—were not the result of "autocratic edits of Stalin" but were "hard fought victories in his defense of a daring program." Lyons asked why Russian affairs had been "so persistently distorted," giving as an example Stalin's being labeled a dictator (a term that he considered had been "band[ied]" about "much too freely"). Stalin told Lyons that dictatorship was impossible under the Soviet system, to which the *Digest* author replied that he had been "convinced [that Stalin] meant what he said."[17]

Another sympathetic piece that described with decided respect the aesthetics and naturalness of Soviet life warned that interference from "the outer world" might "choke" the new country.[18]

Those who were sympathetic to the Soviets often structured their narratives around notions of progressive change, arguing that the country was moving away from poverty and the inequalities of czarism. Versions of this argument suggested that however imperfect Soviet society might be, at least under the Bolsheviks the majority of people had some input into the running of their country. Many of these articles acknowledged the imperfections of the Soviet system and the fact that it had yet to reach American standards of living. However, Soviet society appeared to have great potential. The *Digest* believed that recognition of this potential accounted for the enthusiasm driving the Russian people's willingness to work hard in the USSR. Many *Digest* authors regarded this as a winning formula, looking upon it with respect and, no doubt, a degree of envy. In 1926 one author wrote about economic hardship in Russia but concluded that after his investigation into Soviet society he was "convinced that the average worker feels vastly better off than under the Tsar."[19] In an article commenting on sexual equality in the USSR, a Russian woman said, "I was not a revolutionist. But now that this thing has come, I am happier than ever before."[20]

One author praised the Soviets for putting workers before profits[21] and another saw the country's rapid industrialization as a positive and dynamic force or order with which to construct a new society, "a natural process ... crystallizing the chaos of the land into a world of time and factories and factory farms."[22] For still others, it was the general concept underlying socialist and communist society that would secure Russia a great future. One writer maintained that

> the struggle in Russia is permeated with romance. It may be that capitalism has more to fear from Russia's appeal to the idealism of the young than it has from economic competition.[23]

In general, this position advocated openness with the USSR. Contact between Soviets and Americans was regarded as being mutually beneficial, and Americans were advised to put an end to their scaremongering about the Soviets. A number of articles described the USSR's importance as a trading partner both to demonstrate American goodwill and because of the benefits of trading with such a large and apparently dynamic market. One *Digest* author suggested that in a communist country there would be no commitment to buy goods without sufficient funds to pay for them:

In capitalist nations, on the other hand, instead of this ordered control of imports, there exists a comparative anarchy.[24]

Articles written from a standpoint opposed to changes in Russia saw any spread of socialism or communism as a more aggressive affair, a change that would be propagated by Soviet leaders as a national power-political expansion and not an idealistic-conceptual move. Rather than being spontaneous expressions of the will of the people, socialist revolutions in other countries would have to be instigated by Soviet agents. Indeed, even in the Soviet Union—many authors writing from this position claimed—the revolution was not the expression of the will of the people. Instead, a small group of activists had grabbed power in Russia.[25]

During the years from 1922 to 1945, there was a prevailing sense of doubt over the intentions of the USSR. This explains the prevalence of articles that invoked threats to national security despite the otherwise quite favorable representation of the country.[26] The *Digest* suggested that America should be wary of the Russian state, even in its currently friendly guise. Drawing on Rudyard Kipling's famous imagery, one author suggested that "the bear of the Soviet Republic arouses sinister apprehension throughout the world, even when he comes walking with great sheaves of orders for foreign goods."[27] Another article accused Soviet social change of being detrimental to Russia by producing both "hordes" of homeless children "roaming over the republic" and women who have "fewer protections than a Stone Age mother."[28] With the continuation of narratives such as these and with the rhetorical use of socialism by the American political right to describe the New Deal, it appeared to the *Digest* that there was always the possibility that new red scares would erupt in America.

Despite articles such as this, Russia was never entirely "Othered" from America; commonalities were indicated in even the most negative articles at this time. For example, a highly critical article about religious persecution in Russia in the early 1920s claimed that individuals "of the highest manhood are being martyred in their thousands while the *rest* of the civilized world remains completely indifferent."[29] Soviet behavior was in no way condoned, yet the country remained with America as part of the "civilized world."

Around the mid-1930s, the inequalities of Soviet life were increasingly illustrated. The *Digest* suggested that the communist system was hypo-critical, since despite its rhetoric of equality, "inevitable class distinctions" had reemerged.[30] Perhaps surprisingly, this was not always represented as a negative change. Instead, it was seen as the inevitabilities of reality coming home to the utopian Soviet dream. The article "Russia Bows to Human Nature" portrayed the situation in the Soviet Union as being similar to that faced by other countries:

> Indeed, a main problem of the Soviet Union is to find how much individualism must be conceded in order to make a collective system work, just as the main problem in other countries is to discover how much collective control must be established to make an individualist system work.[31]

This article introduced a narrative that brought the Soviet Union into line with the capitalist project through a narrative that wrote it not as new and different but as a "perversion" of the "natural" (that is, American) way. *Reader's Digest* suggested that capitalism was alive and well in the USSR in the 1930s by ignoring definitions of capitalism that depended upon the relation of workers to the means of production. Instead, capitalism was simplistically redefined as the accumulation of industrial capital. This redefinition allowed the *Digest* to rewrite the Soviet system as capitalism in one sense: the "Bolsheviki have made one change only in the capitalistic system, and that is to bar out all the *ordinary capitalists* and gather the whole capital of the country into their own hands."[32] This *Digest* article continued to explain the unnatural result of this enforced redistribution:

> As soon as the *natural* and *ages-old* opposition between accumulated capital and political power breaks down, and one side engulfs the other, all the rights and liberties of the people are destroyed.... Russia, in truth, becomes a sort of inflated burlesque of the United States with all the evils of capitalism and none of the solid benefits.[33]

Certain characteristics were common to both the predominantly pos-itive and the more negative forms of explanation. Many articles presented the Soviet system as inherently inefficient and wasteful.[34] The Soviet people worked with incredible determination, either from authentic enthusiasm (a natural and commendable result) or through brainwashed misguidance (a manipulation of the natural social order) to achieve the new system. A 1931 *Digest* article critiqued the wastefulness of the Soviet system but nevertheless praised it for putting people before profit. The author approvingly quoted an American working in Russia who claimed that the Soviets were headed in the right direction and that their hard work would pay off in the long run.[35]

An interesting constant in all articles written during this period is in the representation of Soviet interpersonal relationships. One author reflected in 1926 that "communists persistently campaign against the reticences which have surrounded sex life."[36] Such policies were seen to have cleverly avoided the dangerous consequences that upstanding *Reader's Digest* readers might have expected from this secularized society. Despite the easier availability of divorce in the USSR, the magazine reported that marriage was still being strongly upheld. In 1926 it proclaimed that "there is no capital of Europe ... more free from open vice than Moscow."[37] Indeed, one *Digest* author quoted Lenin as a moral authority who advocated sexual fidelity despite his country's liberal sex laws.[38] Not surprisingly, given its prominent role in hegemonic American self-identity, religion was another important focus of attention within this period. Although Soviet disapproval and repression of religion was documented at length, *Reader's Digest* noted that the strength of Soviet character facilitated the preservation of religious values, particularly love. "Godlessness is the creed of communism," stated a 1932 article, "but not lovelessness."[39]

Certainly there appears to be recognition on the part of *Reader's Digest* of high moral standards in Soviet society. In fact, perhaps as a result of their recognition of high Soviet moral standards—higher even than those the *Digest* recognized in America at the time—some authors decided that morality could be taken too far, and that the USSR might be suffering from an unnatural excess of morals. The Soviet Union was sometimes portrayed as morality run riot, as the following movie synopsis reported in the 1930 article "Making Whoopee with the Soviets" indicates:

> The love interest in pictures is always subordinated to the character's obligations to the state and his trade union. I saw only one picture, "The Birth of a Man," that was built completely around a love interest. It told the story of a party member who still harbored what the Soviets term 'bourjui ideas' concerning his wife's obligations to him. When he learns

he is not the father of her child he sulks and chides her until she attempts suicide, from which he saves her. He asks her forgiveness, and the picture comes to a happy communist ending with the child in a public nursery while the mother and her husband return to the whirling steel wheels of industry, happy at serving their state by efficient labor.[40]

Linked to the moral aspects of society were the changes in gender relations in Soviet society. Improved women's rights were seen by the *Digest* as progressive, yet articles were also quick to announce that women's "natural" desire to look attractive had triumphed over zealous efficiency codes in dress: Soviet women demanded fashion in a regime where a "nose that didn't shine was practically counter-revolutionary" and every dress "was tested to see how efficiently it would serve its wearer in reaching for gadgets on a factory belt or throwing switches at a railway crossroads."[41] Lyons applauded Soviet men's chivalry and respect but insisted that the party "*orders* its men to be gallant, its children to be more considerate of their elders, and its families to remain unified."[42]

The *Digest* seemed to be suggesting that human nature would out despite attempts by the Soviet government to "improve" upon it, whether it was the "natural" human inclination to worship the Christian God, or the female inclination to wear attractive dresses and makeup. This was a reminder to readers that despite the changes made by the Soviet regime, some natural behaviors—common values and desires—would inevitably assert themselves, and rightly so. In a different context, Roland Barthes described this type of narrative as producing an image of the "great family of man." Here, the diversity of human life becomes but a superficial appearance and

> a type of unity is magically produced: man is born, works, laughs and dies everywhere in the same way ... diversity is only formal and does not belie the existence of a common mould.[43]

Seen with the aid of hindsight, then, perhaps the most significant commonality between articles written in the early years of *Reader's Digest* was that the USSR was not portrayed as a threat to the United States. There was a prevailing sense that the Soviet experiment would come into conflict with human nature and must, as a result, lose. Articles described the country's poverty, lack of resources, and inefficiency rather than its might. This position changed in the late 1930s, when a more aggressive stance toward the USSR took over.

Doubts

By the mid-1930s the tone of the majority of articles about the Soviet Union had taken a noticeably critical turn. Stalin was frequently compared to Hitler and Mussolini; all three were portrayed as dictatorial and authoritarian. Terror and brutality were central to most of the *Digest's* descriptions of Soviet life. Indeed, one contributor suggested that "violence is the very nature of the communist dictatorship." This, he continued, was confounded by the underhanded and power-hungry tactics of the Bolsheviks who grabbed power in 1917:

> the Russian communists gained power by stabbing a provincial government in the back on the very eve of a constitutional convention elected by universal suffrage of the Russian people—and, by the way, after the communist candidates had been defeated six to one.[44]

From this point onward, the strand of thought that had presented the Russian Revolution as an expression of discontent by "the people" disappeared from the pages of the *Digest*. Erasure of a previously significant conceptualization of the USSR was managed by the magazine through the language of decline; articles implied that although the Russian Revolution had initially adhered to the principles of socialist equality and improvement, there had been a move away from such purity of intent. Whereas a few years earlier, *Reader's Digest* regarded this move away from socialist values as an inevitable and indeed natural movement away from unrealistic goals, now the magazine presented it as a degeneration from commendable, albeit unrealistic, principles toward depravity. Inequalities had arisen, and it seemed that terror alone maintained the Soviet system. Almost as if they were explaining the magazine's change of attitude, two *Digest* writers suggested in 1938 that in their two-year absence from the USSR, "the Communists had staged a Second Revolution." Writing in the same year, another regular contributor claimed that he had "watched skepticism spread like a thick wet fog over Russia, soaking into the flesh and spirits of men and women."[45]

The charge of degeneracy among Soviet leaders was represented most clearly in narratives of show trials, which were described to *Digest* readers as fictitious affairs in which the "*guilt of the accused is never the chief or even an important issue.*"[46] Articles about successes and improvements in Soviet life became much rarer.

In the late 1930s, two significant changes in the representation of the Soviet Union in the *Reader's Digest* had become clear. First, the peacefulness of the USSR was questioned. In a condensation of articles from *Fortune* magazine, published in the *Reader's Digest* in 1937, a piece entitled "The Bear That Shoots Like a Man" spoke for the first time of a powerfully armed Soviet Union and asked whether the country wanted peace or war.[47] Until America and the Soviet Union fought as allies in World War II, the USSR was increasingly regarded as a threat to American security.

A second, and perhaps more subtle, change in the narrative construction of the Soviet Union was in the systemic terminology used to represent that country as different from America. Until the late 1930s, Soviet socialism offered an alternative system to American *capitalism*; the distinction between the two societies was primarily written as one of economic organization. In the late 1930s, however, Soviet socialism was reinterpreted as a system opposed to American *democracy*; in other words, the opposition between the two broadened in scale from the economic sphere to encompass social organization, indeed the mythic history of America's exceptionalism itself. The sense of difference between America and the Soviet Union was made more powerful.

The Depression had shaken American political culture, challenging not only the country's economy, but also the narrative of the American Dream, which promised that anyone could "make it." The Depression highlighted the fragility of this tale. Radical political theorist Mary Kaldor has suggested that the "experience of the depression was to shape profoundly the outlook of politicians in the post-war period." She cites Charles Kindleberger, who argued that the Depression was caused by the absence of a hegemonic power capable of guaranteeing a liberal international economy. What became apparent to politicians by the late 1940s was the need for an injection of government spending both in America and abroad in order to stimulate markets and to overcome the overcapacity of the American economy. Belief in the need for a strong global hegemon and the requirements of the booming American economy, Kaldor argued, both led directly to Cold War policies.[48]

The *Digest*'s emerging belief in a more fundamental difference between the Soviet and American characters was underscored by articles that merged communism with the other significant alternative to democracy of the time, fascism. Numerous pieces compared the Soviet system to Nazism, dismissing both as totalitarian dictatorships. The German-Soviet nonaggression pact of 1939 served in this narrative to illustrate the *total* commonality of interests (and intentions) between the two countries.

Reader's Digest's revision of its image of the USSR in the late 1930s was not confined to descriptions of new events occurring in the Soviet Union but was projected backward into Soviet history. The *Digest* produced new histories of the Russian Revolution and key figures within it. The revolution either became an act of the few, or, if the actions of the Russian people were acknowledged, it was suggested that the Bolsheviks had ruthlessly seized power from the masses who had fought the revolution in the name of freedom from the czarist aristocracy.[49] Lenin was presented as an intellectual and idealistic figure in the revolt, but now Stalin emerged as a power-grabbing incompetent who wrote his way into the revolution after the fact and, having taken control of the country, ruled with tyranny and terror matched only by that of another infamous Asian tyrant: Genghis Khan.[50] *Reader's Digest* claimed that it was the *Soviet* rewriting of history—in other words, state propaganda—that ensured the support of the long-suffering Soviet population. Tales of work in forced labor camps, show trials, and secret police replaced stories of struggle and human triumph. In "Socialism Doesn't Jibe with Human Nature," Max Eastman, "a former prominent socialist," suggested that socialism tried to escape from reality rather than adjust to it. Socialists' good intentions inevitably led to the bureaucratic stagnation and tyranny in evidence in the Soviet Union of the time.[51]

In addition to narrating Soviet decline, then, the *Digest* sometimes utilized a language of timelessness to represent the Soviet system. One author who wrote in the magazine in 1941 insisted that the Soviet system did not represent any improvement over the czarist regime; indeed, he stated, this "new Russia has its roots deep in the ancient ways of the Czarist state."[52] This association with Oriental despotism, added to Russian nationalism, overwork, surveillance, and government control over all aspects of life, led some *Reader's Digest* authors to conclude that the new communist system offered little to attract followers in other countries. This view was in strange tension with a larger number of articles that suddenly uncovered Stalinist plots to infiltrate and initiate revolutionary change in America.

American Entry into World War II

Reader's Digest's merging of communism and fascism into an undifferentiated oppositional presence to American—and, to a lesser extent, European—democracy, became somewhat problematic when Germany and the Soviet Union emerged as opposing rather than allied forces in World War II. Around 1942, the *Digest's* harsh tone toward the Soviet Union began to soften. Although articles no longer went as far as to promote the ends of socialism, a number of authors showered praise on Russian soldiers' bravery in the war.[53] More than one article favorably compared Russians to early American pioneers in spirit and resolve.[54] Stalin's leadership, although still recognized as harsh and severe, was once more rewritten, this time as nothing more than a personal style rather than the result of a deep-seated evil character. Most significantly for *Digest* writers, communism and Nazism were no longer two versions of the same system. *Reader's Digest* narrated Soviet totalitarianism as but a passing stage in the evolution toward full communism, whereas totalitarianism was seen as the ideological end point of Nazism and fascism.

The relationship between the United States and the USSR was presented as traditionally "one of friendship and goodwill."[55] In this revision of the Soviet Union, the *Digest* depicted the inherent *difference* between the U.S. and Soviet systems as an advantage to American security rather than a threat to it. The two systems were scripted by *Reader's Digest* as being so fundamentally different from one another that it was assumed that Stalin would realize that any attempt to promote a Soviet-style revolution in America would be futile. This logic led to the conclusion that the United States had nothing to fear from him. The representation of the USSR again became more balanced.[56]

Plans for the postwar world order were being drawn up in America long before 1945. Like many other commentators at the time, the *Digest* believed that the future world system would be built upon Soviet-American cooperation.[57] Indeed, a number of articles insisted that Russians wanted peace after the war, and some suggested practical measures to overcome political differences between the two states.[58] There was even acceptance of the requirements of geopolitical stability for the Soviet state:

> The Soviet government is as legitimately entitled to promote a regional system of Eastern Europe, composed of co-operative and well-disposed independent governments among the countries adjacent to Russia, as the

United States has been justified in promoting an inter-American system of the 21 sovereign republics of the Western Hemisphere.[59]

Nevertheless, attaining this new world order was not presented as either a simple or an automatic process. A number of authors suggested that ordinary Russian people were much like Americans and should be commended for their bravery in the war. In 1943, however, one indicated that bravery on the part of the people should not also imply accepting the validity of their political system and, less still, its aims. Russia still represented a powerful enemy of democracy, and the *Digest* felt that the true nature of the Soviet Union must be revealed so as to guard against the potential power it could wield over an unsuspecting America attempting to forge international peace after the war:

> Democracy is at a disadvantage in contact with communism because it is more civilized. It believes in tolerance, in free discussion, in popular enlightenment, in the value of life and the dignity of the individual, in honor and truth-telling and the principles of morality.[60]

This argument has run throughout the *Reader's Digest* account of the Soviet threat to the United States ever since.

Some articles insisted that after the war, relations between the United States and the Soviet Union would be dependent upon proactive action by America. Soviets would move into Europe only if America allowed Europe to remain in economic distress or if it allowed a power vacuum to become established there. This reasoning introduced the narrative of "preparedness" that came to dominate the *Reader's Digest* worldview throughout the Cold War and insisted that since the nature of the Soviet Union was inherently expansionary and aggressive, the country would take advantage of weakness. Thus America had to act to contain the USSR and to develop advanced weaponry to curtail the temptation for the Soviets to make the first move. Although this narrative encouraged preemptive action, it did not present America as aggressive. Since the narrative insisted that *by its very nature* the Soviet Union would act aggressively, America would only be *reacting* to an inevitable threat. This illustrates the importance of the predictive element of American geopolitics as presented in *Reader's Digest*. The lessons of history and the laws of geography have consistently been used by the magazine to present a case of inevitable Soviet aggression—that the Soviets will attack is already written by these timeless laws. In this case, the *Digest* wrote American preemptive action not as aggression but as a means of defense.

Distrust was reinforced by the apparent emergence of evidence of "an astute and unscrupulous [international communist] conspiracy to lay the groundwork for eventually seizing power in the United States and transforming this country into a totalitarian communist dictatorship."[61] *Reader's Digest* often claimed that in some ways, infiltration had already occurred: there had been, for example, communist influence of trade unions and New Dealers. Although their ideology might appear innocent, the *Digest* suggested that this was an illusion central to the communist mission of eventual takeover of key American institutions. The communist conspiracy was achieving its initial goals with the support of unsuspecting American citizens who were unaware of its real intentions.

At this point the magazine moved from predominantly using the term *Bolshevik* to using *communist.* Initially *Reader's Digest* demonstrated awareness of the differences between communists and socialists, and the Soviet divergences from orthodox Marxism. Thus, the magazine usually had used *Bolshevik* to refer to the Soviet form of communism. From the end of World War II onward, these distinctions were lost to produce a monolithic presence: communists. Essentializing "the" communist identity was important to the magazine's geopolitics during the Cold War, when the essentializing process was completed, and it intensified the magazine's feelings about American society. Stabilizing of the Soviet Other simultaneously entailed a more singular vision of America, its mirror opposite. What *Digest* readers should do, think, and aspire to was more closely reined in.

Over this initial period, then, *Reader's Digest* presented the Soviet Union in a number of different ways. To an extent, these representations were provoked by events occurring in the USSR, but the changes in terminology, and less subtle rewrites of history, demonstrate that the magazine's representations of the Soviet Union were also dependent on domestic American concerns and changing attitudes toward the role of the United States in the world system.

America and International Society

During its first years of publication, *Reader's Digest* rewrote America's role in the world through a mixture of traditional beliefs in the country's exceptionalism and destiny, and new confidence borne out by its newly emerging power and influence. Although this representation of the American Self should not be seen apart from the magazine's representation of the USSR, it is possible to categorize the two sets of articles at this time. By the end of World War II, however, it became impossible to separate *Reader's Digest* articles concerned with the Soviet Union from those on American mission and destiny.

Throughout the 1920s, *Reader's Digest* was more concerned with understanding the new identity and influence of America than it was with interpreting the implications of a communist state. This changed in the mid to late 1940s, when "America" became constructed largely through its opposition to the Soviet Union. As I did in the previous section, I will examine the *Reader's Digest* production of America's unique role in global affairs in chronological order.

America emerged from isolation to enter World War I, and by the end of the period covered in this chapter, Pax Americana had risen to replace Pax Britannica as the focal point of world order. Needless to say, policies of interventionism were not without critics within American political culture. Indeed, during the interwar period America retreated somewhat from international affairs.

Isolationism can be traced back to the period after the American Revolution when there arose a pervasive belief that to become involved in world affairs would be to compromise or undermine liberty, democracy, and the pursuit of happiness at home.[62] Later, the closing of the western frontier, coupled with expanding businesses and their influence in government, led to privileging of the necessity for new markets over desires for domestic protection. Furthermore, America's evident power and influence, tied to the pervasive influence of belief in the country's "Manifest Destiny" to export its democratic way of life, led many *Digest* writers to believe that it was morally wrong for the country to stay out of world affairs. Accordingly, the first issues of *Reader's Digest* contained rumination and debate over the future of America's role in world society. Although articles have since reflected occasionally upon the necessity and values of American interventionism (especially at the end of the Cold War), the close of World War II effectively represents the end of the isolationism-interventionism debate in *Reader's Digest*.

To some, interventionism reeked of imperialism. In many ways during the first decades of this century, as the United States was replacing Britain as global hegemon, it also was replacing Britain as "chief imperialist."

Reader's Digest entered into this debate with articles that pondered the implications of American intervention. Except during the Depression years, *Reader's Digest* consistently focused on America's role in the development of world order, particularly in the "American" hemisphere. The majority of articles dealing with this subject considered interventionism not a self-interested *choice* of policy, but rather a necessity created by the country's economic power. In the *Digest* in 1927, Walter Lippmann entreated Americans to come to terms with the fact that they had become a world power and should prepare themselves "for the part their power and their position compel them to play."[63] Moral influence was also seen as an inevitable outcome of America's unique geographical and historical location. A 1925 article proclaimed:

> As far as American policy is concerned, it is not a question of choosing between intervention and non-intervention. We are already pledged by our history and our geographical position, to the policy of intervention when certain contingencies arise. The question is whether we are willing to submit over acts of conscience of the world.[64]

Despite acknowledging the moral dangers of imperialism in articles such as "Are We Worthy of Our Destiny?"[65] the *Digest* concluded in characteristically optimistic fashion that, if Americans remained vigilant and unselfish, U.S. intervention would lead to greater development of world society. In the late 1920s, the *Digest* was intrigued by the ascent of America but wrote it as an innocent path to power, drawing heavily on narratives of coming of age. A 1926 article suggested that America "cannot turn back [to isolationism]. We must go forward facing our destiny."[66] Another agreed, insisting that the country was "no longer a virginal republic."[67] A version of Henry Luce's famous "American century" article was reproduced in the *Digest* in April 1941. This piece explained perfectly the magazine's view of the way in which American domination would differ from previous great societies:

> Unlike the prestige of Rome or Genghis Khan or 19th-century England, American prestige throughout the world is faith in the good intentions as well as in the ultimate intelligence and strength of the American people.[68]

This naturalization of American power allowed *Reader's Digest* to overcome its anxiety about whether imperialism might contradict the moral values of equality underwriting the country's identity.

The invocation of nature and morality thus changed the discursive basis of the *Digest's* world geopolitics. The magazine could script geopolitical and international relations not as power-political relations between countries in which disputes were over control of territory or resources, but as an inevitable clash of worldviews. In this narrative, "America" was projected beyond its state territory to become a transcendental force without necessary borders, an embodiment of a certain morality that, merged with the rhetoric of Manifest Destiny, could make necessary the extension of its influence beyond American borders.[69] "To denounce American civilization," proclaimed the *Digest* in 1927, "is to denounce not a country but a way of life."[70]

The grand teleological narrative of Manifest Destiny was naturalized and legitimated in the pages of *Reader's Digest* through a comparison of America to classical societies whose impact on the development of society stood as a model for what the magazine felt the United States could offer the world:

> The art that was Greece and the legal temperament that was Rome reflect the idealism of great peoples who had something within their national souls which became the common heritage of humanity. This is the supreme test of a truly great people.... No fear need be felt that the historians of the future will pronounce national humanitarianism—the will to disinterested human service—the original national contribution of the United States to the higher idealism of the world.[71]

This classical allusion would periodically reappear in the pages of the magazine. The *Digest* celebrated America's rise to hegemonic status, but it is also possible to read fear of degeneracy into these narratives. America's turn at world leadership—following the empires of Greece and Rome, and, more recently, Britain—was destined; the *Digest* wondered if the degeneration that had come to previous empires would also come to the United States. Was there a way to avoid the decline that had brought down America's predecessors? In the following section I will explore some of these imperial anxieties.

The Individual in American Society

Next I will consider the *Reader's Digest* narrative of the individual's role in American society: the magazine's presentation of American society; the responsibilities of good American citizens, and the dangers of neglecting these responsibilities.

In the 1920s in particular, there was a concentration of articles that focused on the dynamics of American society and the individual's place and potential within it. The magazine also discussed the differences between democratic and socialist societies—not in an abstract way, or purely with reference to the distanced case of the Soviets, but in such a way as to explain potential changes that socialism or communism would introduce to the reader's own way of life.

Articles argued the impossibility of realizing true socialism because it was assumed that socialism did not reflect the "natural" order of civilized human society. In socialism individuals are seen as equal, and thus should all be equally provided for by society. Equality was a theme central to American ideology as espoused in the *Digest*, yet the magazine did not try to present America of the 1920s as a society in which all individuals enjoyed the same standard of living, wealth, or access to power and resources. This did not, however, contradict the values of individual equality that *Reader's Digest* held to be of such great importance to American social organization because inequalities arose from differences created by nature. One early article, "Nature's Inexorable Law—Inequality," suggested:

> The great difficulty of realizing socialism is that not only is wealth unequally distributed, but mentality is unequally distributed. Until the socialist can find a way of equalizing mentality his other attempts at equalizing will be futile. . . . Equality or sameness would not only be the shortest road to boredom but the means of impoverishing a nation or race.[72]

The *Digest* saw America as embodying a more natural form of social organization than, for example, aristocratic Europe or socialist Russia. In contrast to the inherited wealth and status *Reader's Digest* saw in the "old" nations of Europe and the political dogma it saw in the Soviet political system, American democracy was presented not as idealistic, but as practical; quite simply, democracy in America stood for "institutionalized self respect" and "a decent regard for the average man."[73]

It could be argued that attention to American democracy in the *Digest* heightened at this time as a result of the particular form of democracy introduced by the emergent culture of consumption. The turn of the century was a period in American history when older forms of authority and prestige were increasingly replaced with the distinction that could be achieved through consumption. *Reader's Digest* celebrated this market-based democratic culture but sometimes regarded the very materiality of this culture as something of a problem. A widespread belief paralleled or implicitly drew upon Christian millennialist arguments that amorality and the "sophistication, irresponsibility, materialism and other results of luxury and wealth," or a "crisis in character,"[74] had emerged from the modern conveniences that American technical developments offered its citizens to make their lives easier. America had the power, wealth, and resources to be a great civilization, but had it "matured" sufficiently to contribute to the development of world culture? A number of articles outlining American wealth and industrial culture reasoned the materialist focus:

> But, after all, is not the material more fundamental? What boots it if we produce a Shakespeare if there are millions living in misery and degradation?[75]

Despite displaying some distaste for the Soviet system and the continued potential for renewed red scares, at this point the *Digest* did not consider socialism and communism to be serious threats to American culture and society. Indeed, although accepting the American Communist Party as an organization that forced business to face "its most glaring inequalities," a condensation from *Fortune* published in *Reader's Digest* in 1935 suggests that America need not fear a communist revolution:

> The American dream of Poor Boy Makes Good leads even the most underpaid drudge to consider himself a potential millionaire. This makes it hard to arouse him to a Marxian consciousness.[76]

Other articles stressed the rejection of class warfare in the United States and point out that the vast majority of Americans distance themselves from class opposition by declaring themselves to be middle-class.[77] Drawing heavily on the prevalent belief that America represented a classless society, one *Digest* author explained that the labor struggle in America *could not* lead to Soviet-style changes because "part of everyday human grievances, rather than 'class war,' is American labor struggle."[78]

During this period, *Reader's Digest* can be seen to formulate what Dana Polan has termed a "discourse of the common person," more commonly known as the American Dream.[79] This is an explanation of the averageness of the American citizen, a social structuring that aims to avoid both the aristocratic hierarchies that the *Digest* perceived to structure European society of that time and the relentless homogeneity that in the *Digest*'s view the Soviet Union offered its citizens. The discourse of the common person is relayed thus: every average citizen is an individual, distinct from others because of this unique individual quality. This array of individuality existed within American society, within which there is equality of *opportunity* for all. Thus, the fact that some people do better than others in American society is not attributable to a fault inherent in the social order but is a result of different talents distributed by nature. It is this end-product differentiation that made America so dynamic, so the story goes; all individuals start off with equal opportunity to make the best of their talents, and their efforts are justly rewarded:

> The mediation of all Americans by a shared quality of averageness thus paradoxically allows the possibility of hierarchy and a division of labor in the narrative: if everyone becomes important through a particular talent, it becomes necessary to maintain social stratifications while claiming that these stratifications make no judgment on specific roles.[80]

Perhaps not surprisingly, given DeWitt Wallace's rise to riches, apparently through his own hard work, ingenuity, and persistence, this narrative is strongly represented in *Reader's Digest* from this early period through to the present. Almost every issue has included at least one story that recounts the rise of an average individual (described to seem to be *just* like the reader) who parlayed his or her natural talents into success.

This is not to suggest, however, that *Reader's Digest* never explored the possibility of a communist turn in America. The fear of communist influence began to reemerge with increasing power after World War II. The *Reader's Digest* narrative suggested that the good life derived from material benefits had made Americans soft, submissive, and thus dependent upon decisions made by others—most damaging of all, by the government. Only one author made a direct connection between such softness and the femininity of American culture, but descriptions using concepts of softness and submissiveness certainly invoke stereotypical characteristics of women.[81] This becomes more significant in the Cold War when the *Digest* was quick to write for itself a strong, warriorlike position with regard to the Soviet threat; in this stance, there is no room for feminine traits.[82]

President Roosevelt's New Deal, with its policies aimed at strengthening government powers, posed a potential threat to American individualism. As a result, initial *Digest* articles on the New Deal asked directly whether it represented a turn toward socialism. At first the answer was no, the New Deal represented a new (or last) chance for capitalism, combining capitalism's efficiency with social responsibility. As one author put it in "Is the New Deal Socialism?":

> The broad policies of the New Deal inject into the framework of capitalism certain principles of social responsibility which the "economic man" of traditional capitalism did not recognize.[83]

Another author writing in the same year—1934—feared that the logical end point of the New Deal would be socialism but remained optimistic that the lessons of American history indicated that this social change would be interrupted if it went too far.[84] Regular *Digest* contributor John Adams agreed, suggesting in 1934 that the broad-scale planning and control required by the New Deal was opposed to the individualism inherent in the American character.[85] He took this argument further still four years later, suggesting that capitalism is an innate feature of human character. He concluded that "the desire for private property, gain and personal advancement is so widespread as to indicate a fundamental instinct in man."[86]

Other *Reader's Digest* writers were not so confident in the resilience of American capitalistic culture. One stated that of "all forms of relief, government relief is the most dangerous and debilitating" because people do not work but expect the government to provide for them.[87] Fears of the effects of "big government" began to take up more space in the *Digest*, and there was a rapid increase in articles concerned with the American way and character, particularly the continuing strength and autonomy of the individual in the *Digest*'s view of "real" American culture.

In the 1920s, the *Digest* had recognized labor unions as an important counterbalance to the power of capitalists; from the mid-1930s onward, it perceived organized workers' actions as a threat to American individualism. Now, instead of being an integral part of the market, organized labor challenged its "natural" workings. The number of articles concerned with labor action increased markedly. Militant unionists were regarded as a minority who had grabbed trade-union power and whose ideological activities would harm the (innocent) remainder of society by threatening the natural balance of power between capital and labor.

A 1937 article was titled "It *Can* Happen Here."[88] Excessively powerful union leaders, the article claimed, were the instigators of the Russian Revolution. "The American people," it asserted, "do not yet realize that they are in the first stage of a revolution."[89] Communist infiltration was not intended to "secure better living conditions for the strikers but solely to disrupt the productive process and lead the strikers into clashes with the authorities."[90] Disruption was masquerading as progressive change. Indeed, the *Digest* did not fear a change of leadership springing from the American people; rather, it assumed that any move toward totalitarian rule would be the result of Americans' being misled by socialist leaders. Fear of unintentional change engendered dozens of articles in the late 1930s and early 1940s elucidating the common interests of American labor and management, repeatedly underscoring the necessity for cooperation. The vast majority of articles concerned with labor disputes emphasized that in America the interests of capital and labor were identical. Drawing from the narrative of the American Dream, *Reader's Digest* suggested that American society did not work on zero-sum principles: one person's success raises the whole of society by offering possibilities to other workers. Strike breakers were depicted by the *Digest* not as good, conscientious citizens but as gangsters brought in under the pretext of destroying the morale of strikers.[91] Articles implored readers to promote cooperation between labor and management, and to keep trade unions focused strictly on economic rather than political concerns. In articles titled "Every Worker a Capitalist" and "Where Workmen Are Capitalists," cooperation and mutual advancement were portrayed as the primarily pillars of capitalism in America.[92]

The early part of the twentieth century was a period of fairly intense social, economic, political, and cultural change in the United States. Most important was the rise in consumerism and a concomitant increase in the average person's standard of living. Alongside this change was a rise in corporate control of American society; with Fordist production techniques, mass consumerism, and the organization of labor came a loss of individualism and autonomy.[93] The political world was increasingly mediated for the average citizen, and the pages of *Reader's Digest* illustrated a sense of anxiety over the loss of self-determination. Within this anxiety over the presence of a socialist way, these parallel losses of individual determination must have struck some as ominous. A number of commentators have also pointed to the effects of immigration on hegemonic American culture at the time: many Americans feared a loss of identity and values with increased immigration from countries outside northern Europe.[94]

Robert Dallek has argued that with the apparent success of the New Deal at the end of the Depression, Manifest Destiny outweighed the immediate concern for security, so that Americans projected Wilsonian universalism into the international arena.[95] The Depression, however, had provided evidence of the fragility of the American economy; many believed it to have stemmed from abroad and so demanded protectionism. On the other hand, the increasing reach of new military technologies made isolationism seem less and less possible, let alone attractive, in the middle of the century. *Reader's Digest* was worrying about challenges to American sovereignty in matters of economy and security, and at the same time it feared a loss of integrity of the "boundaries" of the autonomous individual. The magazine was offering a role for individual Americans as well as scripting a role for the United States in the post–World War II world order. Thus, alongside articles discussing the country's security were articles about the differences between American and Russian society: the *Digest* reader was bombarded with the message that the Russian Revolution was a revolution against the *Russian* aristocracy, not workers versus capitalists per se. The *Digest* often suggested that the USSR inevitably would move toward the American way; a revolution was unnecessary in America, where no class distinctions distorted the natural workings of society.

The effects of the Depression, added to fears of the negative influence of prosperity on American character, produced anxiety in *Reader's Digest* over the American population's imperviousness to socialism. As a result, the magazine attempted to distinguish the utopian goals of the Russian Revolution from the hard realities of everyday life in the USSR.

Nevertheless, at the close of World War II, even *Reader's Digest* did not yet write geopolitical relations as a simple ideological dualism. Before the war, it was not clear in the pages of the *Digest* whether it would be the imperial power of Britain or of socialist Russia that might oppose America at the close of conflict.[96] With the benefit of hindsight, we can see that America's projection of liberal internationalism might inevitably have run up against the Soviet Union's alternative international political-economic presence and find it to be an impenetrable Other.

The importance of the *Reader's Digest* account of this period lies in the manner in which it brings together the domestic and international spheres. Articles on personal issues and on national and global events, appearing side by side, reinforce the impression of important links between these "levels": individual readers had an important role to play in the preservation of American democracy. This provision of a political role for the reader is an important effect of the *Digest's* mediation of the political process. For present-day readers, the *Digest* of the 1920s, 1930s, and 1940s provides insight into the ways in which domestic concerns were projected onto international issues.

With the emergence of the Cold War proper, the linkages between conceptual scales become so tightly woven as to virtually eliminate differences between them; the international becomes the personal, the personal becomes domestic security, and danger is everywhere. At this point, the boundaries between the *Digest's* narratives on domestic affairs, international relations, and conditions in the Soviet Union all but dissolve.

CHAPTER FOUR

The Beginnings of Cold War

If the interwar period could be seen as one in which *Reader's Digest* created an ambivalent political geography, then the period that followed the end of World War II would be characterized by a single-minded obsession with the threat that communism posed to the "free world." In this chapter I explore the ways in which the *Digest* reconstructed the Soviet Union, and communism more generally, as the single alter ego of America, and attempt to explain how this representational shift to an extreme image of the Soviets as Other and evil could be made reasonable and acceptable to the magazine's readership.

The Cold War is generally agreed to have begun immediately after World War II, even though its precedents can be traced much further back in the history of the relations between the American state and communism. Certainly the sheer volume of *Digest* articles on the Soviet Union and communism from 1946 onward would verify this as a starting point (see figure 6). In contrast, there are a number of possible definitions of the extent of its duration. Fred Halliday has written that the "first" Cold War finished in 1953 with, on the one hand, the death of Stalin and the resulting relaxation of Soviet domestic and foreign policies, and, on the other hand, the election of President Eisenhower, who promised to end the Korean War;[1] the following phase of "oscillatory antagonism" lasted until 1969.[2] My analysis of *Reader's Digest*, however, suggests that for this particular voice of America, the unswerving binarism of the Cold War was unsettled only by the public Sino-Soviet split in the wake of the Soviet signing of the 1963 nuclear test ban.[3] After the events of 1963, the enemy of the *Digest*'s conception of Americanness divided in two distinct ways. First, and most obviously, the unitary communist threat of world domination was delivered a significant blow with the breakdown in Sino-Soviet relations. As tensions mounted along the Chinese-Soviet border, the specter of communism clearly fractured and visibly weakened. Second, and more subtly, the *Digest* faced a more insidious threat to its binary scripting of international political praxis: the threat of détente. The "weakening" of American opposition to communism—backing down from the threat of "total war" to accept the possibility of peaceful coexistence—represented a movement of great significance to the magazine. The dis-order that communism had inflicted on international society was not to be eliminated, but to be allowed to exist, albeit in a contained state. The triumphalism of American Manifest Destiny overcoming the Soviet threat to the onward march of freedom and democracy was seen to weaken into an acknowledgment of communism, contained within the sphere of influence of the Soviet state. Both of these themes are central to the narrative of international politics during the period of détente from the mid-1960s to 1979.

But contrary to Halliday's observations, the Cold War truly ended for the *Digest* only with the eventual dissolution of the Soviet Union, and even since then, commentators have recognized a continuation of "Cold War metaphysics," even in the absence of Cold War geopolitics.[4] The

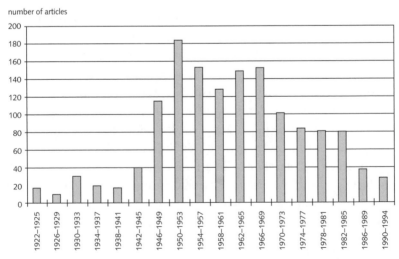

Figure 6. Number of articles about the Soviet Union or communism in the *Reader's Digest*, 1922–1994.

Soviet-communist Other of the Cold War has remained a key anchor in the magazine's narration of international events since the end of World War II and, as I will explain in this chapter, constructed the Soviet Union and communism as the location of America's alter ego and danger.

This chapter is concerned with the rise of the USSR to the position of absolute Other. In the next two chapters I will consider the effects of détente and then the return to extreme Cold War geopolitics in the 1980s under the leadership of Ronald Reagan. In chapter 7 I will analyze the impact of the ending of this binary geopolitics with the formal end to the Cold War.

The "First" Cold War: Othering the Soviet Union

Although *Reader's Digest* had been of growing significance in American popular culture for two decades, its presence became most strongly felt at the height of the Cold War. In many ways it was one of the initiators of American opposition to the Soviet Union as a "Cold War." The *Digest* both picked up on popular American anxieties regarding the postwar world order and helped to maintain popular anticommunism throughout the Cold War years.

No radically new representations of the Soviet Union were introduced to readers after the end of World War II. Instead, there was a silencing of descriptions that had previously been more sympathetic to the *potential* of changes occurring in the USSR and other countries that were undertaking a transition to communism. *Reader's Digest* now presented a more uniformly negative picture.

The magazine's change in representation of the communist system was explained as the result of the Soviets' previous ability to hide the brutality and cruelty of their system from global scrutiny. Propaganda was mentioned in the vast majority of pieces on communist systems, and *Digest* authors portrayed Soviet citizens as slaves whose plight had previously been hidden from view by Soviet leaders pulling down the Iron Curtain to hide their crimes.[5]

With the onset of the Cold War, ambivalence over the origins and potential of the 1917 Russian Revolution disappeared into the rigid ideological binary of freedom versus totalitarianism. Although a 1951 *Digest* article claimed that the Russian Revolution "was a tremendous and spontaneous popular uprising, the end result of a century-old struggle for emancipation," it further disclosed that at the time of the revolution, the Bolshevik leaders were not to be found in Russia.[6] According to the magazine, it was only after the Russian people had chosen a new government at the ballot box that the Bolsheviks returned and rushed in to seize power by force.[7]

Narratives describing the emancipatory potential of the uprising against the czars rapidly faded into the background as descriptions of famine, terror, and gulags came to the fore. The *Digest*'s belief in the unnaturalness of the Soviet system was underscored by articles claiming that despite the *natural* optimism of the Russian people, they were fearful for the future.[8] Thus *Reader's Digest* increasingly wrote the Soviet system as one that lacked public support. One train of thought in the magazine insisted that Soviet morale would drop further if the Soviet population was to hear of conditions in America.[9] This presented the United States with a simple Cold War tactic: instead of posing as an aggressive presence—which would be against the "American way" and more importantly, would prove to be impractical in this situation—America should continue to demonstrate and export the principles of democracy. These principles alone, the *Digest* claimed, would ensure its triumph over the USSR. This clearly demonstrates the importance of ideas in the postwar era: "In the field of ideas," claimed the *Digest* in 1947, "freedom is the atomic bomb."[10]

Before the end of World War II, Soviet territorial ambition was often explained away by the *Digest* as the Soviet state's understandable anxious desire to protect its borders and maintain a sphere of interest in a world mostly wary of its existence. The Soviets' postwar moves to territorial acquisition, however, proved to be too much for this model and were interpreted in the new geopolitical context as inherently threatening, illustrating a blatantly colonial impulse on the part of the USSR.[11]

At this time *Reader's Digest* forged an exclusive link between communism and the USSR. From this point onward, the Soviet Union represented the origin of communism. No longer a mere political ideology, communism was now presented as an essentially *Russian* ideology that disguised Soviet national expansionary tactics beneath its utopian claims. The *Digest* reader could be forgiven for mistaking Karl Marx for a player in the Russian Revolution, so often was he lumped together with Lenin and Stalin as a perpetrator of this demonic Russian ideology.[12] Here the *Digest* can be seen to be drawing upon George Kennan's contention that the Soviets' use of Marxism was simply a rationalization for their own expansionary urges: "Marxism was only a 'fig-leaf' of moral and intellectual responsibility which cloaked their essentially naked instinctive desires."[13] This solidified the *Digest's* transition from capitalism as the opposition to Soviet communism, to democracy, and finally to anticommunism per se. Now there was total opposition between Americans and Soviets; readers had nothing in common with the Russians.

Through repetition of this story of communism's origins, a new "communist" identity was formed in the *Digest*. The origins were power-political ones, but the Russians' continued use of Marxist ideology was simply a strategy to conceal national-expansionary tactics. Repetition of this narrative served to erase earlier accounts and earlier explanations of origins as the will of the people shaking off their aristocratic rulers.

Articles underscored this national origin of communism by highlighting the unnaturalness of communist doctrine when it was implemented in other places. One piece suggested the continued validity of Sir Bernard Pares's 1832 reflection that "Russia could only hold Poland by uncivilizing her."[14] A 1947 article proclaiming "democracy's last chance in Latin America" argued that communists deviously disguised their antireligious attitudes in order to gain support.[15] Other articles described how certain leaders had masked their communist leanings until they took control. This clearly demonstrates the *Digest's* moral geography, which constructed a cartography of good and evil for its readers and illustrated the spaces within which future battles between these forces would be fought.

Having eliminated its earlier ambivalence toward communism, *Reader's Digest* now constructed it as an alter ego for postwar America and the world order it sought to impose. First, the magazine constructed an exclusive communist identity; then it naturalized this different identity. I will explore each of these rhetorical strategies before discussing how the magazine's representation of the USSR remained credible in the face of inconsistencies in its construction of its Other over the years.

The Communist Identity

The effect of the *Digest's* rewrite of the origin of communism was to establish it as an absolute identity. The magazine displayed a belief in the existence of what might be called "ontological communists." In the previous chapter, I described *Digest* narratives in which people either had communist leanings or had suggested possible combinations of communism and capitalism in various social reforms. During the Cold War period, it was not possible, in the eyes of the *Digest*, to be sympathetic to any communist belief without actually *being* a communist. Identities became singular and exclusive: a person had to be one identity or the other, not a combination of them. This offered a lesson to readers and illustrates the magazine's desire to offer normative visions in addition to describing current events.

The desire to know whether or not a person was essentially a communist or a democrat propelled many *Digest* articles, as it had driven the red scare trials in America. Articles about new leaders coming to power around the world posed urgent questions about their political-ideological leanings, paralleling the biographical scrutiny of the American trials.[16] Mere association with known communists would be enough to color the characters of these leaders a deep scarlet hue. The effects of this drive to identify must surely mirror the disciplinary regime of modern subjectivity through sexual revelation and identification, articulated so eloquently by Michel Foucault.[17] In other words, just as Foucault described modern society's obsession with authentic sexual identification, during the Cold War the *Digest* believed that at some "deep" level, the political identity of an individual was either "democrat" or "communist."

The *Digest* attributed the singular communist identity not only to individuals; countries too were essentially either communist or free. It was at this historic juncture that the concept of the three worlds was introduced to world political-economic discourse.[18] Many *Digest* articles of the time scripted the Third World as an empty space of superpower conflict whose fate was to become developed "naturally" in accordance with American principles or "perversely" along Soviet lines. Even when countries had declared their nonalignment, the *Digest* suspected that they must secretly adhere to one systemic principle or the other.

Reader's Digest presented its articles as being of even more immediate personal importance to its readers now that discerning communist from noncommunist identity was a concern. Sometimes the linkages were spelled out blatantly, as in an article that described how, for the author, "communism was the poison that was to canker and destroy our marriage."[19] More frequently, because of the ontological status of communism, the earlier divisions of political scale I have described simply did not exist in articles during the first two decades of the Cold War. The communist peril was writ large in articles that explained the danger to society if individuals did not act as responsible citizens. Similarly, articles that described events in the Soviet Union or geopolitical relations between the superpowers rarely failed to mention what the reader could personally do: write to politicians, send article reprints to friends and colleagues, or simply stay alert.[20]

Increased vigilance was necessary because of communist conspiracies to take over the world. Communists apparently were preparing to attack U.S. government institutions whenever "the interior situation of the United States is suitable for the attack."[21] One author quoted a communist in the United States who stated that socialism would "never come about by the ballot box."[22] A good citizen needed to stay informed not only to vote wisely, but also in order to be alert to the communist threat:

> The unsuspecting American imagines that we are safe from socialism because he knows the people will never vote for it. But socialism can be put over by a small minority.[23]

The *Digest* suggested that communists the world over would take advantage of those who were ignorant of their nature and intentions:

> The power of the Soviet Union, and particularly the Soviet Communist Party, is due to the fact that, while in a sense the Soviet state has moved into a power vacuum in Europe and Asia, the Soviet Communist Party has moved into a moral vacuum in the world.[24]

Intensification of the narrative of communist takeover as a result of ignorance led ultimately to the introduction of the concept of "total war." Communism could never be truly defeated; because of its insidious tactics, its propaganda, and its utter ruthlessness, it would always be ready to reestablish power if Americans dropped their guard.

Communism had made "the morality of war *its permanent single standard*," so that war with the USSR would be "*inevitable* the moment we [Americans] become weak."[25] Americans had to remain vigilant because "for Russia anything is a weapon."[26] Indeed, one 1961 article proclaimed "WORLD WAR III HAS ALREADY STARTED!"[27] *Reader's Digest* had established America as the space opposite to that of communism, so the United States would always be on the receiving end of communist threats: "This country is the Number One target of the communist espionage apparatus."[28] This struggle was usually written in dramatic, even apocalyptic terms: the two systems were "competing for the loyalty of the human race,"[29] so that "either we must correct the imbalance caused by our approach ... or we might just as well write this country off the books."[30] Americans were uniquely placed as the last line of defense of freedom:

> Can we survive? At no time in the history of our nation has this question had more urgent meaning.... A successful attack on us might give the merciless communist leaders control of the world in a week.[31]

In retrospect and taken out of context, these assertions seem rather hysterical and overwrought. The concept of encirclement by enemies, however, has a long history in America. The imperial frontier narrative of heroic pioneers surrounded by "savage" Indians is central to self-imaginings of American national identity, and is often replayed in Hollywood Westerns. The Cold War narrative simply replaced native peoples with Soviets and communists.[32]

Naturalizing the binary of good U.S. system versus bad USSR system—via "objective" language and "common sense"—legitimated the demonization of communism, and especially the USSR.

The Naturalization of Difference

The discourse of the natural runs throughout *Reader's Digest* representation of the Soviet Union and communist systems. During the Cold War, this discourse was used to an even greater extent to render American activity innocent in the face of Soviet ideological practice. The languages of geopolitics, disease, and perversity all invoked the natural-unnatural binary in such a way as to reinforce the American moral high ground in interpreting international political events and gave credence to interpretations that otherwise might have appeared to be hopelessly biased.

Geopolitics

Orthodox geopolitical concepts depend upon apparently nonideological use of geographical process and elements. Geopolitics can thus be regarded as a myth in the sense in which Roland Barthes employed the term in his study of modern society.[33] As an apparently purely factual argument, geopolitics would be unaffected by political bias, cultural norm, or historical situation. The laws of geopolitics could thus be regarded as ahistorical—as rules that could be extracted from context and applied to situations as different as the Peloponnesian Wars and the invasion of North Korea. Furthermore, drawing upon these apparently immutable laws, geopolitical arguments in *Reader's Digest* could be used to predict future situations.

The use of geopolitical reasoning in *Reader's Digest* was intended to *naturalize* arguments by explaining issues via geographical *facts*. This use of geopolitical ideas as commonsense knowledge was seen as incompatible with ideology or political bias. Although during the Cold War there was a distinct increase in the number of *Reader's Digest* articles that relied upon traditional fixed-form or fixed-process geopolitical concepts, the term *geopolitics* was rarely used in the magazine. I would speculate that the reason for this omission was the association of *geopolitics* with German *geopolitik*. In the case of *Reader's Digest*, the association with Nazi Germany per se would not be the only problem with using the term, but more generally the *ideological* underpinnings that the term *geopolitik* might conjure up. When the term was used, it was applied only to communist political geography, as if to reinforce the idea that only communist reasoning was ideological.

Geopolitical arguments were especially useful in conveying the significance of Soviet expansion into countries that previously had little international importance. The broader implications were made manifest in the geographical linkages that geopolitical models foregrounded. A 1947 article on the Soviet takeover of Albania stated that "whoever controls this little country can turn the Adriatic into his private lake and have access to the Mediterranean."[34] Another *Digest* author claimed that "our stake in the future of Japan is vast. It is nothing less than the future of western civilization in the entire Far East."[35] In "Is Russia Prepared to Make War?" the *Digest* claimed that although industry was inefficient, the "menace to peace is appallingly real," for Russia's geographical location was almost impregnable.[36] Soviet actions were usually presented as the result of ruthless strategy, but geography was sometimes cited as a truly deterministic variable, leading Russia into irresistible temptation: "Yugoslavia is hemmed in by three satellite foes, each with an inviting plain to invade."[37] Finally, for more than one *Digest* writer, Soviet character was perceived to be a result of geography.[38] In 1946 one author noted the endurance of certain characteristics in the USSR, claiming that seven hundred years of autocratic rule had made totalitarianism appear normal to the Russians. This argument suggested that they were driven by history to be suspicious of their neighbors and, shifting from geopolitics to chronopolitics, held that they had been separated from "the ways of

Western civilization" by three hundred and fifty years.[39] This and articles
that insisted "Stalin's heart is in Asia" reinforced the Orientalist—and so
uncivilized—nature of the Soviets.[40] Thus, distinct from narratives that
wrote Soviet action in deliberate power-political or ideological terms
were those that made expansionary and repressive Soviet action seem
unavoidable because of the laws of history and geopolitical location.

A parallel line of argument explained why communism was not likely
to be a permanent feature of Chinese society. The Chinese were individ-
ualists, the *Digest* explained, so that "eventually [they] will absorb the
communists, just as they swallowed up the Mongols and Manchus."[41]
The superficial hold that communism had over "real" Asian character
and culture was emphasized in articles that referred to governments as
"puppets" and "dupes."

The courses of action proposed by *Reader's Digest* authors similarly
insisted on recognition of the facts of geography. The magazine said in
1948 that the country's location made the Soviet Union

> almost impregnable. And the defensive strength which it gives her enables
> her to behave towards us in the way she is behaving.[42]

Domino theories and the perils of territorial congruence were the most
obvious cases in which geography in the form of containment could be
used to counter geography as an aid to expansion. Drawing directly upon
both Mackinder's heartland thesis (although without referencing it) and,
particularly, later developments of the geopolitics of airspace, *Digest*
authors urged America to build up its air force in response to the power
of Russia's land advantage. In a 1950 article, American strategist Major
A. de Seversky argued that depending on its geography, "a nation seeks
a clear-cut superiority in a single medium.... This law accords with
common sense."[43]

The *Digest* also recognized geopolitics as based in other geographical
facts such as population distribution, which the magazine related directly
to possible American strategy. De Seversky argued that it would be impossible for America to match "the swarming communist man power"[44]—
"the 800 million people now at the disposal of the Kremlin"—to which
Stalin was preparing to add 700 million Asiatics.[45] Capture of people was
a central aspect of *Reader's Digest* narrativization of the danger in the
spread of communism. The danger was particularly acute when the people in question were skilled: "Capture of Japan's 9.5 million industrial

workers by Communism could seal the fate of democracy in half the world."[46] The logical conclusion of this polemic was that Russians were after not just territorial acquisition but also peoples' minds, thus reinforcing the argument that the idea of communism was a Soviet tactic. This also allowed the *Digest* to bring the threat of communism directly home to all individual Americans:

> This is where *you* come in. No-one is too small or insignificant, too young or too old, to be shackled and regimented, or pauperized and destroyed.... By its all-encompassing timetable sooner or later [the "communist masterplot"] has to reach you. [47]

With this, the *Digest* constructed a conceptual bridge that links events occurring in distant parts of the globe to the future freedom of the reader. Thus, indirectly, *Reader's Digest* was constructing for its readers geographies that linked them with world events. The magazine was constantly presenting a model for its readers to adopt in their understanding of their place and role in American society. This allowed the magazine to introduce more prescriptive statements relating to individual and state action. Some articles called directly for the development of Soviet-style devotion in America. Many authors appeared to admire the Soviet single-mindedness about the value of their system, lamenting the lack of missionary zeal about the U.S. system. This ranged from authors who expressed frustration at others' inability to acknowledge the generosity of American action to those who claimed that all that was needed to improve America's reputation overseas was to find a name for the American system with which to replace the unpopular term *capitalism*.[48]

Some authors clearly thought that nominal action would not suffice. A number of them claimed that American national character was naturally not as aggressive as the Russian national character.[49] Thus, because America was not naturally a militaristic nation, Russia in the next war would "have quantity therefore we need to improve quality."[50] *Reader's Digest* entered the debate on military spending by asking if too many government resources were channeled to defense. The answer was, overwhelmingly, that it was preferable to becoming a "slave of communism."[51]

U.S.-Soviet relations were also written in terms of geopolitical economy.[52] Postwar Soviet economic weakness was simultaneously a comfort and a concern to *Reader's Digest* in this period. On the one hand, the *Digest* believed that systemic inefficiency and scarcity meant that the

Soviet Union could not implement its internationalist goals through aggressive expansion. The magazine's (neo)realist belief in the effect of the world system on individual state character meant that it believed that the primary American concern would thus be how best to aid Russia in order to have it fall into line in its postwar order. Here, if the Soviet Union could be brought into an American-led system of free trade, its internal political and economic character would soon fall into line with American democracy. Although the United States and the USSR could not cooperate politically in the reconstruction of world society, some *Digest* authors thought it imperative for America to bring the USSR into the world system through trade.[53] This represented both fear of the consequences of alienating the Soviet Union and acknowledgment of the power of trade in constructing geopolitical order. Although this was not a major line of reasoning after the early Cold War period, in the 1960s and 1970s, traces of this reasoning could be found running through *Digest* arguments that stated that trade sanctions should be used as a weapon when more overtly hostile action was precluded by détente policies.

Another interpretation of the implications of Soviet economic weakness began to dominate at this time. This second viewpoint argued that the leaders of the USSR recognized their weakness and realized that they needed peace to facilitate growth. *Reader's Digest* recognized the growth potential of the Soviet system, deciding that it might pose a challenge to the United States in the future.[54] Furthermore, the *Digest* argued, it was the USSR that benefited most from peace. The Soviets would cooperate with the United States and Britain until their economy (and military) was strong enough for them to pursue their ultimate goal of world supremacy. The implications of this situation were drawn out by the *Digest* through its use of the "laws of history" and the predictive powers of geopolitics. Citizens needed to be wary even when the communists appeared to have quite peaceful intentions. For the *Digest*, communists could never be peaceful, as this would go against their nature; instead, they would take advantage of peace to build up their economy and military, then openly end the peace.

All of these articles were structured around a belief that Americans would have to act immediately while they still retained a comparative advantage over the Soviet Union. If they waited until Russia actually threatened them directly—when the Soviet Union had built up its economy and military—it would already be too late. *Reader's Digest* laid out

this argument with regard to France. If communism were to be successful in France,

> the smaller states of Europe would succumb one by one ... [and] all
> Europe will be unified under Soviet tyranny.... Our only chance to avoid
> war with the Soviet Union lies in the possibility that today, when we are
> far stronger then the Soviet Union, we shall have the foresight, energy and
> courage to prevent Stalin from dominating new strategic areas, and shall
> ourselves organize the world's free peoples to resist Soviet imperialism, so
> that the Soviet dictator will be constantly confronted by superior force.[55]

This argument was not limited to Europe but applied to the entire world.
Although *Reader's Digest* believed that Stalin could not afford war for the
time being, it saw him as "devis[ing] the diabolically shrewd plan to set
the world afire."[56] In other words, the *Digest* looked at socialist revolutions around the world and saw Stalin behind them; Stalin was the mastermind who left others to do the fighting for him. He took advantage of
discontent and then hijacked protest to employ it to his own ends.

This perception of Soviet involvement led to the development of two
further *Reader's Digest* narratives. First, by externalizing all local conflicts
into interrelated aspects of the overarching global conflict,[57] the *Digest*
was able to support preservation of the status quo in a number of places
in the name of international anticommunism, despite the inequities in
many of these countries. For example, *Reader's Digest* would recognize
the ills of colonialism or dictatorship in a country and would accept the
local population's desire for change; yet oppose political or military protest or revolution because it was assumed to be Soviet-promoted.

Second, this argument witnessed the beginnings of development theory in *Reader's Digest* global rhetoric. The *Digest* explained that communists were able to influence revolutions across the globe by "exploiting
local difficulties."[58] In other words, Soviets took advantage of poor economic conditions that caused political chaos. The *Digest* described dis-
organized societies in terms that made their susceptibility to communism
seem inevitable. One author stated that "poverty is the best breeding
ground for theoretical communism," and another that chaos was "a fer-
tile field for communism."[59] Again the *Digest* was pushing for order and
discipline in societies so that the communist threat could be repelled.
Once again its geographies tied together the necessity for order at a societal level and for the individual American reader.

For America's goal of expanding Western democracy (not to mention free market economics), investment in development, both economic and political, was the answer. This was first achieved via the Marshall Plan to save Europe from "chaos and communism";[60] American aid was then extended to other endangered parts of the world. For example, in Afghanistan it was thought that "poverty attracts swarms of Soviet agents"[61] and that the Philippines might have gone "the way of China" because of the "danger of discontent" there.[62] Similarly, *Reader's Digest* urged Japan to "make the reforms necessary to eliminate the misery on which communism thrives"[63] and argued that the United States needed to use "prosperity as a weapon."[64]

In addition to economic support, America should make available the truth about each situation by introducing "moral literacy."[65] Reinforcing this idea was a 1950 piece that insisted that communism "has no political appeal to individualistic, liberty-loving Latin Americans. Its only appeal is economic."[66] As the *Digest* was never totally negative in its portrayal of any situation, however difficult and challenging, it provided anecdotes of success at halting or turning back communist encroachment: "Libya is a reassuring example of how, by intelligent spending, we can clearly get our money's worth."[67]

Elsewhere, communists themselves covertly created political chaos, which meant that they would later be welcomed to these countries as a result of subsequent overt offers of help. *Reader's Digest* warned that if America did not take control in such instances, the communists would be welcomed by local people as they waltzed in and took control before anyone really knew what was going on.[68] The communists' motives were always represented to be at odds with the (genuine dissatisfaction of the) indigenous people. In a 1962 *Digest* article about his trip to Latin America, Richard Nixon wrote that the "communists joined in the revolution not because of any dislike of dictatorship but only because they themselves wanted to become dictators."[69]

Another *Digest* argument put forward in support of U.S. intervention was also linked to the language of developmentalism in its most "evolutionary" guise stemming from colonialist representations of non-European peoples: political maturity. "The great majority of the responsible people in Guatemala are pro-American" claimed one author, but they were "woefully inexperienced politically."[70]

One of the rhetorical powers of geopolitical reasoning is the transcendence of history. *Reader's Digest* also relied upon rhetorical use of history and its "laws" to naturalize the relationship between the United States and the Soviet Union. A significant number of articles in this period covered issues or events that were identified as key moments in American history. The situations these articles described were presented as potential turning points in history. According to the *Digest*, the showdown in Cuba in the early 1960s represented "one of the decisive moments of the 20th century." Other articles explained that Mao's army was "the most viciously reactionary force in history," and that communist Chinese society represented "the most frightful regimentation in history."[71] Similarly, other articles compared current events with key periods of American history to drive home the importance of the event being described. A 1962 piece on America's potential role in the fate of Soviet people, for example, asserted that "this debate may appear as momentous as the Lincoln-Douglas debate over slavery more than a century ago."[72] This familiar and moral example was used to draw readers into complicity with the narrative and accept the importance of its message.

The *Reader's Digest* use of laws of history was sometimes brought together with geopolitical reasoning to facilitate prediction of future events, often to analyze Russian territorial acquisition in the past as a measure of future threats. Drawing upon what it evidently regarded as the "lessons of history," the *Digest* explained that "Stalin will not stop. He can only be stopped."[73] Other articles claimed that "each day brings us closer to Russia's development of the atomic bomb" and that "when the Soviet stockpile [of atomic weapons] reaches a decisive size, war will probably come."[74]

In short, *Reader's Digest* believed in the limitless expansive potential of communism, that it "will not stop at international frontiers unless it is opposed."[75] Of course, the *Digest* did not see the propagation of communism as coming about solely by political-territorial expansion; it was also driven by the spread of Soviet propaganda. As a result, adding to the predictive nature of geopolitics was the *Digest's* contention that the conflict could not be understood simply by weighing material capabilities. The confrontation was most importantly an ideological one—in the sense that Soviet ideology threatened to suppress (American) truth. This in turn threatened democracy, for *Reader's Digest* insisted that citizens are required to be (truthfully) informed of the facts for democracy to work.

Propelled by claims that the *people* of communist regimes, but not their leaders, wanted peace, the *Digest* said it was U.S. duty to provide the Soviet people with help and support.[76] A 1951 article described the battle over the truth as "the war we are losing" and complained that Americans were unable to win the battle for people's minds because they were up against fanatics ready to die for communism.[77] Other authors used language that implied unnatural devotion on the part of the Soviets: "fanatical crusade; the communist forces have the fire of zealots," "fanatical discipline," "rabid communist."[78] The 1953 article "What Is a Communist?" provided the following answer: "Most simply, [communism] is a militant faith, engaged in a war, now open, now closed, against all others."[79] The most dangerous factor in U.S.-USSR relations, claimed another article, was that "the Russians acted on the assumption that they were at war with us and we acted as though we were at peace with them."[80] This theme reappeared with a vengeance in the détente period.

The *Digest's* fear that American peacefulness was a disadvantage was reinforced by what was apparently a historical example of an open, democratic society falling to communism. In "The First Democracy Destroyed by Communism," Aleksandr Kerensky told of how the communists took over from the provisional government he led in what he claimed was Russia's first democracy. He argued that "the myth that communists overthrew Czarism has been purposely spread to conceal their crime of having strangled the first Russian democracy."[81] For the *Digest*, this was the first of many such stories, the original event that was to be repeated across the globe. Throughout the Cold War, *Reader's Digest* presented endless repetitions of this story in a variety of settings. For example, in "How the Russians Stole My Government," the *Digest* described how communists took control of Hungary despite achieving only 17 percent support in the last free elections.[82] Repetition of this narrative was important to the *Digest's* representational schema. It did not really matter which country was threatened; the tragic structure of the narrative reinforced the message encoded in the details: eventually America too would succumb.

The lessons of history and the facts of geography proved invaluable in the *Digest's* naturalization of the communist presence. This process of naturalization was taken one stage further through the use of disease metaphors.

Disease

Although no disease metaphors were to be found in its pages before the end of World War II, during the Cold War *Reader's Digest* employed a number of them in its narration of communism.[83] The magazine insisted that "disease is bad, but the worst disease of all is communism."[84] The *Digest* favored metaphors of diseases that appear harmless at first but inevitably develop into life-threatening forms: "cancerous intrusion of Soviet agents" and "communist cancer [eating] into the body of exhausted France."*Reader's Digest* also described various types of communist poison, including "the blood virus type, radiating from communist Russia, [which] is today rotting the souls of two-fifths of all mankind"[85] and "slow poison" of socialist influence.[86] Countries that had yet to decide on the political direction that modern development would take them were seen as being not entirely healthy:

> The truth is clear: with China lost for the time to Communism, with India pale with the sickness of neutralism, a free and healthy Japan is not only democracy's best hope in Asia—it is quite probably its only hope.[87]

Within this discourse, resistance to communism was written in the language of the body's *natural* reaction to viral infections, thus reinforcing the naturalness of resistance to communism: "This attempted Russification has generated a passive but strong resistance, as the invasion of a virus generates antibodies in the human body."[88]

The structure of these metaphors mirrors the predictive nature of geopolitics. Yet disease metaphors are more powerful interpellators of subjectivity because they not only naturalize danger and perpetuate fear but do so in language that inscribes global ideological conflict onto the territory of the human body. They thus vividly relate international events to the reader's own familiar terrain. As with its use of geopolitics, in its use of disease metaphors *Reader's Digest* enacted a double move. First, it uncovered a threat or predicted a deleterious change to the body politic. Articles created a sense of dis-ease over future conditions. Second, the magazine provided a therapeutic discourse.[89] It offered, and at times administered, a cure or inoculation against whatever had infected—or threatened to infect—American society. The first move was intended to construct a desire for order and stability; the second offered safety through voluntary disciplining of the reader's thoughts and actions.[90]

The use of disease metaphors here vividly illustrates the role that *Reader's Digest* has projected for itself in American political culture. As I argued earlier, *Reader's Digest* sees itself as providing its readership with the essential information they require in order to "stay informed" about

American society and world issues. Staying informed is central to the role of the *Digest*'s good citizen, for it is believed that only knowledgeable people can understand what is really going on (as opposed to accepting what others tell them is happening or what appears to be happening) and can act and vote accordingly. *Reader's Digest*'s self-projected role within the rhetoric of disease reinforces its more general self-perception as provider of expert knowledge. Medical experts are required not only to find and administer a cure but often also to diagnose a problem: a person can be infected without having any symptoms that an untrained eye can detect.

During the Cold War, *Reader's Digest* scripted communism in much the same way in its insistence that Americans did not realize that changes were already under way, or that American society was already undergoing the first stages of revolution. The *Digest* elevated itself to the status of an expert who could see through the superficial appearance of society to get at what was really happening. The magazine could predict what would develop if society were left untreated. Even apparently healthy people—patriotic, hardworking Americans—could be "infected" with communist leanings (an infection that might be invisible not only to others but also to themselves).[91] To avoid this, people required a course of treatment: a monthly dose of *Reader's Digest*'s clearheaded facts. The magazine explained the symptoms to watch for in others and offered advice on how best to avoid contracting bad morals or communist leanings. As the communist threat had become naturalized and dehistoricized, this prescription was indefinite: regular consumption and digestion of information was required to maintain an effective and ideologically healthy citizenship.

Disease metaphors appear to be quite an extreme form of representation. Some articles went a step further, opposing the natural not with an unhealthy state, but with one that was *completely* unnatural, or perverse.

Perversity

Although "the natural" is a constant measure running through all the *Digest*'s comparisons of the Soviet and American systems, the infusion of articles with the "unnatural" or "perverse" makes the formation of difference that much clearer. Here, concepts of natural and unnatural were explicit: Soviets were labeled as perverse. Unnaturalness was invoked by a number of tropes that extended from a relatively weak aesthetic form to sexual perversity and inhumanity. Readers are left in no doubt about the differences between the Soviets and themselves.

Aesthetic descriptions drew heavily upon the unnatural. Russian people and landscapes were described in language that evoked ugliness or dullness. Simply put, the look of Soviet and communist people and places was unnatural in its unattractiveness. For example, Mao Tse-tung was described as ugly ("a short, fat, stooping man of 53 with a warty chin"), the female "Boss of Rumania" was "shaped like a wrestler," and the "usual Russian countenance is like a hog . . . incredibly filthy and untidy."[92]

Aesthetics were presented in such a way as to imply something about character. Soviet women, for example, were described as having a "plodding submissiveness, more animal-like than human" and lacking feminine grace and "coquetry."[93] General Malenkov, described as fat and having an "extremely repulsive" face, was called the "machine that walks like a man."[94]

Reader's Digest suggested that beauty was scarce in the USSR, and its appearance was written so as to seem incongruous. In 1957 an author remarked that one evening in a Russian restaurant, "I was astonished to see a pretty girl. This is rare in Moscow."[95] "Ivan looks at Iowa" noted how visiting Russian farmers were impressed at agricultural efficiency, the range of products available in shops, and the "beautiful bosoms" of the American women.[96]

This use of unnatural aesthetics was more than a simple attempt to make the enemy difficult to like and identify with and therefore easier to hate. Through reference to antiaesthetics, *Reader's Digest* made Soviet people appear unnatural, and therefore beyond any system used to judge normal people.[97] But the use of aesthetics also implied social process. If it was acknowledged at all, beauty was found in children (who had yet to be fully corrupted by the system) or in women, who were perhaps assumed to have less of a role in official Soviet society than men. Alternatively, the notion of "beauty" could be used to enforce certain "natural" traits of humanity that even Soviet communists could not pervert, such as women's natural beauty or their desire to maintain it as part of their "natural" role within human society. As a result, articles that discussed women who had been successful in the USSR made much of the women's putting their careers ahead of their natural role as mothers.

This binary of natural and unnatural was not limited to the *Digest*'s description of Soviet people. The Soviet landscape too was "shabby and gray."[98] On the other hand, pro-American areas in otherwise Soviet-friendly places were described in almost utopian terms, especially West Berlin, "the free island surrounded by the 'Red Sea'"; it was "an oasis of freedom in the communist desert."[99] Communist takeover of a place inevitably made it appear less attractive to *Digest* writers.

The natural-unnatural discursive structure was also expressed through the concept of rationality and its absence. One autobiographical tale confessed that a "purely emotional reaction to this misery"—rather than rational evaluation—"led me to socialism."[100] *Reader's Digest* described communist education as proof of the existence of a system of rationality different from that of America and the "free world." Communists did not offer "real" education but political education and propaganda. Soviet knowledge was so Other to its American counterpart that even science was irrational. One author claimed that for Russians, "to seek a compromise with the capitalist world is not only disloyal to the working class but also 'unscientific,'"[101] and another quoted from the *Short Philosophical Encyclopedia* (Moscow, 1934) to underscore the "perverted code of conduct sanctioned by communist doctrines":

> From the point of view of communist morality, "moral" is only that
> which facilitates the destruction of the old world and which strengthens
> the new, communist world.[102]

As a result, as far as the basis for making decisions was concerned, the United States and the USSR were portrayed as truly incompatible systems, both scientifically and morally. *Reader's Digest* argued that as a result, appeasement would accomplish nothing; negotiation was futile and would only indicate American weakness.

The *Digest* frequently articulated the Soviet system through an overtly sexualized language. For example, communism was "sterile and quixotic," or a seducer: "The Continent fears Russia will woo frustrated Germany into partnership again."[103] One author described the character of Soviet relations with the rest of world in terms of a repressed sexual encounter: "Nonintercourse is the general rule and fraternization is forbidden, except as part of a planned penetration."[104]

In addition, the *Digest* argued that sex was an integral part of communist schemes of capture: "unrestrained sexual license is the principal means by which the communist regimes today seduce young people and chain them to Moscow's objectives," it claimed in 1955. This was achieved via "a rampant scourge of promiscuity" and the "unique communist institution" of state-sponsored prostitution, both in diametric opposition to the family values of most *Digest* readers.[105] The magazine underscored the unnaturalness of this Soviet policy by explaining in a later article "why and how the communists deliberately destroy family life behind the iron curtain."[106] This line of argument also reinforced the magazine's statements that all aspects of life were politicized under communism: even family life and sexual relations were not free from the all-powerful communist gaze.[107]

At times, the relationship between the superpowers was itself written as a sexual one. This was not an open partnership but one enmeshed in tension and frustration, even when the appearance was of détente: "When I speak of a settlement with the Soviet Union," wrote a *Digest* author in 1951, "I do not mean a marriage. I mean a divorce. I mean the fixing of boundaries between their world and ours."[108]

Discourses of sexuality and geopolitics should not be regarded as separate, since geography was often inferred through sexualized and gendered languages constructing strength, vulnerability, and impenetrability. In some cases, vulnerability was reduced to an embodied essence: nakedness. Nakedness was written in two distinct ways. On the one hand, it was natural, a result of geography, for instance. Russian behavior was often linked directly to its geography and the particular form of sexualized character that its geography promoted. The *Digest* claimed that "another clue to Russian behavior lies in geography. *Naked* plains stretch east and west with no defense barrier."[109] In other cases, places were naked because they had been stripped of protection. One author suggested that in dealing with communism, "we can deter or emasculate attacks on free nations."[110] This represented the most powerful, if somewhat hyperbolic, depictions of America's current, or potential, vulnerability: "The United States is naked—incredibly naked—against a Russian atom-bomb attack."[111] In a similar vein, Carl Spaatz argued in the *Digest* that if Russia were to gain control of the air, Europe would be left "naked and paralyzed."[112] Therefore, there were limited options in this zero-sum game: "submitting to it, crushing it by force, or 'containing' it without war by a steel wall."[113] Some pieces talked of perverse sexual penetration in terms of "rape."[114]

Taken to an extreme, perversity can imply the lack of what humans are supposedly born with, a sense of humanity. In 1948 *Reader's Digest* recounted famine in Russia in the 1920s as inhuman because it led to terror and then the "final degradation of cannibalism."[115] The perversion of cannibalism was also suggested by the "man-eat-man" nature of the Soviet political system.[116] Another author drew upon a different, yet equally powerful, mythology of perverse consumption to declare that Bolshevism "sucks the lifeblood of its victims."[117]

Thus, *Reader's Digest* wrote communist life as degeneration from the values of civilized society. The communist system was often described as treating its citizens like animals, with "policies better fitted to beasts than men."[118] Taking this further, articles claimed that "the communist state breeds informers like maggots in a mass-burial pit" and referred to "bestial crime" or "bestial behavior."[119]

This period also witnessed several reiterations of incompatibility of communism and democracy in *Reader's Digest*.[120] "Red China's war against God" seemed to prove the gulf between good/freedom and evil/communism beyond doubt. The *Digest* suggested that communist behavior should no longer come as a surprise to the informed reader:

> Sadism, depravity, bestiality beyond imagination—these are the end products of a system which must invariably depend upon the dregs of society to protect itself from the wrath of the people it has defrauded.[121]

As the territorial and rhetorical structures of the Cold War became entrenched, the characteristics of the United States and the Soviet Union were represented as being more and more natural to each place. This meant that the essence of each place was abstracted to transcend the moment, rendering the struggle between them an inevitability. As one *Digest* author put it, "Communism and freedom ... two irreconcilable faiths of our time."[122]

Managing Narrative Contradiction

Although overwhelmingly united in their condemnation of all things communist, *Digest* articles did not create a seamless image of the USSR. For example, there was an exception to *Reader's Digest*'s Cold War position on the necessity for high levels of defense spending in 1952. The lone voice of Herbert Hoover warned of the dangers of too much defense spending. Hoover did not display any leftist or liberal concerns over militarization or present more humane ways to spend defense money. Rather, firmly set within Cold War discursive structures, he argued that overspending might adversely affect the American standard of living, and the resulting discontent would leave the country even more vulnerable to the communist menace.[123] Despite the different tack taken by this article, the outcome would be the same, and Hoover concluded in the apocalyptic fashion characteristic of this period: "If our economy should collapse, Stalin's victory would be complete."[124] Other authors challenged defense spending by questioning priorities within the military budget. In particular, *Digest* writers were concerned with America's apparent obsession with winning the moon race. "Are we suffering from moon madness?" asked one author who feared that America's enthusiasm for exploration (and for beating the Russians) was naive compared to the Soviets, whose inner space project was "unblushingly *military.*"[125]

A potentially more significant contradiction within the *Digest's* construction of the USSR lay in its description of the communist system as both hopelessly inefficient *and* militarily superior. This dual representation was possible because any apparent Soviet success was described as dependent upon two factors that distorted comparison with the United States. First, Soviet growth was possible only because of the slavelike conditions that the *Digest* understood workers to suffer in communist countries. Second was the Soviets' "perverse" use of their resources. The Soviets were seen as being so wrapped up in competition with the West that they allowed their citizens few luxuries. The individual was secondary to the requirements of the state, an arrangement that was opposed to the *Digest's* ethos of America. Thus, a discourse of irrationality was employed to explain the apparently paradoxical situation that the Soviet Union, "a nation that 'can't even make a decent flush toilet' is, in terms of war potential, overtaking U.S. industry."[126]

The Othering of the Soviet Union during this period is significant to the construction of U.S. mission and destiny but also to the formation of good citizens to undertake a historic role. The Soviet threat meant that any American intervention could be read as reactive rather than aggressive or confrontational, even when it occurred before Soviet action, because of the predictive power of geopolitics that insisted Soviet action was imminent.

At a time when American intervention—military, cultural, and economic—was spreading throughout the world, the explanation of events in this chapter offered not only legitimation but also urgency to the U.S. role. A new frontier for the American spirit to conquer was drawn.

At the end of the 1950s, the *Digest*'s demonization of the Soviet Union relaxed slightly, but the magazine recognized a new and potentially more damaging threat to America's power: an internal threat from people who believed in the possibility of détente and wanted to relax hostilities between the superpowers. The misguidedness of this view was explained in the 1959 piece "One Trip to Russia Doesn't Make an Expert." This author foreshadowed the *Digest*'s narrativization of détente when he warned of the dangers of believing the stories that tourists were told by official guides in Russia.[127] A subsequent article insisted that visitors became "prisoner[s] of Intourist" and saw only what the Soviet state wanted them to see.[128] In the next chapter I will examine the *Digest*'s construction of a new sense of danger with the relaxation of international relations in détente.

CHAPTER FIVE

The Jeopardy of Détente

Both the number and the tone of articles on the Soviet Union and communism changed around 1964. The Sino-Soviet split following Soviet-American arms talks meant that *Reader's Digest* no longer saw America facing an overwhelming communist force. When Richard Nixon became president in 1969, the *Digest* was further reassured that American interests were being well served. Thus, there was a decline in the number of articles on Soviet and communist topics in comparison with the 1950s (see figure 6). New—although, as I will show, not unrelated—evils were found in the anti–Vietnam War movement, urban violence, and civil rights protests.

This is not to suggest too profound a change in the *Digest's* representation of global politics. *Reader's Digest* did not accept that the Cold War was ending in any significant way. Instead, it feared that détente with the USSR might endanger the United States. The *Digest* was highly skeptical about the possibility of change in the Soviet Union and so could not accept the authenticity of any appearance of improvement. As a result of its demonizing of the USSR, the magazine could not accept that the communists had the ability to behave either honorably or rationally; Soviets would always try to find some way of making détente work to their advantage so that Americans would always lose out. Thus, although the absolute demonization of the USSR was eased, the *Digest* continued to script international politics around the same model of U.S. democratic freedom versus Soviet totalitarian communism.

At the beginning of this period, one of *Reader's Digest*'s primary concerns was the Vietnam War. Articles contrasted the bravery and generosity of American soldiers with the brutality of communist captors[1] and warned of the perils of showing military weakness by negotiating an end to the war. This latter topic, which various authors pursued in warning of the detrimental effects of the appearance of "giving in" to the communists by going to the negotiation table, represented the beginnings of a discourse of jeopardy within the *Digest*'s conservative "rhetoric of reaction." This discourse became increasingly significant when the United States entered further strategic arms talks with the Soviet Union, and more especially as the *Digest* perceived American society to accept the reality of détente. The idea of Americans believing in Soviet goodwill concerned *Reader's Digest*, which believed that America was dropping its vigilance and its citizens were being duped into believing their old enemy. The image of "internal" softness was reinforced by the magazine's inclusion of a large number of articles on changes in American society, especially in the late 1960s and early 1970s. The issues of urban violence, campus radicalism, civil rights, and drug cultures were extensively covered. The approach of America's "bicentennial" provided the *Digest* an opportunity to turn its attention to the changes it perceived had affected American identity and the importance of self-discipline in setting things right. A 1972 article, "Ring Out, Liberty Bell!" called Americans back to their historic mission. An article a year later drew inspiration from the "spirits of 1776."[2] To reinforce its image of the unique American mission, the *Digest* in 1976 included a number of articles retelling the significant moments in the foundation of American identity and purpose. The lasting impression of the détente period, however, was the jeopardy that America faced if its citizens did not "wake up" to the realities of communism. This was articulated through a "rhetoric of reaction."

"The Rhetoric of Reaction"

The *Rhetoric of Reaction*, Albert Hirschman lists three concepts of central discursive power to the arguments of political conservatives: futility, jeopardy, and perversity.[3] Futility is an argument that does not accept the possibility of real change. This rhetoric is based on belief in a highly structured system, in which any apparent change to the underlying structure is merely superficial. In this case, jeopardy represents the danger to national security that will result from the ill-informed actions of well-meaning individuals. Perversity in Hirschman's theorization is an extreme case of jeopardy in which the results of well-intentioned action will not just endanger security but will in fact produce the condition exactly opposite to that the actors intended. Each of these three rhetorics ran through *Reader's Digest* articles on communism and socialism in the détente period. To avoid confusion with the definition of *perversity* I used in the previous chapter, I will consider the last two of Hirschman's rhetorics together as different "degrees" of jeopardy.

Futility

> Peace-loving? Today Red China bristles with training centers for subversion and guerrilla warfare.[4]

> The cold war isn't thawing; it is burning with a deadly heat.[5]

As used by *Reader's Digest*, the discourse or rhetoric of futility assumed the existence of the Cold War binary structure that opposed the "good space" of America and freedom against the "bad space" of the Soviet Union and communist totalitarianism. This assumption was based on the magazine's essentialist belief in the existence of communists and held that there could not be any change in relations between America and the communists unless the communists denounced communism. For the *Digest*, any change people attributed to the Soviets' embracing of détente could only be superficial. Surface relations might have thawed somewhat, but *Reader's Digest* believed that the permafrost of the Cold War structure remained firmly in place. It claimed in 1969, for example, that "Russia has *not* changed," and a later issue suggested that Castro's détente progress was "more cosmetic than basic."[6]

Instead, *Reader's Digest* believed that "communist expansion aims are being pushed as vigorously today as they were under Khrushchev and Stalin."[7] Even when the Soviets were not represented as continuing the Cold War via aggressive military means, they were written by the *Digest* as continuing the war by alternative strategies. According to the magazine, the situation had become more dangerous because the threat was more pernicious. Détente was used by the Soviets to achieve their goals: "Crying peace when they do not mean peace—is a device for promoting communist takeover by every means short of nuclear war."[8] The magazine insisted that the communists saw the negotiation table as part of the battlefield:[9]

> From their new position of strategic nuclear parity with the United States, the Soviets are probing for freeworld weak spots with every weapon at their command—and this includes negotiation. . . . Negotiation is viewed by the Soviets as a weapon, like a ship in the Mediterranean or a strategic weapon.[10]

In the *Digest* in 1975, the dissident Aleksandr Solzhenitsyn described this use of détente as a conscious Soviet ploy. He argued that the communists were taking advantage of American goodwill through nothing more than a sly linguistic turn:

> [When] Khrushchev came here and shouted "We will bury you!" people didn't believe that . . . they took it as a joke. Now, of course, the communists in our country have become more clever. They no longer say "We're going to bury you." Now they say "détente." But nothing has changed.[11]

The words changed, the surface impression was different, but the underlying intention remained the same. Many authors indicated that whatever military treaties were signed, there could never be détente because Soviet ideology could not allow for peaceful coexistence.[12] This clearly illustrates Frederick Dolan's assertion of liberal anxieties over promises made by American enemies; by their very nature, enemies of the United States are unlike Americans and thus cannot be trusted. Not only will they fail to keep their promises, they also will manipulate Americans' willingness to trust their enemies as part of a strategy to undermine the United States.[13]

Within the parameters of the discourse of futility, even the Sino-Soviet split could be written as representing continuity with the height of the Cold War rather than a distinct break from it. The deterioration of relations between Russia and China did not represent a fundamental opposition of worldviews but was defined by the *Digest* as nothing more than an argument about "which is the *best* way to bury the Western world and build a Red world."[14]

Finally, the *Digest* used the newly emerged trade relations between the United States and communist countries to provide new ground for the Cold War conflict to be played out. From positions that still accepted the condition of "total war" between East and West, a number of authors feared the implications of trade. Total war implied that the opposition between the Soviet Union and America transcended all aspects of life rather than being confined to a political or military confrontation. There-fore, trade that aided the Soviet economy *in any way* represented a gain for the communists. Within the zero-sum game of the *Digest's* common-sensical worldview, any communist gain had to be made at the expense of America. The magazine asked, in trade, "Just what *is* non-strategic?" and argued that any difference between strategic and nonstrategic action was more apparent than real.[15]

This argument reached its extreme in articles that claimed the lessons of history show that America should be *most* vigilant against communist subversion during periods of détente: "The Soviet Union ... [took over Eastern Europe] in another period of relaxed tensions—the era of good feeling that followed victory over Hitler."[16] This feeling of continued threat was reinforced by authors' adoption of the "ethnographic present"[17] in their description of communism. These articles talked about the goals of all communists in all times and in all places as if they were a single, unchanging presence. Communism was usually presented as an iden-tity without adjectives. When adjectives were added ("Latin American communism," "Third World communism"), they had no influence on the meaning of the term. Communist, socialist, or Marxist identity was seen to have come directly from its Eurasian heartland source; rarely were national brands indicated. This reified identity appeared to be ahis-torical, devoid of the influence of place, and Marxism offered a single "prescription for ... revolution."[18] The *Digest* claimed to know "what the communists are after—in Vietnam and elsewhere": communist victory and American defeat.[19]

Jeopardy

Jeopardy here refers to well-intentioned social or political changes that inadvertently endanger American security. Jeopardy is best illustrated in the *Digest's* depiction of American détente policies as "the dangerous game of 'let's pretend.'"[20] In the extreme this leads to unintended con-sequences. To the *Digest,* this was where the real danger of détente lay. Failure of foresight in ordinary citizens is shown to produce precisely the opposite of what was intended. Hirschman explains the perverse effect thus:

> Those who started the chain of events that led to the perverse result are
> portrayed as lacking, ridiculously or culpably, in elementary understand-
> ing of the complex interactions of social and economic forces. But at least

their good faith is not impugned—on the contrary it functions as the necessary counterpart of their incurable naiveté, which it is the mission of the enlightened social scientist to expose.[21]

If you replace "the complex interactions of social and economic forces" with "the immutable facts of the communist system," and "social scientist" with "*Reader's Digest,*" the paragraph could well have been written by the *Digest* about its role in American society. American citizens were not mistaken about détente; it was only natural that peace-loving citizens would embrace the possibility of coexistence. But, as the *Digest* argued, "the public is not *indifferent*: it is just not *informed.*"[22] American ignorance of the real stakes threatened the security of America. Once again *Reader's Digest* cleverly wrote itself into the heart of American culture. The *Digest* praised Americans' openness to peace, yet it simultaneously created a sense of danger that would arise if citizens were not properly informed of what was at stake. Despite Americans' love of peace, the *Digest* suggested that if they were properly informed, they could not accept "peace at any price," because at times peace could be achieved only by standing firm. Thus the *Digest* implied that détente did not mean that the individual citizen could be lulled into a sense of security. Détente threatened the *Digest*'s ideal reader in that the end of the overt threat of the Cold War had drawn the American public into a false sense of security in which they were losing touch with the real state of world affairs. Now more than ever, Americans had to know what was really going on in the world. Now more than ever they needed *Reader's Digest.*

Extreme examples of jeopardy became increasingly significant, along with *Reader's Digest*'s fear of the power-political consequences of American withdrawal from the war in Vietnam. When Nixon took office in 1969, the magazine believed a stronger world stance was established and interpreted American withdrawal as being achieved without loss of faith. Thus the use of this discourse dropped significantly in the early 1970s. It slowly entered more and more articles over the 1970s, however, as the magazine perceived a gradual loss of superiority over—even losing parity with—the Soviet Union because, unlike their communist counterparts, Americans had *really* accepted détente.

Digest writers feared a loss of American conviction in the fight against communism. "'The risk of war,'" it claimed, "is not a sufficient reason for refusing to consider the realities."[23] Other authors were more ready to blame Americans for their lack of support. One claimed that those who advocated appeasement had obviously not learned the lessons of history; he cited the violation of the 1939 Hitler-Stalin pact as a reason to distrust the communists' word in negotiation, despite the fact that it was Hitler and not Stalin who broke the agreement.[24] Others argued that some American citizens' desire for peace was producing what Hirschman would call a "perverse effect." In "From Hanoi—with Thanks," a 1970 documentary report presented a "study of how American anti-war demonstrations serve to prolong the war."[25]

As always, the *Digest* invited its readers to become personally involved. At the end of articles on U.S. prisoners of war in Vietnam, readers were told how to register their protests, and they were told to write to tell their congressional representatives that they wanted America to stand strong. In addition, Admiral Stockstill outlined for readers "what you can do for American prisoners in Vietnam."[26] The last page of this article provided the address of the North Vietnamese delegate to the Paris peace talks and specified correct postage for an airmail letter so that readers could easily register their opinions.

Another extreme example of jeopardy *Reader's Digest* feared would materialize at the beginning of this period was linked to the "natural" idealism of youth. The *Digest* claimed that "an organized communist effort has been hijacking the restless idealism of significant numbers of our youth."[27] Although "some are communists ... they are in the minority";[28] in most cases, the *Digest* saw impatient and vulnerable youths looking for answers to poverty and inner-city problems.

Closure was enacted on the rhetorical structure of communist jeopardy in articles that described individuals' realization of the evils of communism.[29] One story of a former American communist told of how a trip to Cuba had turned him away from communism. The story described propaganda and conditions of excessive discipline in Cuba. It also claimed that "hard drugs and wild sexual orgies were stressed as important because they served to break down any links with the 'straight' world."[30] Although the article made no mention of the American youth counterculture, this statement was obviously intended to set up a parallel between *Reader's Digest*'s descriptions of communism and the articles it published in the late 1960s and early 1970s about the character-destroying effects of drug use and sexual promiscuity.

The clearest invocation of discourses of jeopardy was in articles about arms negotiations, which made up approximately a quarter of all pieces on the Soviet Union and communism in this period. *Reader's Digest* described the acceptance of détente in terms that seem to be straight out of Hirschman's characterization of "perverse effect":

> There are some wishful thinkers who ... tell us that we have entered a period of "*détente*," and that the Soviet Union has given us many significant evidences of its desire for peaceful coexistence. These well-intentioned people are completely cut off from the reality of the world in which they live.[31]

The assuredness of claims such as this were based upon belief in the unchanging nature of communism underpinning the discourse of futility: "Russia has *not* changed her ways.... we must not allow ourselves to mask realities with soothing myths."[32] The *Digest* argued that by accepting the parameters of détente, "We're helping the communists win the propaganda war."[33] This ideological setback was all the more significant because of the "slow emasculation of the country's military power," which had come about as a result of the "dangerous failings of our state department"—which *Reader's Digest* saw as capitulating to the Soviet Union.[34]

Taking this argument a step further and reinforcing its impact through a wonderful use of geopolitical language, Solzhenitsyn argued that in fact the USSR was gaining more from the period of détente than it had ever managed to acquire during the more open military confrontation:

> There will not be any nuclear war. Why should there be a nuclear war if for the last 30 years the communists have been breaking off as much of the West as they wanted, piece after piece?[35]

Others agreed, arguing that the inefficient and technically backward Soviet system was rapidly catching up with the United States because it was taking advantage of America's openness in détente to get trade supplies and technology.[36]

All the while, articles catalogued Soviet violations of treaties and continuation of research, development, and investment in new weapons. Even Russia's preparation of its citizens in case of American nuclear attack was perceived by *Reader's Digest* as giving that country a strategic advantage: "Russia's elaborate blueprint for survival in the event of full-scale nuclear war affects the balance of power in the free world's security."[37]

Fractures in the Cold War Binary

Of course *Reader's Digest* is never entirely negative. During the Cold War it readily recognized periods when America successfully offered a barrier to Soviet expansion. In the late 1960s, the magazine's perception that American policy gave the enemy the advantage was paralleled with an understanding of potential to beat the enemy.

Reader's Digest's solution to the jeopardy of America's position was to stand firm:

> Each time, our firmness has led not to escalation, as many feared, but to *de*-escalation. It is when we have shown indecision, disunity and the appearance of fear that escalation has resulted.[38]

This was held to be true in situations ranging from American military action to its treatment of spies ("Releasing spies invites Soviet contempt, not cooperation").[39]

Turning the discourse of jeopardy on its head, *Reader's Digest* argued that America "must arm to disarm."[40] Articles in this period saw a technological fix to American foreign policy and described technological developments in American armament. For example, Trident was presented as "a weapon system potentially so destructive that it could ultimately ensure the peace."[41] This therefore explained and justified American pro-action as reaction.

Although the language of fixed-form geopolitics was much less prevalent in this period, the concept of America as guardian of the free world, and as the last domino in the communist goal of world domination, persisted. The state of American security represented the state of the security of the free world: "Weakness of the United States—in its military capacity and its will—could be the gravest threat to the rest of the world."[42] This sentiment was subtly reinforced by an article on great civilizations, which compared contemporary America to ancient Greece and Rome. It offered a sobering conclusion to those confident of America's greatness: "Lest we forget: *every great nation which has risen to power has declined.*"[43]

The communist presence had fractured before the onset of détente. The state that *Reader's Digest* saw as being in opposition to the American way shifted over the course of the 1960s and 1970s. Initially, communism was split between the "half mad" Maoists[44] and the more reasonable and realistic Russians. After President Nixon's visit to China in 1972, this valorization changed. Russia became the main source of communist subversion, whereas articles on China tended to stress the influence of its ancient civilization and the rationality of its leaders. Two narratives characterized the reduction in threat posed now that the communist presence was split.

From Fear to Boredom

The absolute negativity of articles in the period from 1946 to 1953 gave way in the 1960s and 1970s to articles that mentioned more positive aspects of communist society.

The most radical challenge to the dominant *Digest* take on Soviet-American relations came from former vice president Hubert Humphrey in "We Stand on Common Ground," his part of a two-viewpoint article titled "Can We Trust the Kremlin?" published in 1970:

> There is no doubt that we stayed ahead of the Soviets in the first two decades of this arms race. In the late '60s, however, the goal of "staying ahead" became relative, if not outright illusory. For the fundamental fact of life today is that each side possesses sufficient nuclear weaponry to inflict "unacceptable damage" on the other.[45]

Another author had sounded a lone call for the end of Cold War rhetoric six years earlier: "There is no longer a communist monolith.... the time-worn clichés of the Cold War are becoming obsolete."[46] The *Digest* suggested that rather than worrying about international events, "we should put our own house in order."[47] In 1972 President Nixon agreed that "we are entering the period when the danger of world conflict, of world war, has been very substantially reduced."[48] He tempered his claim by warning that since the communists would not change their position any more than Americans would change theirs, the United States could not afford to fall behind in the arms race.

Other authors started to write about a degree of progress in communist society. In Moscow in 1969 one saw "a notable improvement in the standard of living, although the standard comes nowhere near equalizing ours.... Queues for foodstuffs and other basic articles have virtually disappeared."[49] Some positive socioeconomic changes in Cuba were also recognized and, even more significantly, the *Digest* acknowledged in 1975 that Castro enjoyed the support of about 80 percent of the Cuban people.[50]

For the most part, however, articles with a slightly more positive take on the communist system simply replaced fear with dullness. For example, in 1972 Lawrence Elliott described Brezhnev in contrast to other Soviet leaders:[51]

> Nikolai [sic] Lenin, the visionary, who wrenched a medieval Russia into the 20th century; brooding bloody Joseph Stalin, who slaughtered millions in the name of communism; and flamboyant Nikita Khrushchev, who thrust the nation, ready or not, to the brink of nuclear war. They were revolutionaries all. Brezhnev is about as revolutionary as an average U.S. chamber of commerce. He is the ultimate *apparatchik*, the Soviet organization man, and he is bent on making communism work without Stalin's bloody terror or Khrushchev's wild improvisations.[52]

The *Digest* almost seemed disappointed at the rise of such a boring enemy, prefiguring the boredom of the "end of history"[53] discussed in chapter 8. It also projected onto the Soviet enemy a prevailing fear in American society: the danger of big government. By projecting this onto the negative moral space of the USSR, the *Digest* could portray big government as an evil; this would be more difficult to do if American government were to be discussed directly.

The Representational Economy of the Smile

The characteristic that seemed to indicate the true nature of communist society to *Digest* writers during this period was the (non)existence of the smile.

Both articles on Yugoslavia in this period were accompanied by pictures of Tito, who was depicted as a smiling, grandfatherly figure. In sharp contrast were the stony likenesses of Ho Chi Minh offered in 1968 and of Chou En-lai and Leonid Brezhnev, both published in 1972;[54] none of them made eye contact with the reader (see figure 7).

Each article on Yugoslavia discussed the improvements that this independent communist country had achieved in comparison to Soviet satellites: "Since breaking with Stalin in 1948, Tito has slowly but surely led Yugoslavia out of the bogs of marxism and poverty into the uplands of free enterprise and prosperity."[55] In contrast to "the scarcities, drabness and regimentation elsewhere in the Eastern bloc, [Belgrade] ... is a bustling center of 1.1 million people with 'affluent communism' everywhere apparent."[56]

The importance of the smile did not rest solely with the country's

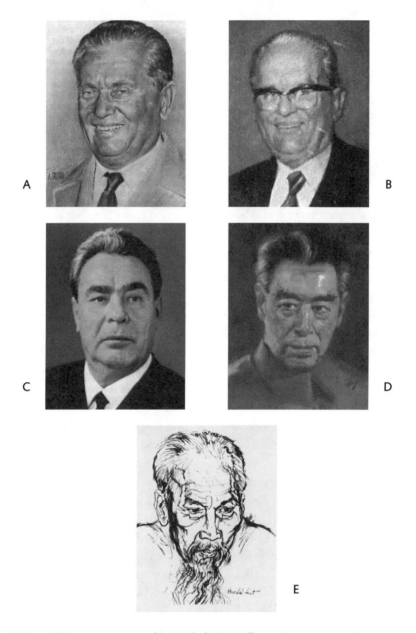

Figure 7. Dictators as portrayed in *Reader's Digest*. Illustrations accompanying two articles on Yugoslavia depicted a smiling Tito (*A and B*) as a kindly patriarch. Other communist dictators were not shown in such a friendly manner: Brezhnev (*C*) and Chou En-Lai (*D*) stare stonily from the pages, while Ho Chi Minh (*E*) looks away (because of the brutality attributed to him in the article?). Images of Tito from September 1967, p. 63, and April 1973, p. 241; Brezhnev from May 1972, p. 85; Chou from February 1972, p. 86; Ho from November 1968, p. 61.

premier. Novelist and travel writer James Michener accompanied Nixon on his state visit to China and reported in the *Digest* that he saw no smiles. More generally, in a ballet performed for him, "not once does any character display any human emotion other than revenge or military triumph."[57] Other travelogues noted the same tendency: Moscow was a "city without smiles," as was Leningrad; an article on the Danube wrote a geography of happiness that claimed that the "laughter of this gay and golden place dies quietly, however, as the river flows under ... the Iron Curtain."[58]

If the smile came to stand for a happy system, then communism was positively glum. The "economic purgatory" communist countries suffered meant that dullness pervaded every aspect of life; one author reported that "Even women's underwear at lingerie counters is coarse and drab."[59] In Cuba, too, individuals were described as being forced to accept drabness for even the most personal or romantic apparel: "Women comb through ads for such items as 'secondhand' brassieres or a 'slightly used wedding gown.'"[60] As is so often the case in *Reader's Digest* and in Western national rhetoric more generally, women—or, more correctly, the bodies of women—were made to stand metaphorically for the well-being of the nation.[61]

The *Digest* saw ideology blanketing the pleasant aspects of cultures and landscapes now dominated by communism. "Bedtime Story, Red China Style" showed how communism had erased happiness and other "human" feelings with its party dogma.[62] In a remarkable show of naïveté, another piece described Cuban signs:

> Ideology is injected into everything. Billboards and posters blanket Havana, urging collective effort rather than individual satisfaction. Instead of "Enjoy the Flavor of Budweiser" it's "When a Communist is Born, Difficulties Die" and "Our Goal—to Increase Production Tenfold."[63]

I believe that both the metaphorical and the actual use of the smile are related to an attempt by the *Digest* to present the subjects of communist governments to the magazine's readership in such a way as to make them seem similar to one another. The smile here signified the underlying unity of the "great family of man" as discussed in chapter 3.[64] This obviously alters the Other in that it is no longer monolithically different.[65] In many ways ordinary Americans and ordinary Russians were seen as the same. The *Digest* no longer presented the people of communist countries as Other, but instead the system itself and those who ran it. Many articles in this period stressed the fact that most people in countries facing communist takeover were anticommunist. Some articles described the vehemence of anticommunist feelings: "Virtually all South Koreans are so bitterly anti-communist that they would rather die than submit to Kim Il Sung's rule";[66] 80 percent of the South Vietnamese population was said to be anticommunist.[67] For other authors, communism was merely a strategy: "Ideology was paper-thin [in Angola].... Neto and his lieutenants were pro-Soviet mainly because the Russians were paying the bills."[68] More often, however, people under communist rule were represented as simple people who cared little for ideology and only wanted a good life for themselves and their families: "*Ours was an attitude rather than an ideology.*"[69]

This strategy of invoking values close to the "ideology-free" American Dream of a prosperous family life made the plight of those under communist regimes all the more real to *Digest* readers. The people described were just like them, but their lives were turned upside down by the imposition of a communist state. If one of the *Digest*'s roles was to articulate the concerns of the individual reader with wider political processes, then surely this process of identification would make communism seem highly relevant to readers in that if communism were to triumph in America, their lives would be similarly affected. A major effect of the magazine's construction of the danger of détente, then, was to make essential a conservative image of politics and values at home—values that the *Digest* itself epitomized.

The End of Détente

The period of détente came to a halt with the Soviet invasion of Afghanistan and Ronald Reagan's becoming president in 1981. The magazine wrote the period as one of intense danger as a result of its fears of the irreversible damage inflicted on the country's security by President Jimmy Carter's appeasement of the Soviets.

Articles in the period from 1964 to 1978 did not reach the hysterical notes of the first years of the Cold War, yet they did not represent a break from this earlier time. Just as had been the case at the beginning of the Cold War, during "détente," communism offered the *Digest* America's principal enemy (although, significantly, not its sole enemy). The *Digest* still offered its readership hope, though, for the American people could resist communism. The magazine's disciplining of its readership continued throughout the détente period more through identification with the lives of similar people living under communist systems than through the tragedy of repeated conquest. The groundwork was in place for reescalation of opposition in the 1980s.

CHAPTER SIX

The "Second Cold War"

The "Second Cold War" refers to the years from 1979 to 1985, a period characterized by rejection of the politics of détente and a return to the political praxis and perceptions of the very first period of the Cold War in American political culture. The rise of the Second Cold War was linked both to perceptions of the relative decline of U.S. hegemony by some groups in the West and to the Soviet invasion of Afghanistan. The election of Ronald Reagan, whose foreign policy was informed by the (geo)politics of the Committee of the Present Danger, reinforced the air of renewed hostility.[1] This heightened perception of danger was underscored by the prominence of Third World political revolutions (most importantly, in Nicaragua and Iran), often viewed in America as movements backed by Moscow. The combination of these factors led to a renewed sense of vulnerability in the United States and a new commitment to halt communist influence around the world. Indeed, for the *Digest,* the Cold War had not in any way ended with détente, and Afghanistan represented confirmation of its interpretation of Soviet nature and intentions. The election of Ronald Reagan as president indicated to the magazine that the country was finally coming to its senses about the reality of superpower conflict.

Reader's Digest anticipated the rise of the Second Cold War mentality in its initial reaction to American moves toward détente in the early 1970s. By the end of the 1970s, *Digest* articles exhibited an intense impression of vulnerability, which the magazine attributed to American weakness in international relations. The Soviets had continued the Cold War by military and propagandistic means throughout détente. In contrast, America had limited itself by the spirit and letter of détente and arms negotiations. To the magazine, this American honesty and Soviet deviousness had led to a reversal of power; during the 1970s, the United States had lost its military dominance to the USSR. This situation provided an innocent motivation for American "re"armament in the face of a superior superpower and facilitated critique of the liberal domination of politics epitomized for the *Digest* in the Carter administration. This weakness had emerged for *Reader's Digest* when America failed to negotiate a fair end to the Vietnam War; it reached an apogee with President Jimmy Carter. The *Digest* presented Carter's policies as wholly idealistic; by operating within this mind-set and "therefore" ignoring realpolitik, Carter had placed the country in grave jeopardy. For example, in "Innocence Abroad: Jimmy Carter's Four Misconceptions," *Digest* regulars Rowland Evans and Robert Novak took the president to task for believing that human rights had to be the cornerstone of foreign policy. Such a policy, they argued, "inevitably led him into a policy of maximum U.S. pressure against friendly tyrants" rather than directing all of its power toward America's *real* enemy, the USSR.[2] With the election of Reagan, the *Digest* had an administration that shared its viewpoint and a president who shared the magazine's rhetorical style and even quoted *Reader's Digest* as a source of insightful information and important opinion. The Reagan administration provided the *Digest* with a potentially happy ending to its long narration of American vulnerability.

Although the heating up of the Cold War at this point did not result in more articles on this topic (see figure 6), a large number of articles represented the Soviet Union, and communist systems more generally, as being entirely different from the American way. In other words, the *Digest's* naturalization of the Soviet Union as America's Other was fully achieved during this period. No longer did the *Digest* have to demonstrate *why* the Soviets were bad, since more than thirty years of demonization had made it "obvious" that the Soviet Union was the enemy; the magazine could expect its readers to know and accept this view. *Reader's Digest's* geo-graphing of international relations had become common sense, obliterating the subtleties of international politics. The complexities of foreign policy decisions were truly condensed to a conflict of good and evil.

In this chapter I will look at the reescalation of the Cold War between

1979 and 1985. First I will examine the *Digest*'s description of what America needed to do to regain its hegemonic status and the dangers that threatened this historic role. Next I will examine the embodiment of the Soviet Union in articles during this period, the techniques used by *Digest* writers to render the operation of world politics relevant to the lives of the magazine's American readership. I will conclude with a description of how the *Digest* portrayed the Soviet Union as entirely different from America.

Restoration of America

From its vantage point in the Second Cold War, *Reader's Digest* dated the moment of American decline to the negotiated end of the Vietnam War. The psychological scars of that event became inscribed into the *Digest*'s description of Soviet involvement in regional conflict. It seemed that if *Reader's Digest* could label contemporary Soviet involvement in regional conflicts as "like Vietnam," this would cancel out the American weakness and dishonor that it perceived as having resulted from America's engagement in Vietnam. A number of articles, therefore, described regional conflicts as new Vietnams: "With modest help from the West, [Savimbi] believes, Angola will become an African Vietnam for the Kremlin and its Cuban mercenaries."[3] Although it talked about Afghanistan as the USSR's Vietnam, the *Digest* had to be careful not to offend the Americans who had served in Vietnam. It thus concluded that in fact the comparison with Vietnam was not fair because, unlike the American campaign, the Soviets were just out for power and so were making "no attempt to win hearts and minds."[4]

The American experience in Vietnam was also used as "evidence" of the necessity of an American presence in regional conflicts in other "strategic" areas regardless of their location or their political-cultural similarity to Southeast Asia two decades earlier. For example, Jeane Kirkpatrick, then U.S. representative to the United Nations, argued that the lessons of Vietnam meant that the United States could not abandon Central Americans in their struggle against communism.[5]

The *Digest* therefore restated its call for investment both in the military and in provision of information to counter Soviet anti-American "propaganda." Détente had not only weakened America's military capability, the magazine argued, but also had led the Soviets into temptation; they saw that they could get away with territorial infringements. For example, one author claimed that "we have led the Russians into irresistible temptation," and another suggested that the Soviets were encouraged "by American indecisiveness," concluding that "history shows that Moscow respects just one thing: counterforce."[6]

The outcome of every regional battle was thus scripted as being key to the strength of America's influence in world events. This was particularly true for conflicts in the Western hemisphere, as the *Digest* insisted that "America's role as a world leader may well rest on how resolutely we deal with this Soviet orchestrated threat in our own backyard."[7] The change of government in 1981 provided the *Digest* with proof that the magazine's views had at last found their way into the practice of American foreign policy. The 1984 article "Grenada: Anatomy of a 'Go' Decision" praised the Reagan administration for taking action to stop the spreading force of Soviet influence rather than being limited by fear of offending the communists.[8]

As we have seen, *Reader's Digest* regarded the Soviet Union as continuing the Cold War through propaganda during the period of détente. The magazine's fear of a Soviet triumph in the war for people's minds persisted into the next period. The *Digest* claimed in "The Freedom Fight We Can't Afford to Lose" that "to communist dictatorships, the struggle for human rights was far more dangerous than hydrogen or neutron bombs."[9] One piece pressed for greater government funding for the Voice of America because "however much the Soviet leaders fear our weapons, they fear the truth even more."[10] Another insisted that the Voice of America become part of America's defense budget because of the anticommunist role that the radio information broadcast played. The *Digest*, arguing that knowledge, and especially possession of the truth, was a powerful weapon in the fight against communism, claimed that even the Soviets were aware that "freedom, even of a limited sort, is contagious."[11] Once again, the magazine wrote American triumph as the natural outcome in its use of a disease metaphor.

The *Digest* wrote its position on defense as both commonsensical and reasonable. The magazine suggested that its concept of American foreign involvement would appeal to those who wanted to stand up to the Soviets but did not want to provoke them unnecessarily: "Extremes aside, cautious people favor defense," it stated. "The less we spend on defense, the greater the risk of war."[12] Again, the magazine wrote American action as reaction.

Although *Reader's Digest* now saw the predominant mood in the United States begin to swing toward its own long-held interpretation of the Soviet Union, the actions of America's European allies appeared to place all countries in the Western alliance in jeopardy. The *Digest* saw growing European peace movements as organizations manipulated by Moscow,[13] and the initial establishment of trade agreements between Europe and the USSR as threats to the security of the continent. In "Europe's Perilous Reach for Siberian Gas" it claimed that

> ever since Lenin said he would hang the capitalists with the rope they sold him, political influence through trade has been a Soviet goal.... If Western Europe ever depends on the Soviet Union for economic security and prosperity, the Western alliance is doomed. NATO will be shattered without the Soviets having to fire a single shot.[14]

Other areas also threatened the security of America and its allies. The Persian Gulf presented a potential threat through a combination of its strategic importance for the supply of oil, for its geopolitical significance, and for the danger that a combination of Islamic fundamentalism and Soviet communism might pose to the *Digest's* conceptualization of an American-dominated world order. Despite the fact that since its inception, *Reader's Digest* had published stories about the incompatibility of communism and religion, at this point the magazine appeared to give the impression that Islamic religious institutions were in collusion with the Soviet Union. I believe that this was possible through the *Digest's* reliance upon an implicit Orientalism in its readers: like communism, Islam represented an Other presence. Americans' general lack of knowledge of Islam and their fear of fundamentalism was part of centuries of Western "Othering" of Islamic societies into a homogeneous, threatening presence. This combination of ignorance of the actual nature of Islam and its positioning as Other made the convergence of Islam and communism quite credible.[15]

Exceptions to this representation of Islam were articles that praised the Afghan jihad for resisting Soviet invasion. When they were fighting the greater evil of communism, it was acceptable to the *Digest* for fundamentalists to become martyrs for Allah.[16]

The Soviet Union was also considered by the *Digest* to be manipulating Middle East conflict more generally. In 1982 the magazine argued that "only the Soviet Union stands to benefit from the growing Arab tensions over the Israeli occupation. The Soviets are entrenched all around the rim of the Middle East heartland."[17] Libya's Colonel Qaddafi was depicted as the "Soviet Union's protégé in the Arab world" with access to "a Soviet war machine."[18]

Reader's Digest indicated that its readership should know—and care—about events occurring in the Middle East because Soviet control of this area would have far-reaching consequences. The *Digest* drew upon classic geopolitical reasoning to argue that if the Soviet Union were to occupy the Strait of Hormuz, it would control the economies of the Western world.[19] Moreover, this action might represent only the first move in a much more important Soviet plan. The *Digest* suggested that although Warsaw Treaty nations would not attack Europe first, they would launch a major offensive in the Persian Gulf and from there advance to the heartland of the Western alliance.[20]

The linkage between the Soviet Union and fundamentalist Middle Eastern powers was extended in Claire Sterling's infamous "Network of Terror," published in *Reader's Digest* in 1981. This article described the formation of a deliberate and unified network of terrorism that included the IRA, the PLO, Cuban-backed insurgents, Basques, and others "whose ultimate beneficiary and undercover patron has been the Soviet Union."[21] The article claimed to provide "proof" for the influence of the Soviet Union on these terrorist groups by describing their ultimate goals. It described the IRA's desires for a united Ireland as "something quite similar to communism"[22] and reinforced the connections between communism and the religious goals of the terrorists by quoting a terrorist who claimed that "Marxism has always been my religion."[23]

Soviet People

One notable difference between the articles in this period and those in the one preceding it was *Reader's Digest*'s view of the Soviet population. During the détente period, the Soviet people were most often seen as being very much like Americans; the only difference between them was that the Russians were forced to live under a communist regime. During the Second Cold War, the Soviet people were divided into different groups. The mass of the Soviet people were described as being quite different from Americans. Either they had become entirely submissive because of years of (Mongol, czarist, and) communist repression, or the harsh Russian environment had influenced their development. For example, one author in 1980 wrote:

> If you were to announce over the [Soviet] radio that now there is to be liberty, people would scratch their heads and try to figure out what this could mean. But if you were to growl loudly that Stalin had chosen to be resurrected, people would quietly exchange glances, sigh secretly and accept it as something normal.[24]

On the other hand, an article entitled "Russian Winter" argued that environmental conditions ultimately were responsible for the authoritarian system and the submissive malleable population characteristic of communist Russia:

> Thanks at least in part to their climate, Russians perceive the outside world as hostile, and yet enviable too. Going deeper, what is usually shrugged off as 'bad luck' can also be seen as punishment; like handicapped children, Russians feel that they are 'not like the others,' and tend to blame themselves for the stigma and hardship.[25]

Reader's Digest provided three exceptions to this picture of a faceless Soviet population. The *Digest* wrote biographies of Soviet leaders, the masterminds behind repressive communist society and aggressive Soviet foreign policy ("Who Is Yuri Andropov?"), of spies, and of brave dissidents ("The Persecution of Andrei Sakharov").[26] The *Digest* represented the dissidents as being most like Americans; they "belonged in spirit to the Western intelligentsia"[27] and thus were placed outside the *Digest*'s neat division of Self and Other. Opposition to the communist system was regarded as an inevitable development and was thus described in naturalizing language ("Poland's Rising Tide of Dissent").[28]

The Embodiment of Politics

The opposition between the Soviet Union and America was often anthropomorphized during this period. This discursive strategy has much in common with the use of metaphors of disease employed in the initial stages of Cold War representation, in that the *Digest* rendered international events in terms of metaphors to which its readers could easily relate; these metaphors used bodily characteristics to explain the realities of the world system. For example, communist tunnels in the Korean demilitarized zone were "all pointing, like daggers, at South Korea's heart,"[29] and Cuba was "the Russian knife at America's throat."[30] In 1985 *Reader's Digest* regular R. K. Bennett provided an "anatomy of a famine" for Ethiopia that described a very unhealthy body. One description of Mozambique provided an even more severe diagnosis: the author described his voyage through "lifeless streets" and claimed that "I had the feeling I was in a dying country."[31]

Of course, "the body" is not a gender-neutral surface. The gendering of the USSR in *Reader's Digest* was very different from the gendering of Europe's Other in the writings of Orientalism;[32] rather than invoking the West's penetration or subjugation of a feminized Other, the *Digest* subjected America and its allies to the whims of an aggressive masculinity. For example, Scandinavian-Soviet relations were written in the traditional language of patriarchal gender relations: invoking rape, one author described "Russian submarines continuing to penetrate these frigid Nordic waters."[33]

Earlier Cold War representation of sexuality reemerged in this period. Homosexuality was written as a weakness the communists could take advantage of. "From Cuba with Hate: The Crime Wave Castro Sent to America" described how, "under threat if they refused [to go], ex-convicts, homosexuals, suspected black-marketeers, vagrants and troublemakers were offered one-way passage to the United States."[34]

Tales of individual exploits used gender identities in a manner that paralleled this systemic gendering. *Reader's Digest* had never given women an important role in creating American security. Women tended to be portrayed as passive victims, anguished wives, or caregivers, whereas men represented dissidents, war heroes, and spies.[35] This should not come as a surprise, for in traditional national rhetoric, men are metonyms of the nation in that the nation is embodied in each man and each man comes to embody the nation. Women are predominantly scripted into the national imaginary in a different manner; women do not embody the nation but are symbolic of it.[36] The Second Cold War period was no exception to this dominant constitution of gendered national identification. Women rarely moved beyond being a passive presence; most often they were objects to be utilized by the male nationalist hero. An article explained how information was attained by spies:

Wolf hit a real espionage winner when he concocted the idea of sending handsome male agents to Bonn ... to bed government secretaries and get them to steal secret documents.[37]

Another article on espionage was illustrated with an image of a woman with a camera seducing a man holding a file marked "secret" (figure 8).[38] A third piece used the female body as a metaphor for what the author considered to be a progressive change in communist China. He stated that the last time he had traveled to China—with President Nixon—he saw a ballet called "The Red Brigade of Women," which he described as "a sterile drama of women storming a reactionary bastion. Beautiful ballet, but no legs showing." On his more recent trip, he said, "above all, I noticed women's thighs in public."[39]

Ultimate Difference

What really distinguishes this period is the construction of absolute difference that *Reader's Digest* presents in Second Cold War articles. Some articles during this period described the Soviet Union and other communist systems in terms that made them appear to be totally alien to the American way and so reinforced the sense of separation and opposition of the two systems.[40]

The Second Cold War period reinforced the *Digest's* view that negotiation with the Soviets was futile. During the détente period, this had been explained as the result of Soviet pathological dishonesty or power-political tactics. Now, however, *Reader's Digest* implied that as a result of their national character, the Soviets were simply unable to negotiate. In "How *Not* to Negotiate with the Russians" the *Digest* explained the problems with attempting diplomatic relations with Soviet leaders:

> *The Soviets do not believe in compromise.* There is no Russian equivalent to the root word of the English "compromise." The Soviets have adopted our word, but not embraced our meaning. The search for a reasonable middle ground of agreement, the heart of the Western sense of negotiation, is foreign to them. Soviet negotiators regard compromise as a sign of weakness.... We failed at the SALT negotiations because we continued to believe that the Russians would or could think like us. While we slipped from strategic superiority to parity to inferiority, the Soviets sought, not to establish a strategic balance but to win a strategic game. And they have at last succeeded.[41]

Our embassies abroad continue to hire local employees who are sometimes as adept at pampering our foreign-service people as they are at espionage

Why Our Embassies Are Nests for Spies

Condensed from
WASHINGTON MONTHLY

PRISCILLA WITT

AMERICANS WHO take assignments at U.S. embassies around the world have always been warned about foreign agents who—through seduction, bribery, bugging or other means—will attempt to recruit them to obtain classified information. In the wake of the recent Marine spy scandal in Moscow, the United States has witnessed just how real the dangers are.

Even more startling, we have seen that these spies needn't hang out in smoky clip joints, waiting to ensnare unsuspecting embassy employees. Instead, today's foreign agents can sometimes be found inside the protective walls of American embassies, as paid employees of the U.S. government.

Our Moscow embassy, which once had 220 Soviets on its payroll,

WASHINGTON MONTHLY (APRIL '87). © 1987 BY THE WASHINGTON MONTHLY CO., 1711 CONNECTICUT AVE., N.W., *111*
WASHINGTON, D.C. 20009. PHOTOS: JAY P. MORGAN

Figure 8. "Why our Embassies are Nests for Spies," by Priscilla Witt. *Reader's Digest,* October, 1987, p. 111.

The *Digest* concluded that there was simply no point in negotiating; America would negotiate in the spirit of compromise, but the Soviets would be *incapable* of doing this. Either the talks would fail or the Soviets would take advantage of the Americans' goodwill.

Thus, portrayal of the opposition between the two systems continued in such a way as to give the impression that there could not be any appeasement between America and the Soviets: "Unless you want to trust Soviet benevolence" claimed one article (and of course, if you were a regular *Digest* reader, you would not), "the only ways to handle them are to surrender, or to keep them at bay with forces sufficient to deter, and with mutual and verifiable arms-limitation agreements that will maintain the balance."[42]

The *Digest*'s portrayal of communist irrationality was mirrored in the non-sense that it saw in the personality cult of Kim Il Sung: "To an outsider, the cult inspires a strange mixture of hilarity and unease." The *Digest* described the hilarity aspect:

> Postal clerks cancel only the corners of stamps showing Kim; the Great Leader must not be defaced. Before a newspaper may safely be used for, say, lining a shelf, Kim's pictures must be removed.[43]

But the irrationality of the cult also posed a threat to America because of Sung's virulent anti-Americanism, which the *Digest* illustrated with reference to North Korean popular culture:

> "Let's mutilate any American soldiers we catch today" is the title of a pop song. Children sing "Our greatest aim in life is to kill 100 Yankees."[44]

Other authors insisted that there was a "lack of respect for human life by those in charge of the Soviet Union."[45] Soviets were thus placed by *Reader's Digest* outside Western standards of behavior, and some articles indicated that Americans would have to take account of this in their preparations to engage with Soviets in any way: "If we allow ourselves the luxury of giving in to our civilized revulsion against [chemical] warfare, we are whistling past what may turn out to be a graveyard for our forces in Europe."[46]

Russian inhumanity was described not just at the societal level; individuals were also presented in this manner. The *Digest* described a twelve-year-old Russian who had come from Russia to live in America. The boy's

American teacher was quoted as saying, "Walter has changed from a robot to a kid learning to laugh."[47]

In short, during the Second Cold War, Soviet society was described as being a different world from what Americans were used to; they were "as different as the moon and earth."[48] Even apparently progressive change ultimately became perverted in this type of system. For example, the 1982 article "Top Secret: Is There Sex in Russia?" suggested that

> to some people in a democratic society, the powerful taboos of a totalitarian state may seem a panacea for raging sexual folly. But illnesses that are covered up tend to rage even stronger and the prognosis grows more dire.[49]

Without any hint of self-conscious irony, the *Digest* even presented the USSR as a perversion of socialism (which itself had been constructed as a perversion of capitalism). In the inevitable 1984 article on the realization of George Orwell's antiutopian vision, the *Digest* claimed that although Orwell was a socialist, "he regarded the Soviet Union and communism in general not as fulfillments of socialism but as its perverters and betrayers."[50]

The *Digest* thus set the stage for the most extreme case of Othering in the magazine over the years of publication covered here: an article that implied Russians and Americans were biologically incompatible. "Russian Blood" told the story of an American, Jim, who required a blood transfusion after surgery in Siberia. The article recounted how Jim was given local blood, which his body appeared to reject. The article indicated that there was not usually any problem when a patient was given "blood of the same type but of different ethnic origin" and admitted that it was possible that the blood might not have been properly screened before transfusion. But, the reader was left to contemplate a more revealing question:

> Is his body rejecting the *Russian* blood?[51]

At the conclusion of the story, the American was airlifted from Siberia before the Soviet surgeons had the opportunity to open him up once more. A transfusion of American blood brought from Germany was successful. The article concluded with the author's statement: "My theory is right! Jim's body is accepting the *American* blood."[52]

Placing a nationality or ideology on a biological characteristic such as blood type is an extreme form of creating difference. The article implied that Soviets and Americans are different to the point of biological incompatibility. I do not believe that this article could have been published earlier in the *Digest*'s career. It was only with the accumulated years of description of communists as America's Other that such an extreme account could be accepted as reasonable by the magazine's readership.

Reader's Digest did not publish as many articles on the Soviet Union and communism during the Second Cold War as it did during the first stage of the Cold War in the late 1940s. I do not believe that this was because the *Digest* saw the Russians as any less evil or any less of a threat. On the contrary, the tone of many of the articles makes the USSR seem much more different from America than the earlier Cold War articles had done. Previously, the Soviets were evil and threatening, and the difference between the two systems was the result of an intentional *choice* of systemic development. By the time of the Second Cold War, Americans and Soviets seemed to have developed so differently that no matter how hard they tried, there *could not* be a convergence of interests of the two systems. In fact, this writing of the relationship between the United States and the USSR could not cope with any notion of positive change. As a result, this period witnessed a rewriting not only of contemporary Soviet behavior, but also of past behavior. The origins of the system—in the Russian Revolution—were rewritten as devious and manipulative, as stealing away the country's one chance of democracy rather than representing a move, however misguided, toward a more egalitarian society, which had been a credible view until the close of World War II.

I believe that because the *Digest* had so clearly characterized the USSR and communism over the years since the beginning of the Cold War, it no longer needed as many articles *explaining* Soviet action—readers knew that the Soviets wore the "black hats," to use Reaganesque terminology. Other periods had established the opposition between America and the Russians; this period demonstrated just how far apart these two systems were.

The initial part of the Cold War period is illustrative of the apparently paradoxical desire of individuals to be disciplined. *Reader's Digest*'s analysis in this period explains why people should live in fear—why people would continue to desire to consume information that fills them with anxiety. *Reader's Digest* simultaneously created fear and offered either preventive measures or solutions: it presented terrible tales of Soviet deeds and possible communist futures, but always offered a therapeutic discourse. The *Digest*, in other words, always offered something that the reader could do (even if it was just staying informed) to help prevent such a tragedy.

The dominant narrative strategy in this period could thus be regarded as tragedy. Roland Barthes described tragedy as the unfolding of a plot, the end of which the reader already knew, yet the reader derived a perverse pleasure from reading on:

> Of all readings, that of tragedy is the most perverse: I take a pleasure in hearing myself tell a story *whose end I know*. I know and I don't know, I act toward myself as though I did not know.[53]

During the Cold War, *Reader's Digest* provided example after example of places and people who endured the tragedy of communist takeover or narrowly missed this finale. Since *Reader's Digest* is not a newsmagazine, the majority of readers presumably would know whether or not a country had in fact turned communist. This would appear to reinforce Barthes's concept of tragedy as a story whose ending is already known to be an appropriate description of *Digest* narrative strategy.

In order to prevent tragedy, the *Digest* could insist upon the masculinist protection of vulnerable lands and ignorant peoples. This legitimated neocolonialist intervention in the Third World. It also led to the insistence on "good citizenship" in the United States to protect American institutions from any weakness that might leave these usually strong pillars of society vulnerable to communist seduction. The good citizen was gendered male, and as such had the effect of reinforcing and legitimating orthodox gender norms. Men were to protect the nation from its enemies, and this protective role was to be replicated in the family through the patriarchal authority of the father figure.

Yet the *Digest* never provides pure tragedy; its underlying optimism demands redemption. Thus articles end up either as comic farces, in which the Soviets' inefficiency or irrationality prohibits them from achieving their goal, or as morality plays in which a path to redemption is offered so that a tragic conclusion can be avoided.

Disease metaphors require the identification of difficulty and pain in order to offer the therapy of a cure. Returning to Fredric Jameson's description of the role of the mass media being to arouse fantasies and desires within structures established to diffuse them,[54] I would argue that at the start of the Cold War the *Digest* constructed perverse desires to be scared, which it then diffused in its therapeutic narratives of (potential) redemption. Later, new fears emerged from détente policies. The *Digest* worried that the American way itself represented a danger in this international setup. Frederick Dolan explained this fear in the context of containment strategies:

> Containment depicts a "dangerous world" in which liberal principles are put "at risk" to the precise extent that liberal policies adhere to them.[55]

Thus *Reader's Digest* managed to maintain—and even increase—a sense of danger even when the threat of communism appeared to be waning. The end of the Cold War, however, presented a more fundamental challenge to the magazine's moral geography, since the very lines of identification of good and evil disappeared before American eyes.

CHAPTER SEVEN

Denying Imperial Decline
at the End of the Cold War

It has now become something of a cliché that with the end of the Cold War and the loss of its alter ego, hegemonic American culture entered a period of crisis that has raised profound questions about both national identity and national purpose.[1] The Cold War, rather than presenting a threat to American self-identity, was constitutive of it. For the right-wing hegemony, to quote one of its doyens, the end of the standoff represented the "end of history":[2] the dynamic dialectic between America and the Soviet Union was lost as capitalism was seen to have triumphed. Most significant was the resultant geopolitical change. America's Cold War goal of containing the USSR can be understood in terms of a moving frontier between the United States and its alter ego, dividing good and evil not unlike the frontier that characterized its initial western expansion. If there is a story about the nation's origins at the origin of every nation,[3] then for America this originary story is of the frontier; its absence at the close of the Cold War must have profound effects on U.S. identity.

With the dissolution of the American Cold War frontier, a new focus on multiple regional enemies and problems arose; as James DerDerian suggested, "This [end] is surely only the beginning: at the end of *the* history comes a thousand, newly re-inscribed ones."[4] Frederick Dolan has noted that the CIA, for example, quickly realized that the postmodern political world would refuse to yield to a clearly defined and marked threat.[5] Intelligence was thus presented as crucial to post–Cold War foreign policy in order to determine what course to follow in a world that might become *more* dangerous because it was *less* predictable.

Reader's Digest had successfully written itself into the heart of American identity constructed around the geopolitics of the Cold War. Like hegemonic U.S. culture as a whole, then, the magazine was desperately searching for a new wor(l)d order within which to script its role in the reproduction of "America." In this chapter I will consider the magazine's engagement with the emergence of the end of the Cold War in order to understand how it has written the changed world order in such a way as to still present itself as a credible guide to America's place in the world. Of course, the *Digest* has also written roles for individual Americans as good citizens. I will also consider the ways in which individual identity has been addressed with the collapse of the Cold War binary.

The Meaning of the Beginning of the End

Many people would date the beginning of the end of the Cold War to the rise of Mikhail Gorbachev as general secretary of the Soviet Communist Party.[6] Just as much of the world was heralding Gorbachev and his reforms as the end of international danger, however, *Reader's Digest* sensed in the new leader an ever more significant threat to American security and the primacy of the democratic world. The *Digest* coded this wary interpretation of the Soviet presence through two distinct narratives.

The first narrative refused to accept the ability of the Soviet Union to change; this Cold Warrior mind-set could not readily comprehend a world order outside the binary cartography of opposing superpowers. This narrative continued to write world politics within the binary structure of the Cold War, acknowledging only cosmetic changes to the Soviet system.[7] Indeed, the *Digest's* insistence on the superficiality of change actually reinforced the Cold War structure in this narrative: Gorbachev's expression of progressive change merely represented a continuation of the "typical" communist tactic of seducing people and nations by projecting positive appearances to deflect attention away from their true (expansionary) intentions. Within the limits of this narrative, it would be impossible for communists to change: a person who was a communist, could not *also* be democratic, open, or progressive, since these characterizations are mutually exclusive. One author stated in 1988 that even if "reforms were broadened substantially, the Soviet Union would remain a totalitarian dictatorship."[8] Implicitly drawing on the traditional Western representation of the Russian empire as an Oriental despotism,[9] this and other *Reader's Digest* articles assumed an essential characteristic of the

Russian people; after so many centuries of dictatorship, submission to absolute authority was lodged deep within the Russian psyche.[10]

The second *Reader's Digest* narrativization of Gorbachev's premiership is of much more interest in the context of the longer-term development of the magazine's map of post–Cold War American identification. *Digest* articles conforming to this second interpretative structure recognized the significance of changes in the USSR but challenged the benign intentions said to drive them. Just as in the 1970s *Reader's Digest* had feared weakness arising from détente policies toward the communist world, now it worried about the effect of "too many Gorbachev boosters"[11] who too readily accepted the intentions of the USSR as benevolent. "Gorbachev's nuclear-weapon-free-world proposal," stated one author in 1989, "was only an attempt to woo public opinion in the west."[12] In an interview with Ronald Reagan, the magazine put it to the president that "it's widely reported that Gorbachev is winning the propaganda war in Europe."[13]

It was, however, not Gorbachev himself nor the changes he proposed that most troubled *Reader's Digest*. Instead, it was widespread public acceptance of Gorbachev's intentions that seemed to threaten an element of American identity that was more important to the *Digest* than simple military or political hegemony. Gorbachev's goal, according to the magazine, was

> the most ambitious ever sought by a Soviet leader, [and it] has profound meaning for the Western alliance. It is nothing less than achieving, in the eyes of the world, full moral equivalence with the United States. . . . It is hugely important to Moscow that the world believe that there is no great difference between us.[14]

The challenge, then, as the *Digest* perceived it, was that America would lose control of its self-proclaimed role as moral cartographer of the world. Although America would stand as the sole superpower at the close of the Cold War, Manifest Destiny might be at stake without a commonly accepted Evil Empire against which to struggle.

The end of the 1980s therefore saw *Reader's Digest* seeking to reinscribe a global cartography of danger against which America's destiny could be mapped out once more. The most overt example of the *Digest's* attempts at post–Cold War geo-graphing, however, came in a series of articles in 1990. Called "Countdown to the Twenty-First Century: Freedom on the

March" and accompanied by a picture of the Statue of Liberty, these articles sought to reestablish America's moral leadership of the new world order.[15] The third part of the triad of articles, titled "Democracy Is Winning," presented a map of world freedom (figure 9). In a remarkable structural parallel to the magazine's Cold War map of the three spaces of First World/democratic, Second World/totalitarian and Third World/contested, *Reader's Digest's* new global cartography divided the world into three blocks: "free," "not free," and "partly free." The accompanying text declared that of ninety-three new states arising from colonial Africa and Asia, only seven "qualify as free today." Without ever defining the terms of freedom and its absence, the text claims an optimistic future in which freedom would spread, propelled by "a fundamental yearning of the human heart, everywhere inborn and inalienable."[16]

The *Digest's* attempt to hold onto a global cartography based on the idea of American leadership is in no way unique. John McClure has suggested that a reconstruction of chaos and uncertainty is central to the state of decline in which the destiny of an imperial power has faded and new challenges have to be scripted in an attempt to reconstruct the nation's role. He sees that embroiled within the narrative structure of identity is a romantic desire for Otherness and chaos that can be tamed or overcome through various trials.[17] McClure's argument is based on an analysis of literature, but I would contend that the desire for a realm of alterity can also be read into the discursive structure of (neo)realist international relations theories.[18] As I have argued, the *Digest's* representation of the dis-order of global spaces outside its definition of normal freedom and democracy allowed the magazine to construct a normative agenda in which order could be projected onto international chaos to create an image of a good American society. Thus the magazine's account of American destiny and identity, and its readers' stake in reproducing them, depends upon the existence of an identifiable threat. The danger to American identity is that the potential for the romantic narration of America's unique destiny will disappear. McClure writes:

> Without the unordered spaces, or spaces distorted by war, it is impossible to stage the wanderings and disorientations, the quests and conquests and conversions, the ordeals and sacrifices and triumphs that are the stuff of romance. The ultimate enemies of romance, then, are not the foreign foes confronted on the field of battle in the test itself, but the foes held at bay by these essential antagonists: the banal, quotidian world of calculation

and compromise from which the heroes of romance are always in flight, and the globally routinized world that only became imaginable about one hundred years ago, a world utterly devoid of romantic regions.[19]

This argument might strike some readers as exaggerated in that state practice and foreign policy, and media coverage of them, are generally accepted as being based upon logic and rational reasoning rather than psychological and intertextual modes of argument.[20] However, the fact that *Reader's Digest* saw the USSR more as an alter ego central to the construction of American self-identification than as a real threat is perhaps indicated by the fact that just when the region became most unstable, when it was most in flux and there would appear to be so much to be explored and discussed, there was actually a *drop* in *Reader's Digest* coverage (see figure 6). Once the unity of the communist world finally crumbled, the magazine did not greatly concern itself about the rise of Yeltsin or Zhirinovsky, or the continued battles for territorial sovereignty or weapons ownership. The USSR no longer embodied the Evil Empire standing in the path of America's Manifest Destiny. Instead the magazine sought new locations within which to stage America's struggles.

New "Others"

As communism declined and the Cold War drew to a close, it was often assumed that other threats would arise in the international arena.[21] *Reader's Digest* did indeed introduce new international threats and also reinforced the danger presented by those already familiar to American society. At first communism still offered a rich source of alterity. If the Soviet Union was becoming a less useful alter ego, then renegade communists could be brought to center stage. Nicolae Ceaușescu, the magazine argued, may have looked "like a daring maverick of the communist bloc" (and, in fact, that is how *Reader's Digest* had generally presented him before), but "he can be seen as a megalomaniac destroying his once-blessed country"—Romania—such that "even by communist standards the project is obscene."[22] But, however deviant other communist leaders may have been, their presence could never match that of the Evil Empire, so that no communist state alone would possess the symbolic power against which to define the American national essence. The *Digest* sought out new representational territory.

In the late 1980s, Third World countries shifted from their Cold War role as spaces of contest between the superpowers[23] to being a source of danger themselves. Tying into rising fears of terrorism and political instability more generally, *Reader's Digest* regular R. K. Bennett claimed in 1990 that the United States was "defenseless against missile terror."[24] Bennett told his readers that "weapons of mass destruction are getting into the hands of Third World tyrants and Middle East madmen" to produce a "new chapter of Middle East instability and global anxiety."[25] He presented an ultimatum that promised acute vulnerability if Reagan's Strategic Defense Initiative were not immediately pursued:

Figure 9. "Countdown to the Twenty-First Century: Freedom on the March," *Reader's Digest*, January 1990, pp. 44–45.

The bottom line for our national security is this: whether it is an accidental or unauthorized launch from the Soviet Union or the terrorist act of another country, we are defenseless against ballistic missiles.[26]

More often, however, it is suggested that at the close of the Cold War, America's new Others would be terrorists, especially Islamic fundamentalists, drug traffickers, and, with the increasing power of international trade, Japan. Each of these themes had been covered by the *Digest* during the Cold War but now took on a new urgency. *Reader's Digest* Cold

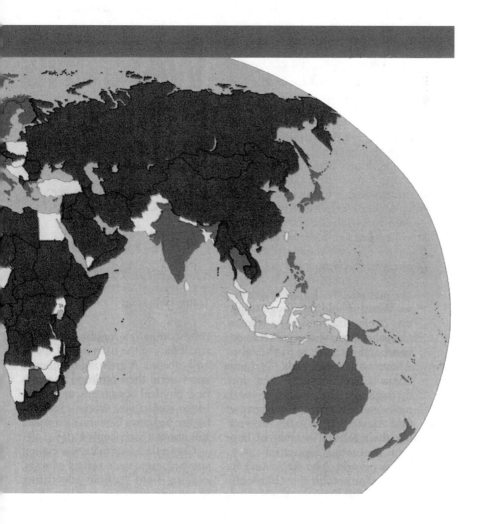

Warriors—including Eugene Methvin, Ralph Bennett, Rowland Evans, and Robert Novak—now turned their attention from communism to these other sources of danger to America.

Terrorists

Terrorism had the potential to present the United States with the same scenario of total war as did the Cold War: perpetual vigilance and pre-emptive action are required to combat what was often described as an incessant threat. Anyone could be a terrorist, just as anyone in the past might have been a communist. Articles helped readers identify terrorists as in the past they had been told how to spot a communist. Like America's fight against communist subversion during the Cold War, antiterrorism in the late 1980s could not be a battle in the military sense; since there is no front line, terrorist intervention might be enacted anywhere. As became evident in media and political discussions following the bombings in the United States over the past few years, terrorist danger permits social disciplining: loss of personal freedom in return for safety from a constantly threatening presence. In the wake of terrorist activity in the United States in the early 1990s, the FBI was granted increased surveillance powers. President Bill Clinton said that although he did not think that Americans would need to give up their liberties in the face of terrorism, "I do think we have to have more discipline."[27]

Reader's Digest compared terrorism both directly and indirectly to communism. For example, one author stated in 1993 that "What Moscow was to world communism, Teheran is to holy revolution and radical international fundamentalism."[28] As with its treatment of communism, *Reader's Digest* was quick to expose the acts of terrorists as being driven not by a higher purpose but rather by much darker, even psychopathic, motivations. The magazine defined terrorism as "the deliberate and systematic murder, maiming and menacing of the innocent to inspire fear for political ends."[29] The *Digest* implied that readers could not expect terrorists to show remorse or any other human trait: "In fact, terrorists are calculating murderers, swaggeringly proud of their acts, and accompanying these acts with clever political propaganda in awfully staged media events."[30] Another author, telling of his kidnapping in Beirut, said he had expected his captors to be "fanatical and devout," but, he insisted, "I never saw them pray."[31] This echoes the magazine's assertion of the hypocrisy of communist leaders who claimed to be devoted to the ideology of communist equality yet enjoyed great wealth at the expense of their people.

Another similarity in the representation between communists and terrorists lies in aesthetic descriptions. Terrorists are almost always described in *Reader's Digest* as unattractive individuals. Evidently, when it is applied to Islamic terrorists, this draws not only upon the magazine's structure of communist versus American but also on the Western tradition of Orientalism.[32] Finally, analogous to its fear of the utopian rhetoric of communism, the *Digest* feared that impressionable teenagers would find the terrorists' cause attractive, that, for example, the young would be "easily seduced by Khomeini's [anti-American] teachings."[33]

An earlier article inscribed the battle lines along a familiar East-West cartography in "Terrorism: How the West Can Win."[34] A report that followed up on the World Trade Center bombing echoed the domino theory by placing the disruption of America once more as the major ambition of evil: "The United States remains the single most important target for international terrorists" whose "hatred of the United States reached psychotic proportions."[35]

Thus, *Reader's Digest* constructed terrorism in a manner similar to the magazine's narrativization of communists and their goals. The magazine can be seen as constructing what James DerDerian has called "A new form of *pure terrorism* . . . [that] has emerged as an international political crisis in which the violent intimidation and manipulation of a global media audience creates a pervasive sense of insecurity and fear."[36] In other words, the total war of democratic America against terrorists is reproduced within the mainstream media so that viewers themselves are terrorized into accepting the kind of social disciplining that had come to characterize Cold War culture.

Nevertheless, terrorists have not presented *Reader's Digest* with the same unity of purpose nor overwhelming power that the magazine saw in communism, so that ultimately, in the immediate wake of the Cold War, terrorism could not replace the USSR as the significant opposition to American destiny.

Drugs

It was a harder task for the *Digest* to suggest that its readership was in immediate danger from illegal drugs. Some articles did attempt to do this by using the disease metaphors that had characterized the height of the Cold War; one suggested that "no-one is immune from [cocaine's] savage infection."[37] Other articles contained anecdotes about the struggles of normal or respectable people with drugs they had thought posed no danger to them (for example, "Champions Who Chose Drugs" in May 1991). A direct connection to communism was attempted in one article that talked of a major dealer as "the nation's drug czar."[38]

To a much more significant extent, *Reader's Digest* illustrated the dangers of the effects of other people's drug abuse on its readership. It suggested that drugs, like communism, would gradually take over American society if they were not checked. The fight against drugs, stated the *Digest*, is "everyone's fight." This warning of the dangers of lack of vigilance was represented in its most hyperbolic form in a 1986 article, "Profiteers of Terror," in which Europe's continued trade with drug-trafficking Middle Eastern countries was exposed and condemned. Europe's failure to see the potential dangers of drugs was compared in this article to its lack of opposition to Hitler in the years preceding World War II.[39]

This comparison with communism meant *Reader's Digest* could suggest that it was not just stereotypical users who would be affected by drugs. Even in apparently "idyllic" villages, drug use could rapidly spread if discipline and moral standards were not maintained, particularly among the young. "Crack invades the countryside" warned a 1989 article.[40] In this tale, a quiet West Virginia village "was engaged in a life-and-death struggle against drugs, and it was losing."[41] The article promised a lesson to all Americans in the ensuing action: citizen outrage and action saved the village. But all areas could potentially be invaded. Just as in the Cold War, readers were advised to act now, before the danger was upon them and it was too late: "If you don't help us now, crack will invade your community too."[42]

In the nexus of fear of drugs and terrorism was "narco-terrorism," the violent blending of drug trade and political power.[43] This proved to be such a powerful threat to hegemonic American culture "because it had taken on the characteristics of a major transnational conglomerate rather than primitive capitalism, with an increase in political power."[44] A new set of powers was added to the international arena and had to be incorporated into the magazine's geopolitical vision. These new agents of power did not easily fit into the (neo)realist world view, which considered states the only significant actors in world politics. Thus, nonstate actors in global affairs could easily be written as a disruptive presence by the magazine.

In "Cocaine King: A Study in Evil" the *Digest* explained the rise of drug lords who had "become a secret government, corrupting entire societies."[45] Just like the *Digest's* tales of communists around the world throughout the Cold War, its stories of drug lords scripted them as having grand ambition:

> His idol: Adolf Hitler. His goal: to destroy the United States, to rule a
> kingdom of cocaine. Here is his story.[46]

For *Reader's Digest*, the real problem facing America was not the drugs themselves but societal attitudes toward them. The magazine's writers evidently believed U.S. institutions to be too permissive in their attitude toward drug use. This laxity could apparently be attributed to the continuing hold of 1960s and 1970s social and cultural permissiveness. In particular, the *Digest* showered scorn on educational groups that advised people to use drugs responsibly, instead insisting with Nancy Reagan that kids should "just say no." This black and white view of drug culture meant that the magazine considered drug users to be as criminal as the dealers and argued that both groups should face criminal proceedings:

> We must never forget that the enemy we are fighting is not a chemical or
> a country or a social condition. Rather, it is each and every individual
> who sells, consumes or condones an illegal drug.[47]

The Economy and "Nippophobia"

Finally, the economy offered an alternative zone of engagement in the reconstruction of the international sphere and American identity in *Reader's Digest* at the close of the Cold War. *Reader's Digest* was determined not to admit to American economic decline, especially decline linked to changes in the culture of work in the United States. Written into the magazine's image of America as world leader is a necessary belief in American economic and industrial superiority, and, more importantly, in the world hegemon's culture as the best example of the industrial spirit.[48] *Reader's Digest* is underwritten by a belief in the power of optimism, a belief that negative thinking and criticism lead to decline, and the American Dream is after all itself a narrative of optimism. *Reader's*

Digest has therefore been scornful of those who have given up on American chances of future economic leadership. For example, a series of articles under the general heading "America on the Rise" in 1989 described American economic buoyancy by way of a series of anecdotes about individuals whose ingenuity, hard work, and persistence had made their businesses successful in the face of "the prophets of doom."[49] Using a rhetorical tool that it had drawn upon many times, the *Digest* dismissed critics of America as simply following fashion. The *Digest*'s historically sensitive approach, on the other hand, explained that America was witnessing a period of restructuring that should be welcomed rather than resisted. Changes in production techniques benefited *Digest* readers as consumer-citizens in addition to revitalizing the American economy; protectionism or resistance to further modernization would only lead to stagnation and further decline in America's relative economic strength. Finally, the magazine suggested that "contrary to what many politicians and academics say, Americans are still admired abroad as people who know how to make a country work."[50] Critics of America were therefore dismissed as being out of touch with reality.

Economic articles often related conditions in America to those in Japan. Some articles suggested that Americans should not envy the Japanese because of the hard work and low standards of living characteristic of life in Japan.[51] One article proclaimed that "the Miyakawas do not expect ever to buy a home, traditionally the dream of every Japanese."[52] This example surely was not random: the Japanese system's denial of a home (a purchase central to the American Dream) to this hardworking couple must have been intended to strike a chord with many readers.

Articles whose worldview considered geoeconomy to be replacing geopolitics as the power behind the shape of international relations required enemies and strategies to drive their narrative. The economy was sometimes rendered in terms of a battlefield in which, for example, Cold Warrior Eugene Methvin suggested that America use "our new defense weapon—competition."[53] On the terrain of economic battles, the "enemy" clearly was written as Japan. Another Cold War *Digest* regular, Fred Barnes, complained that in economic issues, Japan "won't play fair." In the Barnes article, subtitles clearly inscribed the economy along military lines: "Economic warfare," "Targeting for dominance," "Hired guns."[54]

Evidently there were other contenders for economic primacy in the late 1980s, including, most obviously, a reunited Europe following German economic leadership. Japan, however, was already positioned in American culture in such a way that it could more easily be configured as Other. The World War II experience of Pearl Harbor, Japanese mistreatment of American prisoners of war, U.S. internment of Japanese Americans, and America's dropping the atomic bomb on Hiroshima and Nagasaki all placed Japan in the American psyche as a hostile presence and also one that caused discomfort and anxiety. Japan is certainly not represented in *Reader's Digest* as being culturally similar to America, and, although Samuel Huntington's (in)famous "Clash of Civilizations?" paper and the CIA's "Japan 2000" document were not referred to directly, they might have fed into this portrayal of Japanese alterity. In addition, Armand Mattelart had suggested that the recent spate of Japanese purchases of important American industry, perhaps most symbolically Hollywood studios, had left many Americans feeling a loss of their national soul, promoting new levels of "Nippophobia."[55]

Taken to an extreme, this representation of Japan rendered it in terms previously reserved for the imperialist Soviet state. *Reader's Digest* warned of the dangers of American inaction. A 1991 article titled "Don't Remilitarize Japan" proclaimed that if "a warlike nation rises again, we may only have ourselves to blame … Asia tempts them, as it did the Japanese generals whose shades they worship."[56] Just as in the Cold War neutral space offered irresistible temptation to the Soviets, a lapse in the containment of Japan would apparently release the same expansionary desire.

Reader's Digest saw other threats to American identity and values continuing into this period, and new fears—most prominently of AIDS—arose, but none ever came close to occupying the position of communism as America's alter ego. Perhaps the *Digest* realized either consciously or subconsciously that communism was in fact a unique alter ego against which it could construct American identity. In his book *Writing Security*, David Campbell suggests that communism and the threat of Soviet power provided hegemonic American culture with an ideal Other:

> The operations of anticommunism as a prominent discourse of
> danger in the United States throughout the nineteenth and twentieth
> centuries—with its ability to encompass the entire population, inten-
> sively structure the practices of everyday life, and offer a link between
> internal and external threats in ways that circumscribed the boundaries
> of legitimacy—is probably the best example of an effective discourse of
> danger.[57]

This was not true of new dangers. Even in the wake of the World Trade Center, Oklahoma, and Atlanta bombings, terrorism did not have a particularly high profile in America, and drugs failed to sweep through the nation in the biblical proportions suggested in the 1980s; the economy is perhaps too intangible a concept around which to forge a sense of national "us." AIDS too fails to fit the bill. At first it was reported in *Reader's Digest* as a malignant plague ready to course through the American population. Soon, however, the *Digest* decided that it was not the disease most significant to its intended readership and that it had been commonly perceived as a threat because interest groups had used scare tactics to manipulate public fears about AIDS.[58]

In short, despite the evident encoding of terrorism, drug culture, Japan, and other dangers in the language of Cold War opposition, the importance of these themes should not be overstated. Measured by volume of articles, these themes were much less significant than communism was (figure 10). Evidently, unless a new form of identification emerged for hegemonic American culture, one based on inclusion rather than exclusion, the *Digest* would have to pinpoint another source of Otherness against which to construct its normative vision of normal American society. Many theorists and commentators have suggested that multiple regional threats would replace the Soviet threat, and that this combination of Others would produce the greatest danger in the new and chaotic multipolar international world order. However, *Reader's Digest* has tended to shy away from such complexities, instead sticking to its tried and tested dichotomies. Rather than finding its Other outside the territorial bounds of the United States, *Reader's Digest* found it within.

Barbarians within the Gates

The short-lived nature of the oppositional presences discussed here reveal myopia in both orthodox accounts of the international state system and dominant critical theorizing of national identity in its relationship with foreign policy. Both are contained by the structures of (neo)realist theory in that it is the structure of the international state system rather than the historically specific characteristics of the individual state societies that is seen to characterize and shape events. Thus, for the orthodox theorizing of international relations by state elites, it is the dissolution of bipolarity and the apparent chaos of a multipolar state system that shapes the future of the character of America and the shape of the future world system.

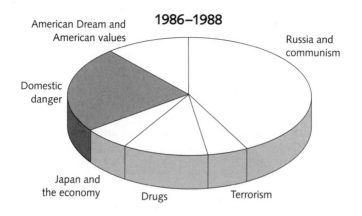

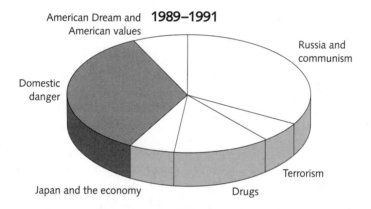

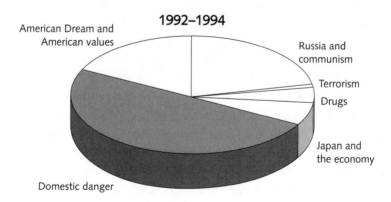

Figure 10. Post–Cold War threats to the United States, 1986–1990.

Many critical analysts are also apparently trapped within this theoretical mold in that they expect the agents of hegemonic U.S. culture to seek an external other to shape American self-identification; with the end of communism, the United States will simply look for another malevolent presence to take over from the Soviet Union.

What characterized American political culture at the end of the twentieth century was its concern not with a new external threat but rather with dangerous groups within America. Analysis of *Reader's Digest* since the end of the Cold War reveals how the magazine turned one of its perennial fears for American society—increased power to central government, and the resulting culture of dependency—to produce a new presence opposing the necessary unfolding of Manifest Destiny. The immediate threat to *Reader's Digest*'s "America" is the morality and resolve of the American people. As one author stated: "The barbarians are not at the gates. They are inside."[59]

Two interlinked themes dominated the *Digest*'s representation of America in the early 1990s: concern with big government and bureaucracy, and fear of moral decline, particularly in what the magazine called a culture of "victimism" (these are classified in figure 10 as domestic danger).

The *Digest*'s tirade against big government is in no way limited to the post–Cold War period. It was a constant complaint for decades, but increased in the wake of the Cold War in both the level of coverage and the magnitude of the stated problem. The magazine suggested that too much government was exacerbating (all) other problems, from stagnation of the economy to America's inability to fight drug dealers and terrorists. Articles about the U.S. government sought to illustrate a range of incompetence ranging from failed good intentions to scandalous excesses. Most of the good-intentions-gone-wrong articles provided anecdotes about the government's ineffectual attempts to help the poor or disadvantaged; in most cases, *Reader's Digest* suggested, people should be left to pull themselves up, since help from the government only leads to dependence ("Wrong Ways to Help the Homeless," May 1993; "A Hand Up—Not a Hand Out," November 1994; "Do We Really Need Corporate Welfare?" March 1992). These articles presented laws they found to be beyond belief and to actually pose significant danger to the workings of normal American society. A 1990 piece asked, "How can cops fight drugs if they are hamstrung by laws that defy common sense?"[60] and the

Digest introduced a new regular series called "That's Outrageous!" that provided examples of ridiculous laws and rampant bureaucracy around the country.

To support its antigovernmental stance, *Reader's Digest* included articles about individuals who had triumphed by standing up to bureaucrats ("You *Can* Fight City Hall").[61] One 1989 article explained the *Digest's* position on the dangers of government "interference" in the voice of a successful expatriate Peruvian who returned to his homeland after the fall of the socialist government. He found on his land two settlements that had been established at the same time; one group was rich and the other poor. The author posed the question of why some people (and, adopting a universalist logic, also some nations) are rich and others poor. Since all the settlers on his land were Indians, the businessman concluded that the difference could not be attributed to either cultural or external influences. Instead, he claimed that the wealthier community was successful because its people had "badgered" government bureaucrats until they were given the title to their land. These lucky peasants invested their wages in improvements to their property and became wealthy.[62] The poor peasants could not improve their lot because of a failure to beat government bureaucracy. Thus, the businessman concluded his report:

> "I now know why some countries are poor and others rich," he says. "We're a world of 169 countries, and only about 25 of them have 'made it' economically. They were able to do so because they stripped governments of the power to deprive the humblest citizens of the fruits of *their* industry and creativity. The answer boils down to one word: *Freedom*."[63]

The American government was frequently berated for its attempts to "limit" personal freedom: "Why are they always trying to take our freedom away?" asked one *Digest* article.[64] Government bureaucracy was also blamed by *Reader's Digest* for "crippling the CIA," increasing spending through taxes, and working against black interests in apartheid South Africa.[65]

Linked to its impatience with government bureaucracy was the *Digest's* disgust at what it perceived to be the state's weakness toward crime. A number of articles told tales of criminals who had been allowed back on the street because of bureaucracy or "misguided" laws. Because of the weak judicial system, criminals were "freed to kill again."[66] These tales were juxtaposed with stories of people getting together to run drugs and crime out of their communities. They refused to allow crime to flourish around their homes; rather than accepting it or moving on, they fought. *Reader's Digest* suggested quite clearly that communities united to protect their property and uphold their values have more power than the government, the police, or, indeed, criminals.[67]

The decline of social morality, most clearly exemplified in the dissolution of communities in the face of troubles, most concerned *Reader's Digest*. Running implicitly through the articles just described, and more obviously through others, was an opposition between the American Dream and a new social condition *Reader's Digest* recognized as the "culture of victimism." During the Cold War, the American Dream was implied in the *Digest's* reporting of the Others of totalitarianism and communist dictatorship. Later, the American Dream emerged either in overt form in narratives of individuals who succeeded despite disadvantages because of their determination and spirit or, more often, from the shadows of articles on "victims."

A 1993 article explained that "stripped of its pretensions, victimism is an ideology of the ego, an impulse to deny personal responsibility."[68] Another author claimed that there was a growing list of things that Americans expect as a right: "There has arisen this insane notion that we deserve a perfect life with nice parents and lots of stuff, and that anything short of that is ground for committing murder or mayhem."[69] When people think their lives are not perfect, claimed the *Digest*, they can act badly without taking responsibility; they have an "It's not my fault!" mentality.[70] Moreover, this was not confined to those who naively expect too much but was being manipulated by "professional victims": "Radical feminists, ethnic minorities, homosexuals and other activists are taking *us* on a guilt trip into a mine field—no matter where *we* step, *we're* in trouble."[71]

This mind-set challenged the *Digest's* utopian view of American society, within which each individual has the potential to "make it." Rather than realizing this potential to succeed, American society seemed to the *Digest* to be lapsing into acceptance of disadvantage and of a view that inequalities mean that not everyone can make it in America, at least not without the aid of the state. If people do not succeed, they blame "the system" rather than their own lack of effort and ingenuity. The *Digest* feared that this attitude fundamentally threatened the ethos of individualism that underwrites American identity. For example, it said of single mothers, a group of people the magazine identified as adopting the term "victims":

> Throughout history, a single woman with a small child has not been a viable economic unit and therefore not a legitimate social unit. In small numbers, they drain the community's resources. In large numbers, they destroy the community's capacity to sustain itself.[72]

A 1992 article explained the decline of individual responsibility as affecting the ability of the American Dream to script a national identification:

> This isn't what our Founding Fathers had in mind when they enshrined in the Declaration of Independence the inalienable right to "Life, Liberty and the pursuit of Happiness." ... Too many Americans have twisted the sensible right to *pursue* happiness into the delusion that we are *entitled* to a guarantee of happiness. If we don't get exactly what we want, we assume that someone must be violating our rights.[73]

Reader's Digest is correct in a sense. En route to the New World, John Winthrop's "A modell of Christian charity" constructed an initial American exceptionalism. In Winthrop's view, a striking fact of humanity was inequality. God's will was for difference and inequality, and although this might seem to provoke antagonism, it made His creation all the more wondrous because the variety of people would be compelled to depend upon each other. This, claimed Winthrop, would strengthen community in the New World.[74] *Reader's Digest* simply secularized this view (although it was often still couched in quasi-religious overtones) to suggest that equality of opportunity should be at the heart of American democracy and not equality per se (which the magazine regarded to be quite unnatural).

Another *Digest* author, writing in 1993, explained why raised expectations had emerged in American society:

> Somewhere in the '60s or '70s we started expecting to be happy.... Why? We have lost the old knowledge that happiness is overrated— that, in a way, life is overrated.... Our ancestors believed in two worlds, and understood this to be the "solitary, poor, nasty, brutish and short" one. We are among the first generation of man that actually expects to find happiness on earth and our search for it has caused such— unhappiness.[75]

This expectation of being provided for worried the *Digest*. Its fear ranged from concern about individuals' increasing reliance upon experts rather than common sense to what the magazine regarded as total dependence on government services. In "Who Says Experts Are Always Right?" one author suggested that the

> world has become so complicated that we've lost confidence in our ability to understand and deal with it. But common sense is as useful now as it ever was. No amount of expertise substitutes for an intimate knowledge of a person or a situation.[76]

Another author feared that practical knowledge was no longer valued in contemporary America, and worried that the "historian of the future, looking back on the past half-century, will be struck by the tyranny of academic and pseudo-academic ideas over commonsense."[77] Given the foundations of *Reader's Digest* rhetorical strategies, it is not surprising that it feared an increase in the perceived value of academic knowledge. The *Digest* has based its worldview on the value of commonsensical knowledge from the very beginning of publication.

In a more critical vein, "Can America's Black Underclass Be Saved?" suggested that people had come to expect too much from the government rather than organizing themselves. The *Digest* feared a loss of self-reliance and individual responsibility. A 1989 article argued that people cannot

> wait for a daycare system to be created; somehow my mother raised seven kids and worked all her days; my father lost a leg in his 20s and kept on working. They didn't have day-care centers.[78]

Reader's Digest counterposed articles on victimism with tales of triumph over adversity and initial disadvantage by the kind of people for whom, like one American hero, "the concept of service to one's country flowed ... as naturally as the American flag flies outside his family's Maryland home."[79] In October 1991 an article told of Colin Powell's rise to power from his lowly background[80], and a new series called "my first job" was introduced; in the series, noted Americans told of humble early employment, claiming that "it's not what you earn it's what you learn." A 1992 article, "From Outcast to Supercop," illustrated the *Digest*'s belief in the power of individual decisions over disadvantage: "Raped as a child, pregnant at 16, Jacklean Davis had every reason to fail. Instead, she chose success."[81] These tales offered *Digest* readers role models of good citizenship, models they could follow themselves for success.

The creation of structures in society—which the notion of victims requires—is inimical to the *Digest's* desire to promote individual potential. Moreover, it runs contrary to the magazine's understanding of society as constructed of nothing more than the sum of its autonomous individual parts. An article asked, "What *really* ails America?"[82] The answer was repeated many times over: America had "lost sight of the moral truths that give meaning to our lives" because of a dissolving of morality and personal responsibility—an acceptance of barriers and hopelessness.[83] America's lost "moral truths" had given way to what *Reader's Digest* perceived to be an "anything goes" mentality. Acceptance of difference—manifest to the magazine's writers as tolerance or promotion of multiculturalism; the presentation of "alternative" histories, religious values, and literary canons in schools; and multilingual U.S. state bodies[84]—suggested to the *Digest* that America's "moral truths" were under attack. Michael Novak claimed in 1994 that "all things are not relative"—sophisticated people think they are cynical, but, he argues, they flatter themselves:

> They do not believe nothing, they believe everything. . . . This is an odorless, deadly gas that is now polluting every free society on earth. It is neither political nor economic, but the poisonous, corrupting culture of relativism.[85]

Another 1994 article quoted an author's greatest fear as "seeing America, with all its great strength and beauty and freedom ... gradually subside into decay through default and be defeated, not by the communist movement, but from within, from weariness, boredom, cynicism, greed and in the end helplessness before its great problems."[86] Yet another author claimed that "the martyrs of our time—victims of fascism and communism—have shown again and again that in fidelity to truth lies human dignity."[87]

In relativism lay the road to moral decline and lack of responsibility. In "Why Nothing Is 'Wrong' Anymore," a *Digest* writer claimed that Americans needed to regain their moral conscience in order to stand up to fashionable beliefs and state that something was wrong.[88] Again, *Reader's Digest* established a fashion-history binary to undermine current popular opinion. It was the belief that individuals were no longer to blame for "deviant" actions that really riled the magazine, however. One author maintained that criminals had been taught to attribute their actions to anger and frustration, or to their disillusionment with a political system in which presidents lied, and colonels ran illegal arms deals under cover of the state. Instead, claimed the *Digest*, these "ethical amputees" had nothing to blame "but their lack of any moral faculty."[89] "The effect of such preposterous statements," it continued—and this was the *Digest*'s real fear—"is to dilute the notion of individual responsibility."[90]

The problem was that America had "lost sight of the moral truths that give meaning to our lives."[91] Much of this was blamed on school systems that threatened to leave students "morally adrift."[92] The *Digest* claimed that children needed lessons in patriotism to appreciate freedom and was horrified that textbooks did not teach about, for example, the failings of the Soviet system. The magazine reprinted part of E. D. Hirsch's *Cultural Literacy* in 1987 to argue the point that schools were not fulfilling their societal role in that they failed to teach "the basic information necessary to maintain our democratic society."[93] Education, claimed the *Digest*, must include cultural literacy to allow people to "make informed civic decisions":

> Cultural literacy lies *above* everyday levels of knowledge that everyone possesses and *below* the expert level known only to experts. It is the middle ground of cultural knowledge writers assume to be possessed by the "common reader."[94]

Cultural literacy was very much in sync with *Reader's Digest* production of knowledge—it is not complex, abstract, or theoretical academic knowledge, but instead is a kind of informed common sense.

Inserted into Hirsch's article was a box about "cultural literacy" at the University of Southern California. This report presented to *Digest* readers the horrific news that "only a few [of the students] could articulate in any way at all why life in a free country is different from life in a non-free country" and concluded that "in a state of such astonishing ignorance, young Americans may well not be prepared for even the most basic national responsibility—understanding what the society is about and why it must be preserved."[95] Hirsch's article concluded with the full implications of this lack in American society:

> I have in mind the Founding Fathers' idea of an informed citizenry.
> This is the basic principle that underlies our national system of education
> in the first place—that people in a democracy can be entrusted to decide

all important matters for themselves because they can deliberate and communicate with one another.[96]

Evidently this posed a fundamental challenge to the *Digest*'s belief that American democracy was upheld by informed voters. Other *Digest* articles suggested that this education was not an unrealistic goal and did not require high levels of government investment in schools. Rather, what was needed was a particular community attitude. This was illustrated in a 1990 article about education in South Dakota. Although the state had the country's lowest teaching salaries and expenditure per pupil, its education rates ranked seventh nationally. The *Digest* attributed this achievement to stable homes, high marriage and birthrates, and low abortion rates, in addition to the benefits of small-community organization, a strong work ethic, and parental authority. The piece concluded with the claim that South Dakota need not be unique and that the rest of the country could easily follow suit:

> But if we really want these things, we cannot pretend that all lifestyles are equally valid or that the answer to every social problem is more government bureaucracy. We have to give small-scale, time-tested social institutions [family, community] our active support; we have to consciously resist their cultural delegitimation.[97]

Needless to say, given the *Digest*'s unrelenting optimism, a solution was in sight. A 1993 article titled "No More Victims, Please" suggested a way to overcome victimism while acknowledging individual injustices:

> We must reinvigorate a "culture of character" in our nation.... Holding people responsible for their behavior means restoring social stigmas that shrink the zone of acceptable conduct.... The weight of law should be brought to bear against individual acts of discrimination rather than be used to create blanket group entitlements.[98]

With this and similar narratives, *Reader's Digest* rescripted an American mission within which the moral triumph of good over evil would be assured through hardworking, law-abiding citizens and their families.

Seeking a New Role

No longer facing a single, overwhelmingly powerful adversary, at the beginning of the twenty-first century the United States lacks both a map of its own identity in global affairs and a workable image of gamesman-ship to define its role.[99]

The change in America's role to the international community's merce-nary army does not provide as secure a basis for national identity as did its Cold War personification as global policeman or sole guardian of free-dom. Despite its attempts to map out freedom and repression, *Reader's Digest* has been unable to redraw the world system in such a way as to reinscribe a significant moral territory for the United States.

Perhaps it is not surprising that *Reader's Digest* should be focusing on domestic issues. After all, the United States in the early 1990s was led by a president voted into office for his promise to turn attention back to domestic affairs. The Reagan-Bush global agenda had less urgency once the USSR was reduced to a handful of states more concerned with resolv-ing regional territorial conflict and reinvigorating their economies than with becoming superpowers. Whatever physical or ideological threat the Evil Empire posed has now more or less disappeared. A new isolationism appears to be descending on America as the major news stations reduce their international coverage and instead devote their attention to lifestyle issues.

The most important challenge to Clinton has been over not his han-dling of foreign policy but his attempts at domestic change—witness the rise of Newt Gingrich's very traditional version of American morality and the "Contract with America." Perhaps Christine Todd Whitman, Republican governor of New Jersey, expressed the attitude most clearly. In an interview with the British newspaper *The Independent*, she dis-cussed conservative reaction to the excesses of power accumulated into the Federal Government. When she was asked, "Why has the anti-Washington clamour grown so loud now? Was it a post–Cold War phe-nomenon?" she replied:

> Yes. Everyone wants an identifiable enemy.... When communism went away you lost it, and everybody had to look back and say "OK, where is it?" So now it's Washington. And it's the social issues, it's welfare—that's bad and we've got to change it, that's kind of the enemy now, the welfare state as we have known it. Domestic issues. People in America feel it's time to look inside.[100]

The *Digest's* 1988 claim that Gorbachev's rise presented a moral threat to the United States has appeared to be valid from the magazine's point of view. In the post–Cold War period, not only has the "moral void" of the

Soviet Other, against which the magazine defined American identity and mission, eroded from its Cold War heights; America's global moral leadership of the "free world" has also faded.

David Campbell claims that the set of practices constituting the Cold War represented a series of boundaries between civilization and barbarity, and as a result rendered a contingent identity of "America" secure.[101] Thus, argues Campbell, containment is more than a historically significant foreign policy strategy; rather, "containment is a strategy associated with the logic of identity whereby the ethical powers of segregation that make up foreign policy constitute the identity of an agent in whose name they operate, and give rise to a geography of evil."[102]

The territoriality of today's "geography of evil," however, is not so easy to define as its Cold War counterpart was: terrorists, drug dealers, and U.S. government power as often compound the breakup of Cold War identities as repair them. Without popular recognition of a powerful and ideological opponent, *Reader's Digest's* ability to define, map, and therefore contain the Other is greatly limited. It is very difficult for the magazine to present a mirror image of American identity of equal coherence. As the Other of "America" fragments, so does hegemonic identity. *Reader's Digest* believes that America is no longer internationally respected as a moral leader; perhaps even more significantly, the American people too seem to have abandoned this historic role.

Thus the *Digest's* double fear: loss of international recognition of American moral superiority and imperial decline as American culture itself falls from its high ground. Like Francis Fukuyama, then, *Reader's Digest* must regard the end of the Cold War as "a very sad time." In Fukuyama's words:

> The struggle for recognition, the willingness to risk one's life for a purely abstract goal, the worldwide ideological struggle that called forth courage, imagination, and idealism, will be replaced by economic calculation, the endless solving of technical problems, environmental concerns, and the satisfaction of sophisticated consumer demands.[103]

The end of Cold War culture for Fukuyama, the end of Cold War romance in McClure's terminology, is characterized by boredom as the great challenges of previous decades—the challenges that defined "America" for the *Digest*—fall away. As one commentator on Fukuyama's work suggested, "His comment of boredom was meant to indicate that liberal states do not refer their citizens to 'higher aims' leaving a vacuum that can be filled with sloth, self-indulgence, banality and the desire for wealth."[104] Containment of the USSR simultaneously contained "America": it disciplined the myriad possible characterizations of "America" into a coherent moral agent and provided that power of authority to those who upheld and espoused these characterizations. Now that the geopolitical containment no longer operates, this naturalized subjectification cannot continue in the same manner; hence *Reader's Digest*, in its continued attempts to promote its version of American identity, first attempts to reintegrate containment in its narrativization of terrorism, drug dealing, and the economy, then eventually faces the question of individual character directly.[105] As before, the new mission would have the effect of recreating the *Digest*'s view of American society based on the values it had espoused for decades.

"Moral equality" with the Soviet Union, wrote a 1988 *Digest* author "erodes our values and visions and compassion; that is its greatest danger."[106] Even in 1988, then, *Reader's Digest* seemed to realize the moral dangers of the end of communism. Morality is perhaps the key concept to understanding *Reader's Digest*'s "America": it is what the magazine's notion of American mission and destiny is all about. But this is a morality that has been pulled through the magazine's lens of "common sense" into the binary logic of right and wrong. If the world could no longer tell Soviet from American morality, then America's moral role would be lost in the ensuing moral relativism. The loss of America's high ground in the wake of a new moral geopolitics means that the authority of *Reader's Digest*, as supporter of the old geopolitics, is also under renewed challenge. The *Digest* has written its way into a particular history and identity of America. With the decay of the moral geopolitics of this old order, *Reader's Digest*, like the America it supports, is struggling to redefine its role.

Conclusion

At eight p.m. eastern standard time on the evening of October 30, 1938, ...
[f]or a few horrible hours people from Maine to California thought that
hideous monsters armed with death rays were destroying all armed
resistance sent against them; that there was simply no escape from
disaster; that the end of the world was near. Newspapers the following
morning spoke of the "tidal wave of terror that swept the nation." It was
clear that a panic of national proportions had occurred....

Long before the [radio] broadcast [of *War of the Worlds*] had ended,
people all over the United States were praying, crying, fleeing frantically
to escape death from the Martians. Some ran to rescue loved ones. Others
telephoned farewells or warnings, hurried to inform neighbors, sought
information from newspapers or radio stations, summoned ambulances
or police cars. At least six million people heard the broadcast. At least a
million of them were frightened or disturbed....

I have often been asked whether I thought such a thing could happen
again.... Since ... 1938 we have seen the development and use of atomic
weapons; we know about the existence of Intercontinental Ballistic
Missiles (ICBM) and their immense destructive power. And we hear talk
of satellites spinning about our tiny globe carrying atomic warheads that
could quickly be guided to any target on earth. Such destructive forces
against which there seems to be so little protection can only enhance the
possibility of delusions that would be even more plausible than the
invasion of Martians—and that would not require the combined talents
of H. G. Wells and Orson Welles to set off.[1]

Sadly for the social theorist, few occasions illustrate the direct influence
of the media on their audience's perceptions and actions as dramatically
as Orson Welles's infamous radio broadcast of *War of the Worlds* in 1938.

Now the number of media feeding Americans information has multiplied many times over. Audiences have perhaps become too sophisticated, too knowing about the media and their effects and imagined worlds, ever again to be taken in so completely by media creation. Despite the incredible effects and realism of contemporary audio and visual media, audiences know that they are being entertained; they are aware of the technologies of (re)production, of the special effects that allow directors to summon natural disasters and believable alien invasions apparently as easily as they can get their actors and actresses to act. This does not mean that the media are less important in the creation of worlds and individuals' places within them, simply that this positioning is somewhat more complex than when Welles broadcast his "imagined geography" of alien attack.

Nevertheless, *Reader's Digest* could be seen to provide for its readership "delusions" similar to those in Welles's broadcast. At times the magazine offered gross overstatements of political threat or subversion, or extremist interpretations of events, yet the presentation of such material in a realistic mode rendered the *Digest* plausible, just like Welles's radio broadcast was. It is indeed probable that *Reader's Digest* reports of Soviet aggression, inhumanity, and perversion, and the imminence of the communist takeover of America, in fact scared far more than the million affected by *War of the Worlds*—and for more than a few hours. The *Digest* has been especially successful at this as a result of its mixture of prophetic geopolitics, moral guidance, commonsense reasoning, and direct address to its readership as active American citizens. The magazine has produced for its readers a set of "imagined geographies" to show how politics works at a global level, what America's role is in these political geographies, and where the readers themselves are actually positioned relative to the events being described. This results in the construction of a model of an active subject through these geographical imaginations.

These imagined geographies are important to all political cultures around the world as they clearly articulate—unequivocally in the case of global political maps—the sense of "our place" and "their place." At perhaps the most basic of levels, this division of territory and of daily existence runs through representations of different national groups.

Nowhere, however, is this of more importance than in the United States, given the formation of national myths in the narrative of the frontier and the expression of America as geographical expansion rather than as a constant historical presence. The narratives and images of nation are constantly being reworked and rewritten and provide a vibrant discursive repertoire for political action. The narratives and images reproduced daily in popular culture provide the background level of national sentiment that can be drawn upon in times of crisis.

Although the role of the *Digest* in creating imagined geographies of the world and America's place within it cannot be illustrated with the force of Welles's impact on the American population in 1938, its presence is many times more significant in the construction of national identity and destiny. Reading the *Digest* is not a spectacular event but a mundane part of everyday life. It is read and reread without much notice and without much attention. This perhaps explains why it has stayed out of the spotlight of critical investigators. Yet it is this mundaneness that makes it so successful; it is because it is read without any fanfare and attention that its ideas are so powerful. The constant reproduction of the United States and the USSR as opposites both resonated with and reinforced *Digest* readers' sense of national identification. Although it is a seemingly mundane process, this narrative repetition of national belonging and national purpose is central to the reproduction of American identity.

Most studies of nationalism have focused on minority struggles for sovereignty. When dominant nationalisms have been examined, it is usually for the spectacular events that are seen to both epitomize and enforce identity. The Vietnam and Gulf Wars, for example, have come in for particular attention from theorists of American national identity. As theorists such as Benedict Anderson and Michael Billig have insisted, however, such spectacular nationalisms can only be performed because of the everyday processes that reproduce national identity, not as a conscious and heroic concept, but as a natural and unquestioned element of individual identity. As Billig has suggested, "The unwaved flag, which is so forgettable, is at least as important as the memorable moment of flag waving."[2] Waving flags would not be the same powerful symbol of Americanness if it were not for the silent ubiquity of flags flying in front of public offices, gas stations, and suburban homes.

This is also true for the role of *Reader's Digest* in American political culture. The magazine provides its readers roles of citizenship and nationalism to play, and presents information on noteworthy international events and America's role in them. The *Digest* offers its readers a guide to American subjecthood: a nonspectacular, mundane, everyday guide that positions its readers to accept—even anticipate—the spectacular events of national flag waving and going to war. The reservoirs of national identity can be tapped in times of conflict or national trial not because of the power of these spectacular events, but as a result of the daily affirmation of narratives of American identity and mission repeated and reinforced in popular culture sources such as *Reader's Digest*. This everyday level of national reproduction makes possible the more spectacular versions. The *Digest* is especially powerful here because of its conscious articulation of the everyday with a sweeping vision of America's myth-history.

The *Digest* not only renders these political geographies as natural orders but also gives them an air of inevitablity. The power of this particular voice of America is its ability to write events into the myth-history of the nation to make certain geopolitical events seem preordained, even God-given. In essence, America does not have a choice, but has to oppose threats to its God-given role to lead the world. In this self-appointed role as moral guardian, the *Digest* is continuing a long tradition of religious-political discourse, the jeremiad:

> The ritual of the jeremiad bespeaks an ideological consensus—in moral, religious, economic, social, and intellectual matters—unmatched in any other modern culture. . . . Only in the United States has nationalism carried with it the Christian meaning of the sacred.[3]

Sacvan Bercovitch describes the "American jeremiad" as "a ritual designed to join social criticism to spiritual renewal, public to private identity, the shifting 'signs of the times' to certain traditional metaphors, themes and symbols."[4] *Reader's Digest* can be seen to perpetuate the jeremiad tradition in American political culture through a normative geopolitical worldview that unites the lessons of history and the facts of geography to make sense of the changing international political scene and America's place—and role—within it.

The *Reader's Digest* jeremiad informs people of events occurring around the world, not simply to give them the facts of the situation (although the rhetoric of *Digest* articles is heavily factual) nor detailed academic analysis, but by revealing the significance of contemporary events within the context of a mythohistorical vision. This vision, peculiarly American, involves a heady and persuasive mix of moral and theological pronouncements of American destiny and exceptionalism. There is a moral to every *Digest* story—whether the subject is an average individual triumphing over adversity or an international event of global significance. The *Digest*'s moral narration relates both to the individual who is reading the article and also to the well-being of the American nation, the world, or both. For the *Digest*, then, what links together the actions of individuals and the fate of nations is moral geography.

For *Reader's Digest*, the world is a moral landscape in which various countries provide the settings as a testing ground for American authority. As Gertjam Dijkink has said of American geopolitics more generally, there is a need for a great purpose, for a danger over which America can triumph.[5]

The *Digest* has created a powerful geography of danger for its readers, and it offers an image of trials against which the country and American citizens must test themselves. The language suggests that these struggles are central to the survival of America and the free world. The challenges must be met because of America's unique role and destiny in world affairs. They can be surmounted if *Digest* readers and America more generally heed the advice offered by the magazine, which paints its role as moral guardian in its narrating of the unfolding of American history. I am arguing not that the *Digest* should be seen as an apolitical voice in American political culture, but that it cannot be reduced to partisan politics or the bare necessities of profit.

Reader's Digest has a concept of American national citizenship that centers on a nexus of values relating to gender, class, and race. It presents a clear image of how good American citizens should act. This image of national subjecthood is not presented directly, however, as that would seem too much like the *Digest* telling the reader how to act, which in turn goes against the individualism inherent in the magazine's understanding of American identity. Instead, readers must feel as if they have made their own choice of identity. This choice can come about as a result of reading the *Digest*'s anecdotes of what happens to people who do not follow these values. Readers are warned of the crushing and dehumanizing effects of bureaucracy and "big government" not only through descriptions of dangerous trends in the United States but also, more importantly, in descriptions of the degeneration of the human condition in the Soviet Union and in other places where socialist and communist government bureaucracy has run riot. This structure of identity is reinforced by other tales. For example, readers are reminded of the naturalness of the nuclear family, again not directly but through tales of the disruptive effects of Soviet women who put their careers first, or who have children out of wedlock.

This verifies the importance of the popular angle taken in this book. The national narratives and texts replicated throughout everyday culture are inherently geographical, drawing a map of belonging and exclusion for national citizens. This is reinforced by apparently ageographical arguments about the difference of others, which again presuppose a geography divided by lines of national character. The boundaries that separate domestic space from the international, or one nation's territory from another's are not natural or inevitable, but the outcome of political praxis. This not only occurs within the rarified atmosphere of state meetings but also on television, in newspapers, at school, and so on. It is through the naturalization of certain metageographical concepts (the Cold War binary moral geography being a perfect example) within the realms of popular culture that these political geographies are rendered politically inoffensive, as common sense.

The Cold War provided an important global map of moral geography from which American purpose and destiny could be reflected. The danger of communism, it must be said, provided an exceptionally efficient example of identity formation in that it linked internal and external threats that legitimized the establishment of physical and moral boundaries separating and protecting the "free world" from the communist threat.[6] But the exaggeration of the threat of communism found in American Cold War discourse has led political theorists such as David Campbell to argue that the Cold War was not an isolated or idiosyncratic event in the history of American foreign policy. The contingencies of Soviet-U.S. systemic differences produced one particular configuration of danger for American foreign-policy makers. This configuration, although empirically unique, was underlain by a Self-Other dichotomy inherent in any modern (Western) formation of identification. Communism did not represent the only threat against which an idealized American identity was established: communism was the most powerful Other in the nexus of Others that centered the production of identity through the practice of foreign policy. Alternative threats have been nurtured in the shadow of communism—drug use, terrorism, Islamic fundamentalism, the breakup of the nuclear family, the specter of "big government," and a culture of victimism—and as the explicit threat of communism faded, these other threats in various combinations came to dominate the nexus of danger.

This argument suggests, therefore, that for the most part, the threat to America from communism was more hyperreal than material. Although it would be ridiculous to claim that the Soviet and communist presence was entirely benign, or that the American powers that be simply invented the communist threat to discipline the American populace,[7] the military threat of the Soviet system probably was never as overwhelming or apocalyptic as the *Digest* claimed, nor was the seduction of "men's" minds so sweeping. The Soviet state did make aggressive moves, and did present "a particularly nasty model of socialism,"[8] but this was always already interpreted through a set of representations of Otherness that positioned America and the USSR as binary opposites, and so escalated the material stakes in the superpower standoff. Mary Kaldor has pointed out the irony of such a binarizing of the countries; she claims that "to typify Stalinism as socialist or Atlanticism as capitalism is, in itself, misleading."[9] The Soviets never attained true socialism, but instead a form distorted under Stalin's leadership. Neither has America ever been entirely capitalist in the true sense of the term: government investment has been significant to the operation of the economy, most so during the height of the Cold War.[10]

The Soviet Union offered an alternative to the American system—it presented a political-economic system that threatened to disrupt the world order the United States was attempting to establish at the end of World War II. But for *Reader's Digest* to mark the borders of the USSR as lines demarcating a "moral void"[11] moves the Soviet presence from realpolitik into the realm of a hyperreal spectacle of alterity. The image of America that was reflected from this phantasmagoria was equally illusory; it was an image *Reader's Digest* wished to impose upon the populace, rather than a reflection of the heterogeneities of American society. This has led to a particular form of social behavior being replicated as normal and essential through the pages of the *Digest*. DeWitt Wallace's image of society required active and informed citizens to ensure that laxness and ignorance did not allow the Soviets to enter through the back door. In addition to articles that celebrated this form of American life were those that demonstrated what happened when this natural social order was overturned. Many different images were offered—stories of divorce, promiscuity, lawlessness—but most powerful was the image of communism, which represented all that America (as defined by the *Digest*) was not, and so reflected back Wallace's ideal world.

Ironically, in many ways, it appeared that *Reader's Digest* envied the societal unity of the USSR. The magazine demanded unity in the face of the Soviet threat, yet freedom and individuality are (to be) the mainstays of the American system. American social order is supposedly established through voluntary discipline, a concept that has a history in American political culture stretching back to America's pre-Revolutionary pamphleteers. In *Plain Truth*, a conservative response to Thomas Paine's *Common Sense*, James Chalmers urged the American people to embrace Montesquieu's definition of liberty as "a right of doing whatever the laws permit."[12] This represents a paradox that runs throughout the pages of the *Digest*: it has a clear vision of a good society to which it feels all individual Americans should submit, yet by its very nature, this model of American life must be adopted voluntarily. Threats to this moralistic model of American society are encountered when it appears that some people adopt an alternative lifestyle, and so lose faith in, or lose sight of, the nation's unique historic mission. It is this sense of danger, rather than anything imposed from outside America's boundaries, that steered the *Digest*'s political writings throughout the period studied here.

So it was during détente and then at the end of the Cold War—periods when a sense of danger from communism retreated for much of American political culture—that *Reader's Digest* scripted American society to be in the greatest danger. Albert Hirschman's "perverse effects," the paradox that well-meaning people may make a given situation worse, offers the *Digest* a powerful rhetorical device.[13] This rhetoric positions as naive those who disagree with the *Digest*'s conservative view. Although meaning the best, people adopting this other view simply do not understand the reality of the situation. Only the *Digest*, unswayed by fashionable explanations and informed by knowledge of history, could really understand what was happening and to what end. The *Digest* is able to predict future outcomes because of its knowledge of history and the unchanging Soviet character. The magazine can see beyond the moment, beyond the faddish thinking of détente, peaceful coexistence, and so on, to see what is really happening.

During the Cold War the threat of communist insurgence or outright war made necessary unity and strength in opposition. When the threat appeared to fade, however, the argument for this disciplined attitude also retreated. On a more metaphorical level, perhaps the excitement and even romance of the height of the Cold War had gone.[14] The danger to the *Digest* was that Americans might become bored or disinterested, might turn to other things and so lose sight of the mission that united the country in its heroic struggle.

The magazine perceived that the USSR had maintained its Cold War unity and purpose, yet American resolve had disappeared. While the Soviets appeared resolute in their vision for the future, the very nature of American identity promoted difference, freedom of expression, and individuality, and so seemed to the *Digest* to be losing coherence. The rhetoric of its own identity threatened to overwhelm America, as the *Digest* saw it, in that dissent and rebellion seemed to be threatening the nature of American character and the inspiring vision of Manifest Destiny. Although during détente the *Digest* published fewer articles on communism and the Soviet Union, this was accompanied by an intensification of the magazine's production of a sense of danger generated from changes in American society rather than actions by Soviets (whose character had remained unchanged). The greatest danger lay in the Self, not the Other.

In contrast to the periods directly before and after, during the reintensification of the Cold War in the early 1980s, and especially at the time of Ronald Reagan's presidency, America was apparently saved from this dangerous divergence from its historical mission and destiny. During the early 1980s, it seemed to *Reader's Digest* that once again a dominant sector of American society had come to its senses to regard the USSR as the ultimate threat to the continued existence of freedom around the world. The American mission to contain this threat to the free world order was accepted again by a dominant element of American society now coded as the ultimate struggle between America and the Evil Empire. During this period, the *Reader's Digest* role—keeping its audience informed of the communist threat—was once again vital to national well-being. And now the magazine no longer had to explain that there were differences between the United States and the USSR, or that communism was an evil perversion of the social order. As a result of the established Cold War narration of the Soviet Union, Americans were well aware of this difference; they merely had to be informed about *just how different* the Soviets were. In many respects, this was when the *Digest*'s "America" was safest. At this time there seemed to be general acceptance of the need for resolve, discipline, and moral authority in American society in the face of the threat from the Evil Empire.

The analysis of *Reader's Digest* in this book suggests that the conventional division of postwar international politics into Cold War, détente, and Second Cold War—periods of intense opposition sandwiching a time of negotiation and coexistence—may be rather clearer in the minds of state and academic observers than in the minds of average citizens during the postwar years. If my analysis of the *Digest* can be accepted as being representative of hegemonic American culture (or at least some form of conservative consensus within it), then far from coming to accept the Soviet Union and communism during détente, many Americans came to be even more distrustful of them. Now the threat was more acute because it was within America: liberals who naively accepted the Soviets' claims of peace were heightening danger by dropping their guard.

This difference indicates the importance of studying popular accounts of geopolitics and imagined geographies in tandem with studies of more formal or official versions. The difference in interpretation between conventional accounts and those provided by *Reader's Digest* might be the result of the conventional focus on official speeches and actions to provide an explanation of international political relationships. The analysis of popular geopolitical discourses presented in my work implies that the intellectual focus on diplomatic negotiations and attempts at arms negotiations provides only one aspect of Cold War relations. My study of *Reader's Digest* suggests that for a large section of the American public, the détente "thaw" did not occur.

The effects of the end of Cold War binary geopolitics have not led to a more fluid or vectoral geopolitical view in the case of *Reader's Digest*. Rather than abandon the concept of the territorial nation-state for a more deterritorialized worldview, as some commentators have suggested is characteristic of the "New world order," the *Digest* has, if anything, attempted to reinforce the unity of the United States in a new isolationism within which there is less room for non-American issues. Readers of the *Digest*, however, no longer see themselves simply as Americans, a community of all people within the territory of the United States. Instead, they are now part of a select group of Americans who inherited the values that made the country great: a group who understand the value of the American way and the dangers to it from their fellow citizens who do not seem to value American history and destiny. So now, rather than seeing identity reflected back from what happens in other places, the *Digest* increasingly sees this reflected in changes within American society itself. Rather than having a neat picture of American society reflected back from the image of communism the *Digest* had established, now it was reflected back from a shattered mirror. The image was no longer coherent but offered a disjointed image both of threats to the United States and of the kind of society toward which Americans should be striving. Readers are told of the effects of American "multiculturalism" that suggests some individuals are at a disadvantage, thus allowing some to abandon the ethos of individual hard work, effort, and the American Dream and instead sit back and await government help to overcome apparent barriers to their success.

As threats to the *Digest*'s image of American society now came from within and outside its borders, the boundary separating "us" from "them" no longer lay directly on the country's borders. In this sense at least, *Reader's Digest* was more in touch with the reality of the fragmentation and lack of territorial cohesion of the new world order than it might like to acknowledge. This raises questions about the ubiquity of Campbell's assertion that identity is always formed around the territorial exclusion of difference. Campbell and other commentators of varying political positions have suggested that new external threats such as terrorism, Islam, and drug cartels would simply take the place of the USSR as America's Other in the structure of binary geopolitics. My reading of *Reader's Digest*, however, suggests that certainly for this voice of American popular culture, the geopolitics of the new world order are more complex, and that a much more powerful danger now threatens the country, this time from within its boundaries. Post–Cold War identity for conservative American political culture is not arranged primarily around territorial divisions of "us" and "them." These boundaries of good and evil have become blurred, making it a difficult task for voices such as *Reader's Digest* to articulate a coherent American identity. There have always been dangers to America from inside the country, but the magazine has usually explained this as the result of foreign influence and subversion. Now that the rot is inside America and there seems to be no clear danger without, there is no common enemy against which to forge a sense of national identity and purpose. It would seem that now, more than ever before, American identity is in trouble. But, with the *Digest*'s leadership, all is not lost: "We can reverse the tide of social degeneracy" it has insisted. "We've done it before."[15]

Appendix

Reader's Digest Readers:
Demographic Profile, 1991

A. Percentage of American population in each age and sex group who
   read *Reader's Digest*

	18–24	*25–34*	*35–44*	*45–54*	*55–64*	*65 and over*
Men	19.2	18.0	22.9	25.1	29.8	33.2
Women	20.1	22.7	28.7	33.5	38.7	37.0
Total	19.6	20.4	25.8	29.5	34.5	35.4

B. Percentage of Americans who read *Reader's Digest* by education
   achieved

Education level	*Percentage*
Graduated college or more	26.9
Attended 1–3 years of college	30.4
Graduated from high school	28.3
Did not graduate from high school	14.4

C. Percentage of Americans who read *Reader's Digest* by occupation

Occupation level	Percentage
Professionals	25.3
Executives, administrators, managers	28.7
Clerical, sales, technical	25.9
Precisions, crafts, repair	22.2
Other employed	24.9
Not employed	29.0

D. Percentage of Americans who read *Reader's Digest* by geographical region

Region	Percentage
Northeast	24.4
North Central	29.8
South	26.8
West	25.4

Source: *Reader's Digest* Demographic Profile, 1991.

Notes

Introduction

1. G. Feifer, "Russian Winter," *Reader's Digest*, Feb. 1984, p. 99.

2. M. Ledeen, "Standing Up to the Russian Bear," *Reader's Digest*, April 1980, p. 73, emphasis mine.

3. C. Rowan and D. Mazie, "Why the Voice of America Is in a Jam," *Reader's Digest*, March 1984, p. 178.

4. L. Stowe "Conquest by Terror," *Reader's Digest*, June 1952, p. 137, emphasis mine.

5. Throughout this book, I will use the terms *America* and *United States* interchangeably.

6. Martin Lewis and Karen Wigen, *The Myth of Continents: A Critique of Metageography* (Berkeley: University of California Press, 1997), p. ix. By "metageography," Lewis and Wigen mean "a set of spatial structures through which people organize their knowledge of the world" (p. ix).

7. *Reader's Digest* uses the terms *Russia* and *Soviet Union* interchangeably.

8. See David Campbell, *Writing Security* (Minneapolis: University of Minnesota Press, 1992); Simon Dalby, "Geopolitical Discourse: The Soviet Union as Other," *Alternatives* 13 (1988); Gearóid Ó Tuathail, *Critical Geopolitics* (Minneapolis: University of Minnesota Press, 1996); James DerDerian and Michael Shapiro, eds., *International/Intertextual Relations* (Lexington, Mass: Lexington, 1989).

9. Benedict Anderson, *Imagined Communities: Reflections on the Origin and Spread of Modern Nations* (London: Verso, 1983/1991).

10. Campbell, *Writing Security*. The quotes are from p. 251.

11. Ibid.

12. Garry Wills, *John Wayne: The Politics of Celebrity* (London: Faber, 1997), p. 29, emphasis in original.

13. One could look to other genres for similar narratives of American identity. Action movies and science fiction are especially focused on this idea of the continuing frontier. See Joanne Sharp, "Reel Geographies of the New World Order: Staging Post–Cold War Geopolitics in American Movies," in *Rethinking Geopolitics*, ed. Simon Dalby and Gearóid Ó Tuathail (London: Routledge, 1998), pp. 152–69.

14. I am surprised by the lack of academic attention focused on *Reader's Digest*.

There has been no critical examination of the magazine's content save one chapter in Ariel Dorfman's *The Empire's Old Clothes*. The remainder of work has been in the form of biographies of *Reader's Digest* founders DeWitt and Lila Wallace. I think that this can be explained by the magazine's middlebrow nature. Middlebrow culture in general has missed out in recent academic trends. Middlebrow is somewhat ambiguous in that its aim is both to entertain and to educate. It thus slips through analyses of the glossy "Disneyfied" development of Western advanced capitalism. Middlebrow is too pedestrian for postmodern chic. It is also left out of intellectual examination of the arts because of the more obvious profit motive that necessarily underlies the institutions producing middlebrow culture.

15. Some have used critical geopolitical approaches to compare different views of places in order to uncover biases in the geographical imaginations of the media: Thomas Klak's comparison of news coverage of the wars in Bosnia and Rwanda illustrated the continuing power of Orientalist images of the latter, for example. See Thomas Klak, "Havana and Kingston: Mass Media Images and Empirical Observations of Two Caribbean Cities in Crisis," *Urban Geography* 15, no. 4 (1994): 318–44.

16. George Kennan, quoted in Mary Kaldor, *The Imaginary War: Understanding the East-West Conflict* (Oxford: Blackwell, 1990), p. 84.

17. The term is from Robert Dallek, *The American Style of Foreign Policy: Cultural Politics and Foreign Affairs* (New York: Knopf, 1983).

18. Albert O. Hirschman, *The Rhetoric of Reaction: Perversity, Futility, Jeopardy* (Cambridge, Mass.: Harvard University Press, 1991).

1. Consumption, Discipline, and Democracy

1. Christopher Wilson, "The Rhetoric of Consumption: Mass Market Magazines and the Demise of the Gentle Reader, 1880–1920," in *The Culture of Consumption: Critical Essays in American History. 1880–1980*, ed. Richard Fox and T. J. Jackson Lears (New York: Pantheon, 1983).

2. Matthew Schneirov, *The Dream of a New Social Order: Popular Magazines in America 1893–1914* (New York: Columbia University Press, 1994); Wilson, "Rhetoric of Consumption." The new magazines included, for example, *Munsey's, McClure's, Saturday Evening Post,* and *Cosmopolitan.*

3. Frank Munsey, a contemporary magazine publisher, saw advertising as part of the magazine revolution that allowed people to keep in touch with the dynamic spirit of the times. Earlier magazines had regarded advertising as incompatible with the purity of the artistic material in the journals. Schneirov, *Dream*, pp. 91–92.

4. Ibid. p. 71.

5. Ibid. p. 203.

6. Ibid. p. 4.

7. Benedict Anderson has highlighted the central role of print capitalism in the collective imagining of national communities in *Imagined Communities: Reflections on the Origins and Spread of Nationalism* (London: Verso, 1983/1991).

8. Schneirov, *Dream*, pp. 219, 97–98.

9. Armand Mattelart, *Mapping World Communication: War, Progress, Culture*, trans. Susan Emanuel and James A. Cohen (Minneapolis: University of Minnesota Press, 1994).

10. John Trebbel and Mary Ellen Zucherman, *The Magazine in America, 1741–1990* (New York: Oxford University Press, 1991), p. 163.

11. Joan Rubin, *The Making of Middle-Brow Culture* (Chapel Hill: University of North Carolina Press, 1992), chapter 5.

12. Wilson, "*Rhetoric of Consumption.*" The quotations are from p. 61.

13. Laura Mulvey, "Visual Pleasure and Narrative Cinema," *Screen* 16, no. 3 (1975): 6–18. Quotation from Ann Kaplan, *Regarding Television*, American Film Institute Monograph Series, vol. 2, 1983, p. 228.

14. Schneirov, *Dream*, p. 161.

15. Ibid., p. 201.

16. Fredric Jameson, "Pleasure: A Political Issue," in *The Ideologies of Theory: Essays 1971–1986*, vol. 2, *Syntax of History* (Minneapolis: University of Minnesota Press, 1988).

17. Quoted in Richard Fox and T. J. Jackson Lears, introduction to *The Culture of Consumption*, p. xiv.

18. Ibid., p. xiii.

19. On the surveillance of the self, see Michel Foucault, *Discipline and Punish* (New York: Vintage, 1977), and "The Repressive Hypothesis," in *The History of Sexuality*, vol. 1, *An Introduction*, trans. R. Hurley (New York: Vintage, 1978), pp. 15–50.

20. Fox and Lears, introduction to *Culture of Consumption*.

21. Schneirov, *Dream*, p. 7.

22. The classic expression of this argument is found in Max Horkheimer and Theodor Adorno, "The Culture Industry: Enlightenment as Mass Deception," in *Dialectic of Enlightenment* (New York: Herder and Herder, 1972).

23. Fox and Lears, introduction to *Culture of Consumption*.

24. Quoted in Schneirov, *Dream*, p. 55.

25. Ibid., p. 42.

26. Virginia Woolf, "Middlebrow," in *Death of the Moth and Other Essays* (New York: Harcourt, Brace, 1942), p. 183.

27. Homi K. Bhabha, "Signs Taken for Wonders," in *The Location of Culture* (New York: Routledge, 1994).

28. Schneirov, *Dream*, p. 87.

29. Charles Ferguson, *Unforgettable DeWitt Wallace* (Pleasantville, N.Y.: Reader's Digest Association, 1987), p. 1. This pamphlet was reprinted from the Feb. 1987 issue of *Reader's Digest*.

30. Ibid., p. 4.

31. Ibid., p. 3.

32. Ibid., p. 8.

33. Ibid.

34. Ibid., p. 13. I have not yet seen *Reader's Digest* referred to as the "pocket university" in any other place, despite Ferguson's assertion that this was the magazine's nickname.

35. Ibid., p. 9.

36. Ibid., p.15. Schreiner suggests a different motivation for their generosity: "Keeping as much of their excess money out of the hands of government as they can and directing it toward their own causes harmonizes with the tonic chord of individualism that rings through half a century of *Digests*" (Samuel Schreiner, *The Condensed World of the Reader's Digest* [New York: Stein and Day, 1977], p. 203).

37. Trebbel and Zucherman, *Magazine in America,* p. 182.

38. Demographic statistics on *Reader's Digest's* 1990 and 1991 readership are provided in the appendix.

39. Emphasis in original.

40. Common sense appeals through the obviousness of its claims; it makes the world simple and manageable.

41. The argument that the representation of an Other is generally a projection of the Self seems to be well illustrated in a July 1946 article about the expansionary nature of the Soviet Union. The author describes the Soviet government's tactics of finding victims for conquest: "If it finds a digestible victim, it flows around and digests it" (W. Bullitt, "Approach to the Soviet Union," *Reader's Digest,* July 1946, p. 173).

42. Rubin, *Making of Middle-Brow Culture,* p. 92.

43. The "expert" label was used rather liberally. For example, the popular novelist Tom Clancy ("Common Sense about Strategic Defense," *Reader's Digest,* Aug. 1988, pp. 49–52) was deemed to be as authoritative a source on American arms requirements in the 1980s as members of government defense agencies.

44. Lowenthal quoted in Rubin, *Making of Middle-Brow Culture,* p. 236.

45. For a discussion of the unifying effects of the statistical average in American political culture, see Warren Susman, "The Culture of the Thirties," in *Culture as History* (New York: Pantheon, 1984), pp. 150–83.

46. The classic expression of fear of the culture industry is Max Horkheimer and Theodor Adorno, "The Culture Industry," pp. 120–67.

47. John Heidenry, *Theirs Was the Kingdom: Lila and DeWitt Wallace and the Story of the Reader's Digest* (New York: Norton, 1993), p. 83.

48. The importance of staying informed about political issues and events can be traced back to early American debates between Federalists and Anti-Federalists over which territorial power arrangement would best ensure the flow of information and preserve democratic politics. See Clinton Rossiter, ed., *The Federalist Papers* (New York: Mentor, 1961), and Ralph Ketcham, *The Anti-Federalist Papers and the Constitutional Convention Debates* (New York: Mentor, 1986).

49. *Reader's Digest* had, in reproducing American identity over the course of thirty years, managed to write itself into the heart of that concept.

50. Heidenry, *Kingdom,* p. 358.

51. "The Country That Saved Itself," *Reader's Digest,* Nov. 1964, p. 159. Reader response to the *Digest's* claims of the importance of particular articles is impressive: approximately 7 million reprints are sold each year (*Reader's Digest* Fact Sheet, Spring 1991).

52. At the end of the article were two sets of instructions. "How You Can Use This Article to Best Effect" suggested whom to send the article to and told how to acquire reprints. "How to Mail It" listed both surface and air postal rates to different parts of the world.

53. Samuel Schreiner, *The Condensed World of the Reader's Digest* (New York: Stein and Day, 1977), p. 49.

54. Even foreign editions are closely monitored and constrained by the central office. Although most material in each foreign edition is chosen to be of specific interest to the region served rather than simply reprinting American articles, content is subject to approval.

55. Heidenry, *Kingdom*, p. 81, emphasis mine.

56. "And it is an art," Edward Thompson, editor in chief from 1976 to 1981 told me with great passion in a personal communication in 1991.

57. Matthew Lynn, "Revolution in Pleasantville," *Management Today*, April 1996, p. 63.

58. Antonio Gramsci, *Selections from Prison Notebooks*, trans. and ed. Q. Hoare and G. Nowell Smith (London: Lawrence and Wishart, 1971), p. 297.

59. Heidenry, *Kingdom*.

60. Ibid.

61. Ibid., p. 564.

62. On the Spanish edition of *Reader's Digest*, see Mattelart, *Mapping*, p. 83; on the Italian version, see Heidenry, *Kingdom*, p. 473.

63. See Ariel Dorfman, "The Infantilization of the Adult Reader," in *The Empire's Old Clothes: What the Lone Ranger, Babar, and Other Innocent Heroes Do to Our Minds* (New York: Pantheon, 1983); Fred Landis, "The CIA and the Reader's Digest," *Covert Action Information Bulletin* 29 (1988): 41–47.

64. In a telephone interview in 1991, Edward Thompson indicated rather warily that such restrictions on promoting differing viewpoints "may have had something to do with [his] leaving."

65. "Pangloss Goes Public," *Economist*, June 10, 1989, p. 26.

66. Lynn, "Revolution in Pleasantville," p. 64.

67. Alexandra Biesada, "Lessons from Pleasantville," *Financial World*, April 16, 1991.

68. "Pangloss Goes Public," p. 26.

69. Dorfman, "Infantilization," p. 153, passim; quote from p. 144.

70. *New York Times* eulogy for DeWitt Wallace, 1981; Heidenry, *Kingdom*, p. 547.

2. Reading the *Digest* Writing the World

1. Gearóid Ó Tuathail, *Critical Geopolitics* (Minneapolis: University of Minnesota Press, 1996).

2. Hayden White, *Tropics of Discourse* (Baltimore: Johns Hopkins University Press, 1978).

3. John Agnew and Stuart Corbridge, "The New Geopolitics: The Dynamics of Geopolitical Disorder," in *A World in Crisis?*, 2d ed., ed. Ron Johnston and Peter Taylor (Oxford: Blackwell, 1989).

4. Christopher Norris, *Uncritical Theory: Postmodernism, Intellectuals and the Gulf War* (Amherst: University of Massachusetts Press, 1992).

5. Ibid., p. 23.

6. Terry Eagleton, *Literary Theory* (Minneapolis: University of Minnesota Press, 1983), p. 145.

7. Simon Dalby, "Geopolitical Discourse: The Soviet Union as Other," *Alternatives* 13 (1988): 416.

8. Martin Lewis and Karen Wigen, *The Myth of Continents: A Critique of Metageography* (Berkeley: University of California Press, 1977), p. xiii.

9. Eagleton, *Literary Theory*, p. 132.

10. Geoffrey Bennington, "Postal Politics and the Institution of the Nation," in *Nation and Narration*, ed. Homi K. Bhabha (London: Routledge, 1990), p. 121.

11. The classic example of geopolitical reasoning is Halford Mackinder's "heartland thesis," which insisted on the importance of the Asian heartland to the unfolding history of great powers. For Mackinder, the conquest of this territory provides an almost impenetrable position. Later theorists accepted changes to geopolitics wrought by air travel and ICBMs, yet the concept of favored locations leading to certain political outcomes remained. For a discussion of classic geopolitics, see Ó Tuathail, *Critical Geopolitics,* and John Agnew and Stuart Corbridge, *Mastering Space: Hegemony, Territory and International Economy* (New York: Routledge, 1995).

12. David Campbell, *Writing Security* (Minneapolis: University of Minnesota Press, 1992), pp. 69, 273.

13. Dalby, "Geopolitical Discourse," p. 420.

14. Campbell, *Writing Security,* p. 105. The classic examination of nations as imagined communities is in Benedict Anderson's *Imagined Communities: Reflections on the Origin and Spread of Modern Nations* (London: Verso, 1983/1991).

15. Frederick Dolan, *Allegories of America: Narratives-Metaphysics-Politics* (Ithaca, N.Y.: Cornell University Press, 1994).

16. Simon Dalby "American Security Discourse: The Persistence of Geopolitics," *Political Geography Quarterly* 9, no. 2 (1990): 172.

17. Robert Cox, "Social Forces, States and World Orders: Beyond International Relations Theory," in *Neorealism and Its Critics,* ed. Robert O. Keohane (New York: Columbia University Press, 1986) p. 216.

18. Simon Dalby, "Gender and Geopolitics: Reading Security Discourse in the New World Order," *Environment and Planning D: Society and Space* 12, no. 5 (1994): 534.

19. See Ó Tuathail, *Critical Geopolitics.*

20. Richard Ashley, "The Geopolitics of Geopolitical Space," *Alternatives* 1987: 407.

21. Antonio Gramsci, *Selections from Prison Notebooks,* ed. and trans. Q. Hoare and G. Nowell Smith (London: Lawrence and Wishart, 1971), p. 241.

22. Ibid., p. 245.

23. Renate Holub, *Antonio Gramsci: Beyond Marxism and Postmodernism* (New York: Routledge, 1992), p. 104.

24. Cynthia Enloe, *Bananas, Beaches and Bases: Making Feminist Sense of International Politics* (Berkeley: University of California Press, 1989), and *The Morning After: Sexual Politics at the End of the Cold War* (Berkeley: University of California Press, 1993).

25. Enloe, *Bananas,* p. 3.

26. Pierre Bourdieu, *Outline of a Theory of Practice,* trans. R. Nice (Cambridge: Cambridge University Press, 1977), p.188.

27. James DerDerian, *Anti-Diplomacy: Spies, Terror, Speed and War* (Oxford: Blackwell, 1992), pp. 12–13, note 1.

28. Ibid., p. 41.

29. Michael Edelman, *Constructing the Political Spectacle* (Chicago: University of Chicago Press, 1988), p. 1.

30. D. Nimmo and J. Combs, *Mediated Political Realities* (New York: Longman, 1983), p. xv.

31. Robert Denton, series foreword to *Visions of Empire: Political Imagery in Contemporary American Film,* by Steven Prince (New York: Praeger, 1992), p. xiv.

32. James Gibson, *Warrior Dreams: Violence and Manhood in Post-Vietnam America* (New York: Hill and Wang, 1994), p. 266.

33. John Hartley, *The Politics of Pictures* (London: Routledge, 1992).

34. Gearóid Ó Tuathail and John Agnew, "Geopolitics and Discourse: Practical Geopolitical Reasoning in American Foreign Policy," *Political Geography* 11, no. 2 (1992): 190–204.

35. Quoted in Dolan, *Allegories*, p. 74.

36. Michael Vlahos, "The End of America's Post-War Ethos," *Foreign Affairs,* Summer 1988, p. 1091.

37. Frances FitzGerald, *America Revised* (New York: Vintage, 1979).

38. Ibid., chapter 1.

39. See Michel Foucault, *Discipline and Punish: The Birth of the Prison,* trans. Alan Sheridan (New York: Vintage, 1979); Anthony Giddens, *The Nation-State and Violence,* vol. 2 of *A Contemporary Critique of Historical Materialism* (Cambridge: Polity, 1985).

40. Benedict Anderson, *Imagined Communities: Reflections on the Origin and Spread of Nationalism* (New York: Verso, 1991).

41. Armand Mattelart, *Mapping World Communication: War, Progress, Culture,* trans. Susan Emanuel and James A. Cohen (Minneapolis: University of Minnesota Press, 1994), p. 71.

42. Michael Shapiro, "The Sports/War Intertext," in James DerDerian and Michael Shapiro, eds., *International/Intertextual Relations* (Lexington, Mass.: Lexington, 1989), p. 87.

43. Campbell, *Writing Security,* p. 40.

44. Samuel Schreiner, *The Condensed World of the Reader's Digest* (New York: Stein and Day, 1977), p. 169.

45. John Heidenry, *Theirs Was the Kingdom: Lila and DeWitt Wallace and the Story of the Reader's Digest* (New York: Norton, 1993), p. 53.

46. Ibid., p. 119, passim.

47. Ibid., p. 456.

48. Ó Tuathail, *Critical Geopolitics.*

49. Halford Mackinder, "The Geographical Pivot of History," *Geographical Journal* 13 (1904): 421–37.

50. Paul Boyer, *When Time Shall Be No More: Prophecy Belief in Modern American Culture* (London: Belknap, 1992), p. xi.

51. Ibid., p. 175. Boyer also suggests that in this prophecy belief system, the producers of knowledge in American society were diffuse: "Albert Einstein, Paul Harvey, the *New York Times, Reader's Digest* and the *South Bay Daily Breeze* of Torrance, California, . . . were on an equal plane in prophecyland" (p. 311).

52. Andrew Ross, *No Respect: Intellectuals and Popular Culture* (London: Routledge, 1990), p. 9.

53. Roland Barthes, *Mythologies,* trans. A. Lavers (London: Paladin, 1973), p. 143.

54. It could be argued, however, that there are in fact structural barriers to success in the *Digest*'s presentations of American society, barriers that are most clearly invoked by the specter of interventionist government and bureaucracy.

55. Edward Thompson, personal communication, 1991.

56. J. Dulles, "Thoughts on Soviet Foreign Policy—and What to Do about It," *Reader's Digest,* Aug. 1946, p. 12.

57. Michel Foucault, "What Is an Author?" in *The Foucault Reader,* ed P. Rabinow (New York: Pantheon, 1984), p. 107.

58. Wolfgang Iser, *Prospecting: From Reader Response to Literary Anthropology* (Baltimore: Johns Hopkins University Press, 1989), p. 7.

59. All figures from the *Reader's Digest* Fact Sheet, Spring 1991.

60. Heidenry, *Theirs Was the Kingdom,* p. 556.

61. C. Lutz and J. Collins, *Reading National Geographic* (Chicago: University of Chicago Press, 1993), p. 229.

62. It is of course impossible to be certain of this contention without undertaking extensive reader surveys. However, given the historical nature of this study coupled with the national reach of the *Reader's Digest* American edition, sufficient coverage to give representative readings would be impossible.

63. D. Carmody, "The Lifeblood of the Reader's Digest Is 40-Year-Old Data Base," *New York Times,* 1994, p. c1. This list, which covers more than half of all U.S. households, is a gold mine for targeted mailings of information about other products manufactured for the *Digest* and as information sold to other companies. This demarcation of people into socioeconomic groups can be seen to be producing publics—clearly delineated subsections of the populace. The *Digest* can be thought of as creating "publics" in the way in which John Hartley has suggested for the media.

64. Statistics from Richard S. Teitelbaum, "Are Times Tough? Here's an Answer," *Forum,* December 2, 1991, p. 101.

65. The *Reader's Digest* editor receives over half a million letters each year (*Reader's Digest* Fact Sheet, Spring 1991); as many of the writers complain that the magazine takes too liberal a stance as complain that it is too conservative (Edward Thompson, personal communication, 1991).

66. Wolfgang Iser, *The Act of Reading: A Theory of Aesthetic Response* (Baltimore: Johns Hopkins University Press, 1978), p. 38.

67. White, *Tropics of Discourse.*

68. Iser, *Act of Reading,* p. 35.

69. Ernesto Laclau, *Politics and Ideology in Marxist Theory* (London: New Left Books, 1977), p. 100, emphasis in original.

70. Louis Althusser, "Ideology and Ideological State Apparatuses," in *Lenin and Philosophy and Other Essays,* trans. B. Brewster (New York: Monthly Review Press, 1971), pp. 121–73.

71. Quotes from *Reader's Digest* articles as follows: C. Malik, "Is It Too Late to Win Against Communism?" Sept. 1960, p. 39, emphasis in original; C. Romulo, "America, Wake-Up," Nov. 1960, p. 46; V. Tchernavin, "I Speak for the Silent," May 1935, pp. 111–26; B. Carter, "Why I Became an American," June 1937, pp. 21–23.

72. Anderson, *Imagined Communities.*

73. Creation of a coherent sense of national identification was of special importance in the federal United States. Mathew Schneirov has argued that magazines more than any other medium seemed to represent an American national identity at the turn of the century (*The Dream of a New Social Order: Popular Magazines in America, 1893–1914* [New York: Columbia University Press, 1994], p. 4).

74. Quotes from *Reader's Digest* articles as follows: L. Marin, "How Latin America Can Save Itself from Castroism," May 1962, pp. 231–36; J. Hibben, "Are We Worthy of Our Destiny?" March 1933, pp. 5–7; M. Eastman, "To Collaborate Successfully—We Must Face the Facts About Russia," July 1943, pp. 1–14.

75. See Michael Billig, *Banal Nationalism* (London: Sage, 1995).

76. Ariel Dorfman, "The Infantilization of the Adult Reader," in *The Empire's Old Clothes: What the Lone Ranger, Babar, and Other Innocent Heroes Do to Our Minds* (New York: Pantheon, 1983), p. 139.

77. Judith Butler, *Gender Trouble: Feminism and the Subversion of Identity* (New York: Routledge, 1990), p. 145.

78. Ohmann quoted in Lutz and Collins, *Reading National Geographic*, p. 17.

79. *Reader's Digest* illustrations often reduced the moral of the tale to a bold graphic. Propaganda maps were popular: Russia as a bear hovering over Eastern Europe (A. Ross, "Iron Curtains for Czechoslovakia," May 1948, pp. 36–39); the capture of various countries by a Russian sickle (E. Johnston, "A Satellite Is Born," Sept. 1948, pp. 31–35); R. Wheeler, "Stalin's Target for Tomorrow," March 1951, pp. 65–68.

80. Subtitles are from J. Van Fleet, "The Truth about Korea," July 1953, pp. 1–16; W. Hard, "Labor and National Unity," Nov. 1939, pp. 1–9; A. Nevis, "Tyrannies Must Fall," Jan. 1952, pp. 51–56; H. Hoover, "The Effective Military Policy for the United States," May 1952, pp. 40–44.

81. In researching this book, I read all *Digest* articles between 1922 and 1994 that mentioned threats to the United States (during the Cold War these were primarily concerned with the Soviet Union, communists, and socialists), discussed America's role in global politics, or presented an image of good American citizenship. A breakdown of editorial content for 1990 can be seen in figure 1. Although this figure represents only one year, I believe that this snapshot is fairly representative of the content of the magazine throughout its years of publication. It should be noted, however, that since comparisons between the Soviet Union and America are so prevalent in *Reader's Digest,* some articles that did not immediately seem to be concerned with this topic did include some relevant material. I gauged relevance from titles and subtitles, but it is inevitable that I missed some material. Nevertheless, I base my discussion here on an analysis of several thousand articles.

As I read, I collected representative and interesting quotes, but also attempted to summarize the topical content and the narratives and discourses that constituted the piece in order to provide some sense of consistency or change over the period being discussed, and to ensure that the quotes I present in my text are representative of the general mood in the magazine at the time.

In my research, I spoke to only one person who was actually involved in the magazine's production. Despite a number of attempts in person, on the telephone, and in writing, there has been little response from the *Digest* to my questions about selection policy and editorial process, although I was lucky enough to speak to former editor in chief Edward Thompson in 1991. John Heidenry's discussion of the problems of researching his excellent biography of *Reader's Digest* founders Lila and DeWitt Wallace suggests that I was not alone in facing this problem. I do not consider this to be a barrier to the project at hand. There have been a number of biographies of the Wallaces and of the *Digest*, and the magazine has periodically discussed its perceived role within American society. What has been missing—and what I hope to achieve— is an account of the content of the magazine and of how changing representations of global geographies on its pages have resulted from changing conditions and anxieties in American culture.

82. Anthony Giddens, *The Constitution of Society* (Oxford: Polity, 1984).

3. Ambivalent Geography

All references in this chapter are to *Reader's Digest* except where noted otherwise.

1. C. Hoover, "Socialism in Practice," Sept. 1931, p. 464.

2. Alan Trachtenberg, *The Incorporation of America: Culture and Society in the Guilded Age* (New York: Hill and Wang, 1982).

3. There is obviously overlap between these three "scales," but articles generally addressed one of them as its dominant focus.

4. Following convention, I have taken 1945 as the year to end this section. Articles in this year and even the next were not uniformly negative in their representation of the Soviet Union; some positive images persisted. However, 1945 does, I think, illustrate a decisive shift in focus, and from this time onward images of the USSR in *Reader's Digest* became progressively less positive. Furthermore, it is conventional wisdom that the end of cooperation in World War II made U.S. relations with the USSR less ambivalent.

5. J. Davis, "Pre-Revolutionary Russia," July-Aug. 1922, pp. 343–44, and "The Russian Revolution," Sept. 1922, pp. 401–2.

6. Quotes from Davis, "Russian Revolution," pp. 401 and 402.

7. William Pietz, "The 'Post-Colonialism' of Cold War Discourse," *Social Text: Theory/Culture/Ideology* 19/20 (1988): 58.

8. See Edward Said, *Orientalism* (London: Vintage, 1978).

9. See, for example, M. Sullivan, "Is Capitalism Passing in Europe?" Sept. 1923, pp. 21–22; C. Sarolea, "Bolshevist Propaganda in the East," Feb. 1924, pp. 749–50; K. Powers, "The Receding Tide of Democracy," May 1924, pp. 121–24.

10. D. Houston, "Every Worker a Capitalist," Feb. 1925, pp. 589–90.

11. "The communists cannot be expected to be 'realistic.'" Condensation, "The Communist Party," May 1935, p. 35.

12. For example, E. Lyons, "Russia Postpones Utopia," June 1936, pp. 17–19, and "Assignment in Utopia," Jan. 1938, pp. 111–27.

13. This strategy again found its roots in Orientalism. Many Orientalist writers admired ancient Islamic scholars and explained their disdainful attitude toward contemporary conditions in the Orient as a result of cultural degeneration caused by a deviation from the written words of high culture. See Said, *Orientalism*.

14. S. Günther, "What Moscow Reads," March 1932, pp. 70–72, and R. Little, "The Daily News, Russian Style," July 1934, pp. 60–63.

15. O. Villard, "Our Attitude Towards Russia," Oct. 1930, p. 537.

16. H. Pell, "Preparing for the Next War," Oct. 1931, pp. 488–90; quote from p. 490.

17. E. Lyons, "Russia's Man of Steel," Aug. 1931; quotes from pp. 323, 324, 325.

18. W. Frank, "Russian Nights," Sept. 1932, p. 73.

19. J. Davis, "Russia Today," Nov. 1926, pp. 437–38.

20. H. Bennett, "Meet the Smiths—of Russia," Jan. 1931, p. 798.

21. O. Villard, "The Russian Industrial Vision," Jan. 1930, pp. 853–55.

22. Frank, "Russian Nights," p. 73.

23. F. Reed, "Going to School in Russia," May 1931, p. 75.

24. M. Sherover, "America and the Russian Market," Oct. 1933, p. 41.

25. The first expression of this view can be found in E. Martin, "Are We Going Communist?—Rebuttal," Feb. 1937, pp. 109–10.

26. In his book *World Politics and Personal Insecurity* (New York: Whittlesay,

1935), published during this period, Harold Lasswell explains the perceptions and effects of insecurity through uncertainty thus: "The flight into action is preferable to the torment of insecurity; the flight into danger becomes an insecurity to end insecurity" (p. 75).

27. T. Knappen, "The Russian Bear Walks Again," March 1931, p. 1040.

28. General P. Krasnoff, "Russia—the Travesty Republic," Aug. 1928, pp. 227–28.

29. R. Urch, "Bolshevism and Religion in Russia," April 1923, p. 74, emphasis mine.

30. J. Abbe, "Moscow Goes to the Races," Oct. 1934, p. 50.

31. W. Chamberlain, "Russia Bows to Human Nature," Nov. 1934, p. 75.

32. H. Menchen, "Capitalism Won't Die," July 1935, p. 12, emphasis mine.

33. Ibid., pp. 13–14, emphasis mine.

34. For example, Villard, "Russian Industrial Vision," pp. 853–55, and V. Tchernarin, "I Speak for the Silent," May 1935, pp. 111–26.

35. Villard, "Russian Industrial Vision."

36. R. Blanshard, "Sex Standards in Moscow," July 1926, p. 181.

37. Ibid., p. 182. See also M. Hindus, "Russia Bans 'Mrs. Warren's Profession,'" Jan. 1934, pp. 85–87.

38. M. Hindus, "Marriage in Russia," Aug. 1929, pp. 328–30.

39. Condensation, "Communist Life," June 1932, p. 38.

40. B. James, "Making Whoopee with the Soviets," Sept. 1930, p. 452.

41. E. McCormick, "The Cosmetic Urge in Russia," June 1934, p. 51.

42. Lyons, "Russia Postpones Utopia," p. 17.

43. Roland Barthes, "The Great Family of Man," in *Mythologies*, trans. A. Lavers (London: Paladin, 1973), p. 100.

44. E. Martin, "America Rejects Communism—Rebuttal," Feb. 1937, p. 110.

45. J. Littlepage and D. Boss, "In Search of Soviet Gold," Oct. 1938, p. 121, and E. Lyons, "Assignment in Utopia," Jan. 1938, p. 122.

46. E. Lyons, "Russia's Rehearsed Trials" June 1937, p. 58, emphasis in original.

47. Condensation, "The Bear That Shoots Like a Man," Oct. 1937, pp. 67–69.

48. Mary Kaldor, *The Imaginary War: Understanding the East-West Conflict* (Oxford: Blackwell, 1990), pp. 79–80; quotation from p. 79.

49. For example, see E. Lyons, "Stalin: Czar of All the Russias," May 1940, pp. 119–40.

50. Ibid., p. 121.

51. M. Eastman, "Socialism Doesn't Jibe with Human Nature," June 1941, pp. 41–49.

52. B. Wolf, "The Silent Soviet Revolution," July 1941, p. 90.

53. See M. Hindus, "Report on Russia," Nov. 1942, pp. 90–92; M. Hindus, "The Price That Russia is Paying," April 1943, pp. 47–50; Lt. Col. P. Thompson, "The Nazi's Own Appraisal of the Russian Soldier," June 1943, pp. 15–18; B. Voyetekhov, "Last Days of Sevastopol," Aug. 1943, pp. 74–81.

54. J. Davies, "What We Didn't Know about Russia," March 1942: "The Russian people . . . have endured the same conditions as our own pioneers and have developed many of the same virtues" (p. 46). See also W. Wilkie, "Life on the Russian Frontier," March 1943, pp. 1–7.

55. See, for example, Davies, "What We Didn't Know," pp. 48 and 49.

56. Some greater levels of enthusiasm for the Soviet Union persisted in this

period. One author elevated the USSR to "one of the most effective societies of modern times" (Wilkie, "Life on the Russian Frontier," p. 1).

57. For example, K. Smith, "The American Plan for a Reorganized World," Jan. 1943, pp. 39–45; W. Lippmann, "US Foreign Policy: Shield of the Republic," July 1943, pp. 119–44.

58. For example, Wilkie, "Life on the Russian Frontier"; W. White, "Report on the Russians," part 1, Dec. 1944, pp. 101–22; part 2, Jan. 1945, pp. 106–28. The articles that discussed the potential for overcoming prewar differences between the United States and the USSR included E. Johnston, "To Bridge the Gulf Between the US and Russia," Aug. 1944, pp. 33–36; E. Johnston, "My Talk with Joseph Stalin," Oct. 1944, pp. 1–10; S. High, "An Open Letter to the Russians," July 1943, pp. 3–7.

59. S. Welles, "What Russia Wants," Nov. 1944, p. 23.

60. M. Eastman, "To Collaborate Successfully—We Must Know The Truth about Russia," July 1943, p. 14. See also A. Barmine, "The New Communist Conspiracy," Oct. 1944, pp. 27–33, and Welles, "What Russia Wants," pp. 20–24.

61. Barmine, "New Communist Conspiracy," p. 30.

62. Paul Cerny, "Political Entropy and American Decline," *Millennium* 18, no. 1 (1989): 47–63.

63. W. Lippmann, "America as an Empire," June 1927, p. 78. See also R. Niebular, "Awkward Imperialists," June 1930, p. 106.

64. L. Buell, "American Imperialists," Nov. 1925, p. 458.

65. J. Hibben, "Are We Worthy of Our Destiny?" March 1933, pp. 5–7.

66. H. Kattenborn, "America's Place in the World," May 1926, p. 50.

67. Lippmann, "America as an Empire," p. 78.

68. H. Luce, "The American Century," April 1941, p. 48. The reference to Genghis Khan is significant given the multiple comparisons between this leader and Stalin in the *Digest* at the time.

69. Gearóid Ó Tuathail and John Agnew, "Geopolitics and Discourse: Practical Geopolitical Reasoning in American Foreign Policy," *Political Geography* 11, no. 2 (1992): 190–204.

70. G. Cutten, "America under Fire," Oct. 1927, p. 378.

71. L. Blayney, "American Ideals and Traditions," June 1922, p. 262.

72. G. Cutten, "Nature's Inexorable Law—Inequality," July 1923, p. 290.

73. W. White, "Cheer Up America!" May 1927, p. 59, and D. Houston, "Every Worker a Capitalist," Feb. 1925, p. 590.

74. W. White, "Our Shifting Modes and Morals," Feb. 1929, p. 602, and J. Adams, "The Crisis in Character," Sept. 1933, pp. 7–10.

75. T. Wertenbaker, "What's Wrong with the United States?" Nov. 1928, p. 387.

76. Condensation, "The Communist Party"; quotations from p. 37.

77. Johnston, "To Bridge the Gulf," p. 34. For a more thorough discussion of Americans' perception of class, see Paul Fussell, *Class* (New York: Ballantine, 1983).

78. W. Williams, "What the Workers Really Want," March 1938, pp. 60–62; quotation from p. 60.

79. Dana Polan, *Power and Paranoia* (New York: Columbia University Press, 1986), pp. 68–69.

80. Ibid., p. 70.

81. R. Helton, "The Inner Threat: Our Own Softness," Oct. 1940, pp. 6–9. Helton considered submissiveness to be a "feminine" trait. This article presents the first

coding of the masculinity of American resistance of the seduction of communism that underwrote much of U.S. Cold War discourse. It is also possible that fear of the feminization of American culture may have been a reaction to the improving status of women in American society.

82. For a discussion of the importance of warriorhood in American political culture, see James Gibson, *Warrior Dreams: Violence and Manhood in Post-Vietnam America* (New York: Hill and Wang, 1994), and Susan Jeffords, *The Remasculinization of America: Gender and the Vietnam War* (Bloomington: Indiana University Press, 1994).

83. Condensation, "Is the New Deal Socialism?" June 1934, p. 34.

84. M. Sullivan, "Old ghosts and the New Deal," Nov. 1934, pp. 1–3.

85. See J. Adams, "The American Character," Dec. 1934, pp. 98–101.

86. J. Adams, "Is Capitalism Doomed?" Nov. 1938, p. 76.

87. N. Baker, "The Decay of Self-Reliance," Feb. 1935, p. 21.

88. G. Sokolsky, "It *Can* Happen Here," May 1937, p. 30, emphasis in original.

89. Ibid., p. 32. See also W. Pegler, "But What of Soulless Unions?" July 1937, pp. 57–58.

90. J. Vatlin, "Academy of High Treason," Aug. 1941, p. 54.

91. E. Levinson, "Strikebreaking Incorporated," Dec. 1935, pp. 68–72.

92. See, for example, Houston, "Every Worker a Capitalist," Feb. 1925, pp. 589–90, and W. Saunders, "Where Workmen Are Capitalists," Dec. 1925, pp. 499–500.

93. Trachtenberg, *Incorporation of America.*

94. For example, see Robert Dallek, *The American Style of Foreign Policy: Cultural Politics and Foreign Affairs* (New York: Knopf, 1983).

95. Ibid., chapter 4.

96. For an elaboration of this view, see Peter Taylor, *Britain and the Cold War: 1945 as Geopolitical Transition* (New York: Guilford, 1990).

4. The Beginnings of Cold War

All references in this chapter are to *Reader's Digest* except where noted otherwise.

1. Fred Halliday, *The Coming of the Second Cold War* (New York: Verso, 1983), p. 4.

2. Ibid., p. 3.

3. J. Strohm, in "How They Hate Us in Red China," Jan. 1959, pp. 30–39, described the root of the split as follows: "China is attempting to move towards 'pure' communism, while Russia, having failed at it, is backing away" (p. 39). As usual, however, the *Digest* advocated caution since the "feud does not, of course, make either power less 'communist'" (M. Frankel, "The Bitter Feud That Splits the Communist World," Aug. 1963, p. 143). Another author (H. Jackson, "The Cold War Isn't Over," Nov. 1963, pp. 99–102) reminded readers of the Russians' lack of fidelity to the nonaggression pact with Hitler as further reason to be wary.

4. The term is from Frederick Dolan, *Allegories of America: Narratives-Metaphysics-Politics* (Ithaca, N.Y.: Cornell University Press, 1994).

5. M. Eastman, "The Truth about Soviet Russia's 14,000,000 Slaves," April 1947, pp. 139–46.

6. J. Steinberg, "The Real Soviet Story," March 1951, p.,157.

7. Ibid., p. 159.

8. See, for example, "If You Worked in Soviet Russia," April 1951, pp. 34–37.

9. J. Fischer, "No Rest for the Weary Russians," Dec. 1946, pp. 101–8.

10. W. Bullitt, "The Strength of Our New Foreign Policy," June 1947, p. 29.

11. Using the language of colonialism to describe Soviet expansion into Eastern Europe (and communist ascendance to power elsewhere) provided additional legitimacy to the *Digest*'s narrative and continuity with coverage of the USSR before the Cold War. Both America and voices within it such as the *Digest* had called for the end of European colonialism. The ideology of colonialism had come to be seen as a trait of the Old World, which America must fight against.

12. For example, see W. Lippmann, "The Rivalry of Nations," April 1948, pp. 15–18.

13. Jan Nijman and Gearóid Ó Tuathail, "George Kennan," in *Dictionary of Geopolitics*, ed. John O'Loughlin (Westport, Conn., Greenwood, 1994), pp. 134–35.

14. W. Bullitt, "Approach to the Soviet Union," July 1946, p. 153.

15. M. Scully, "Democracy's First—and Last—Chance in Latin America," Jan. 1947, pp. 113–16.

16. For example: "Khrushchev is red / Macmillan is blue / Harold Wilson—what color are you?" P. Webb and S. Hagerty, "Harold Wilson: Britain's Question Mark," Oct. 1963, p. 109.

17. See Michel Foucault, *The History of Sexuality*, trans. Robert Hurley (New York: Vintage, 1980). The linkages between these identities was forged with the Cold War association of communism (that is, political perversity as viewed from the position of the American right) with homosexuality (sexual perversity).

18. Carl Pletsch, "The Three Worlds, or, The Division of Social Science Labor, circa 1950–1975," *Comparative Studies in Society and History* 23 (1981): 565–90.

19. M. Maleter, "Hungary's Proud Rebel," Jan. 1959, p. 56.

20. A significant number of articles were available as reprints because their importance made them worthy of further circulation; as I mentioned in chapter 2, some even included instructions for disseminating the article's important message.

21. D. Thompson, "A Nightmare World," June 1949, p. 112.

22. S. Shalett, "The Trial of the Eleven Communists," Aug. 1950, p. 66.

23. L. Miller, "What Does the CVA Mean to You?" Aug. 1950, pp. 100, 103. This quote also demonstrates the *Digest*'s gendering of the active citizen as male.

24. J. Dulles, "Moral Force in World Affairs," Aug. 1948, p. 106.

25. W. Chambers, "What Is a Communist?" Oct. 1953, p. 20, emphasis in original; P. Palmer, "Soviet Union vs. U.S.A.," April 1958, p. 42, emphasis in original.

26. F. Franco quoted in D. Lawrence, "Why Fear Russia?" Oct. 1955, p. 179.

27. M. Eastman, "The Communists' Master Plan for Conquest," Jan. 1961, p. 36.

28. J. Hoover, "Red Spymasters in America," Aug. 1952, p. 83.

29. R. Littell, "Berlin—Divided She Stands," Oct. 1955, p. 85.

30. L. Root, "Are the Russians Ahead of Us in Nuclear Science?" June 1956, p. 32.

31. F. Drake, "A Realistic Plan for National Survival," Feb. 1958, pp. 43–44.

32. See Ella Shohat and Robert Stam, *Unthinking Eurocentrism: Multiculturalism and the Media* (New York: Routledge, 1994), especially p. 123.

33. Roland Barthes, *Mythologies*, trans. A. Lavers (London: Paladin, 1973).

34. B. Raditsa, "How the Communists Took Over Albania," Oct. 1947, p. 103.

35. C. Willoughby, "Tribute to Japan," Feb. 1952, p. 59.

36. H. Taylor, "Is Russia Prepared to Make War?" June 1948, p. 29.

37. Q. Reynolds, "Yugoslavia Stands Resolute," Jan. 1951, p. 105.

38. See J. Fischer, "The Scared Men in the Kremlin," Oct. 1946, pp. 4–10.

39. Bullitt, "Approach," p. 150.

40. W. Hard, "Eight Things to Do about the Soviet Union," Sept. 1945, p. 8.

41. J. McEvoy, "Hold'em! Harass'em! Hamstring'em!" Oct. 1949, p. 25. Despite the *Digest*'s insistence that "ordinary" Soviet citizens were being misled by their leaders and were not to be feared, there was never any labeling Soviet citizens as either Red Russians or Russians, as was done in the case of the Chinese, suggesting a totalizing Communist identity in Russia.

42. Taylor, "Is Russia Prepared to Make War?" p. 29.

43. A. de Seversky, "The Military Key to Survival," Sept. 1950, pp. 1–9.

44. Ibid., p. 7.

45. E. Mowrev, "Who Is with Uncle Sam?" Feb. 1951, p. 121, and W. Bullitt, "No Peace in the Philippines," March 1952, p. 97.

46. F. Gibney, "The Birth of a New Japan," Dec. 1951, p. 59.

47. L. Stowe, "Conquest by Terror: The Story of Satellite Europe," June 1952, p. 137; emphasis in original.

48. F. Allen, "The Unsystematic American System," Aug. 1952, pp. 107–11.

49. See H. Baldwin, "We're Not the Best in the World," Oct. 1950, pp. 1–6.

50. Ibid., p. 6.

51. G. Crowther, "Are We Buying Defense or Disaster?" April 1952, p. 122.

52. On geopolitical economy, see John Agnew and Stuart Corbridge, *Mastering Space: Hegemony, Territory and International Economy* (London: Rouledge, 1995).

53. A. Visson, "To Understand the Russians," May 1946, pp. 18–23.

54. Of course, this growth was explained as the result of sheer hard work rather than the outcome of Marxist or Stalinist social praxis (see V. Kravchenko, "A Soviet Official in America," June 1946, pp. 135–40).

55. Bullitt, "Strength," pp. 27–28.

56. C. Boldyreff, "We Can Win the Cold War—*in Russia*," Nov. 1950, p. 10.

57. For a discussion of the tendency of geopolitical arguments to reduce the causes of regional conflict to the essence of global affairs, see Agnew and Corbridge, *Mastering Space,* p. 75.

58. J. Burnham, "How the United Nations Can Be Made to Work," Jan. 1948, p. 84.

59. L. Yutang, "Why Don't We Take the Offensive in the Cold War?" March 1959, p. 83, and H. Matthews, "Let's Stop Taking Latin America for Granted," Aug. 1959, p. 182.

60. H. Hazlitt, "Will Dollars $ave the World?" Jan 1948, p. 147.

61. W. Hard, "The American Way Goes Abroad," March 1948, p. 27.

62. B. Clark, "Are the Philippines Going the Way of China?" June 1950, pp. 28–34.

63. P. Douglas, "Why Not Defend Freedom *Everywhere We Can?*" Aug. 1951, p. 15.

64. Condensation, "Prosperity as a Weapon," Nov. 1950, pp. 1–4.

65. W. Bullitt, "No Peace in the Philippines," March 1952, p. 98.

66. M. Scully, "Don Pepe's Private War against Communism" June 1950, p. 115.

67. S. High, "How the United States Has Aided a New Nation," Jan. 1958, p. 108.

68. One example would be Greece. See P. Poster, "Wanted: A Miracle in Greece," Dec. 1947, pp. 83–87.

69. R. Nixon, "When the Reds Mobbed Nixon in Latin America," June 1962, p. 67.

70. J. McEvoy, "Trouble in Our Own Back Yard," Aug. 1950, p. 10.

71. "Anatomy of the Cuban Showdown," Jan. 1963, p. 94; D. Norton-Taylor, "The Sword at the Belly of Red China," Sept. 1963, p. 130; J. Bell, "The Nightmare of Life in China's Communes," March 1959, p. 37.

72. Stowe, "Conquest by Terror," p. 136, and E. Lyons, "The Great Debate: How to Fight the Cold War," Nov. 1962, p. 170. This use of historical reference was particularly astute as it linked together the Soviet present with perhaps the major issue clouding the democratic character of American society—slavery. Lyons implied that this was an issue that America had dealt with over one hundred years ago, yet now a similar situation had the potential to exist on a global scale: "Then the question was whether a nation could survive half-slave, half-free; now whether the *world* can survive half-slave, half-free" (p. 170, emphasis in original).

73. W. Bullitt, "We CAN Win the War in Korea," March 1953, p. 31.

74. Bullitt, "Strength," p. 26, and S. Alsop, "Stalin's Plans for the U.S.A.," Oct. 1951, p. 19. Alsop's piece promised to tell "the story of a man who heard Stalin utter his private intentions regarding America—and lived to tell us about them."

75. C. Chennault, "Why We Must Help China Now," April 1948, p. 121.

76. *Reader's Digest* did not just publish this rhetoric but became actively involved in its implementation. Copies of *Reader's Digest* were sent to Eastern Europeans. In return, the magazine got letters that were "evidence that the *Reader's Digest* is helping to keep free thought and discussion alive in troubled parts of the old world" (editorial collection, "From the Lands of the Iron Curtain," April 1948, pp. 161–62). As I mentioned in chapter 2, it was projects like this that spawned rumors of the *Digest's* collaboration with the CIA.

77. G. Gallup, "The War We Are Losing," April 1951, pp. 121–24, quotation from p. 121.

78. W. Douglas, "Indo–China: A House Divided," March 1953, p. 148; Hoover, "Red Spymasters," p. 85; W. Douglas, "The Man Who Saved the Philippines," Jan. 1953, pp. 93–96.

79. Chambers, "What Is a Communist?" pp. 17–22; quotation from p. 20.

80. H. Hazlitt, "No Time for Hysteria," Dec. 1957, p. 118.

81. A. Kerensky, "The First Democracy Destroyed by Communism," Aug. 1947, p. 97, emphasis mine.

82. F. Nagy, "How the Russians Stole My Government," Nov. 1947, pp. 80–96.

83. This could also be related to a more general medicalization of popular discourse in the United States, illustrated in *Reader's Digest* by the series of articles "I am Joe's . . . ," which examined the workings of various body parts.

84. J. Ratcliff, "Radio Medicine Pierces the Iron Curtain," March 1956, p. 96.

85. H. Hoover, "Herbert Hoover on the Protection of Freedom," Oct. 1954, p. 146.

86. R. Hirsch, "The Soviet Spies: The Story of Russian Espionage in North America," May 1947, p. 134; W. Bullitt, "France in Crisis," Sept. 1947, p. 122; J. Flynn, "The Road Ahead: America's Creeping Revolution," Feb. 1950, p. 13.

87. Gibney, "New Japan," p. 59.

88. Alsop, "Stalin's Plans," p. 56.

89. A piece titled "A Link with Home," printed on the inside back cover of the July 1951 issue, wrote this therapeutic role directly: Korea veterans talked of the place of *Reader's Digest* in their daily routines. "Another said 'After a hard day flying over Red territory one needs relaxation and refreshment and I find it in the *Digest.*'"

90. Disease metaphors were usually drawn from the language of physical ailment, although one article described the USSR as inflicted with a mental illness. The *Reader's Digest* insistence on the domination of ordinary citizens by communism meant that Soviet foreign policy at times became a psychological projection of Stalin's personality disorders: "The Soviet dictatorship enabled Stalin to find fullest expression for the frustrations, jealousies, inner conflicts and painful inferiorities which fed the fires of his personality from an early age" (L. Ascher, "Joseph Stalin," July 1948, p. 153).

91. For example, one article suggested that if a reader thought that communist successes were inevitable, "*then you are already a Marxist*" (C. Malik, "Is It Too Late to Win against Communism?" Sept. 1960, p. 39, emphasis in original).

92. M. Knight, "Red Realm in China" May 1947, p. 48; H. Lehrman, "The Most Overpowering Woman in Europe," April 1949, p. 11; A. Orme, "Comes the Comrade!" Nov. 1950, pp. 164–65.

93. L. Kirk, "Postmarked Moscow," Dec. 1952, p. 143, and J. Novak, "The Future Is Ours, Comrade," Aug. 1960, p. 216.

94. A. Visson, "Malenkov—the Machine That Walks Like a Man," June 1953, pp. 137–44.

95. J. Gunther, "Inside Moscow," Dec. 1957, p. 167.

96. J. Strohm, "Ivan Looks at Iowa," Jan. 1956, pp. 173–77, quotation from p. 175.

97. In some places, though, articles hinted that appearances could be deceptive. Khrushchev's "apparent flabbiness seems to mask a powerful physique" (E. Lyons, "Khrushchev: The Killer in the Kremlin," Sept. 1957, p. 104).

98. Littell, "Berlin—Divided She Stands," p. 87.

99. N. Muhlen, "Top Secret," Feb. 1952, p. 71, and R. Jaesrich, "Berlin's Fighting University," Dec. 1952, p. 70.

100. E. Lipper, "Eleven Years in Soviet Prison Camps," June 1951, p. 143. This underwrote *Digest* fears that recently decolonized countries might be tempted to follow communism; they too might be led by emotion or wooed by ideology due to their location in an earlier—and therefore less rational—phase of development rhetoric.

101. O. Anisimov, "Education in Soviet Russia," Oct. 1950, pp. 57–58.

102. Quoted in E. Lyons, "'Negotiating' with the Kremlin," April 1958, p. 76.

103. Editorial, "The Only Way to Deal with Russia," Oct. 1947, p. 31, and D. Boss, "Europe's Old Nightmare Returns," July 1950, p. 49.

104. J. Dulles, "Thoughts on Soviet Foreign Policy—and What to Do about It," Aug. 1946, p. 7.

105. L. Stowe, "Sexual License," March 1955, pp. 27–32.

106. L. Stowe, "Farewell to 'Home, Sweet, Home,'" June 1955, p. 156.

107. One could argue that although the *Digest* did not actively or directly view all aspects of its readership's private lives, the self-knowledge it promoted in its techniques of self-disciplining and improvement produced a sense of surveillance not entirely dissimilar from the Soviets'; the difference was that *Digest* readers were engaging in self-surveillance voluntarily.

108. W. Lippmann, "Total War and Co-existence," Sept. 1951, p. 98.

109. Fischer, "Scared Men," p. 6, emphasis mine.

110. A. de Seversky, "Military Key to Survival," p. 10.

111. H. Taylor, "No Watchdog for America," Feb. 1951, p. 85.

112. C. Spaatz, "The Air-Power Odds against Us," June 1951, p. 12.

113. Mowrev, "Uncle Sam," p. 121.

114. See, for example, C. Hall, "The Rape of Tibet—A Challenge to the Free World's Conscience," Oct. 1962, pp. 96–100.

115. W. Haskell, "How We Fed the Starving Russians," Aug. 1948, p. 68.

116. L. Fischer, "The Fatal Mistake of Marshall Zukov," March 1958, p. 96.

117. A. Kalme, "Soviet Terror in the Baltics," Dec. 1948, p. 33.

118. N. Bailey, "Nonsense and Foreign Aid," March 1961, p. 47.

119. Stowe, "Conquest by Terror," p. 145; G. Hudson, "Who Is Guilty of the Katyn Massacre?" July 1952, p. 131; G. Kent, "The Red Rape of Austria," March 1956, p. 34.

120. W. Chamberlain, "The Permanent Crisis," Sept. 1947, pp. 39–43.

121. J. Michener, "The Prison at Resch," May 1957, p. 93, and P. Durdin, "Red China's War against God," Sept. 1952, pp. 15–18.

122. W. Chambers, "I Was the Witness," May 1952, p. 113.

123. H. Hoover, "The Effective Military Policy for the United States," May 1952, pp. 40–44.

124. Ibid., p. 42.

125. F. Drake, "We're Running the Wrong Race with Russia!" Aug. 1963, p. 50, emphasis in original.

126. J. Alsop and S. Alsop, "The Race We Are Losing to Russia," Oct. 1956, p. 127.

127. E. Lyons, "One Trip to Russia Doesn't Make an Expert," Oct. 1959, pp. 213–20.

128. N. White, "'Nyet' to Tourists in Soviet Russia," Dec. 1960, p. 96.

5. The Jeopardy of Détente

All references in this chapter are to *Reader's Digest* except where noted otherwise.

1. In fact, descriptions of torture of American soldiers in *Digest* articles in this period were remarkably graphic. Detailed explanations of torture techniques and mutilation (accompanied in one case by diagrams) stood in sharp contrast to the magazine's calls for censorship of violence in other media.

2. R. O'Brien, "Ring Out, Liberty Bell!" July 1972, pp. 49–53, and E. Sloan, "Spirits of 1776—and 1976: I. What We Have Lost," Sept. 1973, pp. 61–66.

3. Albert O. Hirschman, *The Rhetoric of Reaction: Perversity, Futility, Jeopardy* (Cambridge, Mass.: Harvard University Press, 1991). I am using Hirschman's concept of "rhetoric" interchangeably with "discourse."

4. W. Judd, "Keep Red China Out," Nov. 1964, p. 115.

5. R. Nixon, "Khrushchev's Hidden Weakness," Jan. 1964, p. 59.

6. H. Jackson, "Russia Has *Not* Changed Her Ways," June 1969, pp. 91–95, and J. Reston, "Castro's Changing Cuba," Jan. 1976, p. 73.

7. L. Velie, "The Week the Hotline Burned," Aug. 1968, p. 44.

8. R. Drummond, "The New Forward Thrust of Freedom," Aug. 1965, p. 133.

9. A. Burke, "The Hazards of Negotiating with the Communists," Oct. 1968, p. 124.

10. M. Mackintosh, "Era of Negotiations," Jan. 1971, p. 57.

11. A. Solzhenitsyn, "No More Concessions!" Oct. 1975, p. 74. See also R. Thompson, "Are We Now Engaged in World War III?" Nov. 1974, pp. 141–46, and E. Lyons, "The Great Debate: How to Fight the Cold War," Nov. 1962, p. 120.

12. C. Rowan, "We're Helping the Communists Win the Propaganda War," Nov.

1966, pp. 106–10; M. Laird, "Let's Not Fool Ourselves about U.S.-Soviet Détente," Feb. 1974, pp. 57–60; Thompson, "World War III."

13. Frederick Dolan, *Allegories of America: Narratives-Metaphysics-Politics* (Ithaca, N.Y.: Cornell University Press, 1994), pp. 85–88.

14. H. Taylor, "Peking and Moscow—Will They Get Back Together?" May 1976, p. 142.

15. N. Busch, "Should We Be Trading with the Reds?" July 1966, p. 84.

16. L. Velie, "The Soviet Design for Free-World Labor," April 1975, p. 107.

17. See Johannes Fabian, *Time and the Other: How Anthropology Makes Its Object* (New York: Columbia University Press, 1983).

18. P. Harvey, "Prescription for a Revolution," Jan. 1971, pp. 93–94.

19. M. Padev, "Communism's Common Goal," July 1967, p. 142.

20. A. Drury, "The Dangerous Game of 'Let's Pretend,'" March 1964, pp. 37–42.

21. Hirschman, *Rhetoric*, p. 76.

22. J. Schlesinger, "The Continuing Challenge to America," April 1976, p. 65.

23. Drury, "Dangerous Game," p. 37.

24. D. Lawrence, "The Road to World War III," Jan. 1968, pp. 19–20.

25. "A Documentary report," "From Hanoi—with Thanks," Feb. 1970, pp. 51–55.

26. L. Stockstill, "What You Can Do for American Prisoners in Vietnam," Nov. 1969, pp. 61–66; and, in a follow up article, " Don't Ever Forget," May 1971, pp. 117–20.

27. E. Methvin, "Behind Those Campus Demonstrations," Jan. 1966, p. 43. See also P. Luce, "What the 'New Left' Did to Me," Feb. 1967, pp. 93–97.

28. R. Sanger, "Is Insurrection Brewing in the United States? An Expert's Appraisal," April 1968, pp. 127–28.

29. For example, "Our Son Is a Campus Radical," April 1969, pp. 71–75.

30. T. Mosher, "Inside the Revolutionary Left," March 1971, p. 54.

31. T. Dodd, "Communists Never Give Up," March 1965, p. 61.

32. Jackson, "Russia Has Not Changed," p. 91.

33. Rowan, "We're Helping the Communists."

34. H. Baldwin, "The Alarming Decline of Our Military Power," Dec. 1968, p. 87, and F. Lausche, "The Dangerous Failings of Our State Department," June 1964, pp. 55–60.

35. A. Solzhenitsyn, "Wake Up! Wake Up!" Dec. 1975, p. 72.

36. J. Barron, "Soviet-American Trade: Trick Or Treat?" Oct. 1977, pp. 67–79.

37. J. Hubbell, "Soviet Civil Defense: The Grim Realities," Feb. 1978, p. 77.

38. W. Judd, "No 'Surrender' in the Vietnam Peace Talks," Sept. 1968, p. 86.

39. J. Barron, "Espionage: The Dark Side of Détente," Jan. 1978, p. 82.

40. Condensation, "Why We Must Arm to Disarm," June 1974, pp. 130–34.

41. J. Hubbell, "Trident: Super-Deterrent of the Deep," May 1973, p. 110.

42. J. Winchester, "Is the Soviet Air Force No. 1?" Sept. 1973, p. 90.

43. H. Prochnow, "Proud Ruins, Sobering Thoughts." March 1974, p. 108, emphasis in original. This shows neat parallels with Christian prophecies of the end of American dominance through cultural decline as consumerism and apolitical behavior have undermined American morality (see chapter 3).

44. M. Padev, "Communism's Common Goal," July 1967, p. 143.

45. H. Humphrey, "We Stand on Common Ground," March 1970, p. 90.

46. E. Griffiths, "World in Change: A Trip through Eastern Europe March 1964, p. 120.

47. W. Griffith, "Summitry and the Prospects for Peace," Jan. 1973, p. 54.

48. R. Nixon, "Toward a Generation of Peace," Feb. 1972, p. 61.

49. J. Gunther, "Moscow Revisited," Jan. 1969, p. 95.

50. T. Morgan, "Cuba's New Look," March 1975, pp. 79–83.

51. The author refers to Vladimir Lenin as Nikolai; interestingly, Ronald Reagan made the same mistake.

52. L. Elliott, "Brezhnev: Russia's New and Undisputed No. 1," May 1972, p. 86.

53. Francis Fukuyama, "The End of History," *National Interest* supplement, Summer 1989.

54. The text praised Chou En-lai's leadership, but the reception of a picture is hard to contain, so that, couched in Orientalism, the image could also be seen as evil.

55. C. Thayer, "Yugoslavia: the Bellwether Keeps Turning Right," Sept. 1967, p. 63.

56. D. Reed, "Yugoslavia: Time Bomb in Europe," April 1972, p. 242.

57. J. Michener, "China Diary," May 1972, p. 253.

58. R. Schiller, "Fabulous, Fascinating, Frustrating Moscow," Nov. 1973, p. 126; C. Lucas, "Leningrad Love Story," Oct. 1974, pp. 170–77; J. Grant, "Down the Beautiful Danube," July 1972, p. 142.

59. J. O'Donnell, "Walter Ulbricht: the Unsinkable Satrap," March 1969, p. 118, and Condensation, "Khrushchev's Monumental Economic Mess," June 1964, p. 71.

60. M. DeMedici, "The Cost of Eight Years of Castro," July 1967, p. 91. Once again the *Digest* refers to women in their capacity to symbolize the nation. Here women's unattractiveness and their inability to improve themselves refers to the nation's poor state.

61. See Joanne Sharp, "Gendering Nationhood: A Feminist Engagement with National Identity," in *BodySpace: Destabilizing Geographies of Gender and Sexuality,* ed. Nancy Duncan (London: Routledge, 1996).

62. T. Bolton, "Bedtime Story, Red China Style," July 1976, pp. 181–86.

63. Morgan, "Cuba's New Look," p. 82.

64. Roland Barthes, "The Great Family of Man," in *Mythologies,* trans. A. Lavers (London: Paladin, 1973), p. 100.

65. *Reader's Digest*'s creation of the "great family of man" was cross-cut with Orientalism. Chinese people, for example, were not presented as being as much like Americans as Eastern Europeans were. The *Digest*'s representations of Asian communists tended to be infused with Orientalistic barbarism and evilness.

66. K. Shin-jo, "Mission: To Murder a President," July 1968, p. 145.

67. D. Reed, "Up Front in Vietnam," Sept. 1967, p. 225.

68. DeMedici, "Eight Years of Castro," p. 93, and D. Reed, "Angola's Made-in-Moscow War," June 1976, p. 85.

69. Luce, "New Left," p. 95, emphasis in original.

6. The "Second Cold War"

All references in this chapter are to *Reader's Digest* except where noted otherwise.

1. Gearóid Ó Tuathail, "The Second Cold War," in *Dictionary of Geopolitics*, ed. John O'Loughlin (Westport, Conn.: Greenwood, 1994), pp. 214–15. See also Simon Dalby, *Creating the Second Cold War* (New York: Guilford, 1990).

2. R. Evans and R. Novak, "Innocence Abroad: Jimmy Carter's Four Misconceptions," May 1980, pp. 103–7, quotation from p. 106.

3. S. Hempstone, "Angola: Where the West Can Still Win," Feb. 1981, p. 105. See also R. Bennett, "El Salvador's Made-in-Havana Revolution," July 1981, pp. 85–89.

4. P. Collier and D. Horowitz, "Reflections from Yesterday's Radicals," July 1985, p. 43. See also C. Malhuret, "Afghanistan: The Secret Terror," May 1984, pp. 147–50.

5. J. Kirkpatrick, "Facing the Facts in Central America," July 1983, pp. 87–90. See also Malhuret, "Afghanistan."

6. M. Ledeen, "Standing Up to the Russian Bear," April 1980, p. 73, and W. Griffith, "The Real Stakes in Afghanistan," June 1980, pp. 148, 149.

7. D. Reed, "High Stakes in Central America," Aug. 1983, p. 39.

8. R. Bennett, "Grenada: Anatomy of a 'Go' Decision," Feb. 1984, pp. 72–77. American reluctance to become militarily involved in regional conflict was often presented by the *Digest* as the result of fear of offending the Soviets and therefore provoking a confrontation. *Reader's Digest* did not, however, consider the risk of war to be a reasonable argument for staying out of a confrontation with communist governments around the world.

9. M. Mihajlov, "The Freedom Fight We Can't Afford to Lose," Jan. 1979, pp. 37–42; quotation from p. 42.

10. M. Laird, "Why We Need Spies," March 1979, pp. 87–92, and C. Rowan and D. Mazie, "Why the Voice of America Is in a Jam," March 1984, p. 178.

11. W. Griffith, "Poland's Strike For Freedom," Jan. 1981, p. 101.

12. J. Koster, "What You Should Know about America's Defense," May 1983, p. 91.

13. F. Chapple, "Perspectives on the Peace Movement" II: "Masters of Manipulation," June 1982, pp. 68–70.

14. J. Harriss, "Europe's Perilous Reach for Siberian Gas," March 1982, pp. 97–100; quotation from p. 100. This quote, among others, clearly exemplifies the *Digest*'s belief in the necessity for America to retain its position as global hegemon—not simply in terms of providing security, but also to ensure the maintenance of markets.

15. There was one more surprising incidence of the *Digest*'s linking of religion and communism in J. Harriss, "Which Master Is the World Council of Churches Serving … Karl Marx or Jesus Christ?" Aug. 1982, pp. 130–34. The pro-Soviet leanings of religious institutions described in this article stand in stark contrast to the antagonistic relationship *Reader's Digest* usually depicted. Ultimately, however, the article attacked the organization—the World Council of Churches—rather than religion itself.

16. A. Paul, "Will We Hear Their Cry?" April 1981, pp. 123–28, and S. Erskine, "Massacre in the Tunnel," Aug. 1983, pp. 33–39.

17. W. Griffith, "Countdown in the Middle East," Feb. 1982, p. 124.

18. D. Reed, "Qaddafi: Libya's Lord of Terror," June 1981, pp. 110, 106.

19. Ledeen, "Russian Bear," p. 72.

20. D. Robinson, "NATO: A Candid View from the Top," Dec. 1980, pp. 103–7.

21. C. Sterling, "Network of Terror," May 1981, pp. 244–45.

22. Ibid., p. 267.

23. Ibid., p. 246.

24. E. Kuznetsov, "From Labor Camp to Liberty," Sept. 1980, p. 132.

25. G. Feifer, "Russian Winter," Feb. 1984, pp. 97–100; quotation from p. 99. Another *Digest* author also used environmental characteristics to reinforce the

systemic differences between the Soviets and Americans. He described Soviet-backed "North Yemen: Cuba of the Arab World" as a "dark and bloody land" but placed American-backed Saudi Arabia next to the "sun sparkled Persian Gulf" (D. Reed, "Russia's *Real* Target: The Middle East Oil Fields," July 1980, pp. 61–66; quotations from p. 65).

26. J. Barron, "Who Is Yuri Andropov?" April 1983, pp. 65–69; J. Barron, "The Spy Who Knew Too Much," June 1983, pp. 124–230; L. Elliott, "The Persecution of Andrei Sakharov," Nov. 1984, pp. 81–87.

27. G. Feifer, "Russian Scenes, Russian Voices," Oct. 1980, p. 208.

28. E. Hughes, "Poland's Rising Tide of Dissent," May 1979, pp. 164–68.

29. D. Reed, "North Korea's Secret Invasion Tunnels," March 1980, p. 90.

30. R. Bennett and J. Mallin, "The Russian Knife at America's Throat," Aug. 1982, pp. 88–92.

31. R. K. Bennett, "Why Ethiopia Is Starving" I: "Anatomy of a Famine," May 1985, p. 95, and D. Lamb, "Mozambique's Move away from Marxism," April 1985, pp. 94–99.

32. See Edward Said, *Orientalism* (New York: Vintage, 1979), and Rana Kabbani, *Europe's Myths of Orient* (Bloomington: Indiana University Press, 1986).

33. J. Harriss, "Scandinavia: Newest Soviet Target?" April 1984, p. 95.

34. P. Wilhelmore, "From Cuba with Hate: The Crime Wave Castro Sent to America," Dec. 1982, pp. 221–48; quotation from p. 226.

35. In fact, the only article in my entire study that addressed "What women can do for peace" was concerned with population growth rates, and suggested that women should promote small families (J. Fischer, "What Women Can Do for Peace," June 1963, pp. 55–59).

36. See Joanne Sharp, "Gendering Nationhood: A Feminist Engagement with National Identity," in *BodySpace: Destabilizing Geographies of Gender and Sexuality,* ed. Nancy Duncan (London: Routledge, 1996).

37. D. Reed, "East Germany's Sinister Superspook," Dec. 1980, p. 178.

38. P. Witt, "Why Our Embassies Are Nests for Spies," Oct. 1987, pp. 111–14.

39. T. White, "China: After The Terror," Oct. 1983, p. 246.

40. Gearóid Ó Tuathail has argued that this form of "hyperreal" politic-ing was characteristic of the Reagan administration, whose hyperbolic images, stereotypes, and intertextual references to cinematic genres obscured "real" political events to the extent that "the triumph of image over substance marks the postmodernity of the Reagan administration" (Ó Tuathail, "Ronald Reagan," in *Dictionary of Geopolitics,* ed. John O'Loughlin [Westport, Conn.: Greenwood, 1994], p. 206). While this period does rely upon intertextual knowledge of the Otherness of the Soviet system, *Reader's Digest's* geographing may be considered to have been "hyperreal" for some time before the rise of Reagan.

41. E. Rowny, "How *Not* to Negotiate with the Russians," June 1981, pp. 66–67, emphasis in original.

42. Koster, "What You Should Know about America's Defense," p. 95.

43. A. Paul, "Inside North Korea, Marxism's First Monarchy," Feb. 1982, p. 75.

44. Ibid., p. 76.

45. T. Armbister, "El Tigrillo: Portrait of a Contra," Oct. 1985, p. 98.

46. R. Ichord, "The Deadly Threat of Soviet Chemical Warfare," Sept. 1979, p. 214. See also J. Hamilton-Merritt, "Gas Warfare in Laos: Communism's Drive to Annihilate People," Oct. 1980, pp. 81–88.

47. J. Barron, "Never I Go Back!" March 1985, p. 67. Laughter as a symbol of Walter's place in the "great family of man" was opposed to his earlier mechanized—almost robotic—existence in the Soviet Union.

48. J. Barron, "MiG Pilot: The Final Escape of Lt. Belenko," Jan. 1980, p. 223.

49. M. Popovsky, "Top Secret: Is There Sex in Russia?" Dec. 1982, p. 138.

50. N. Podhoretz, "1984 Is Here: Where is Big Brother?" Jan. 1984, p. 36.

51. W. Knaus, "Russian Blood," July 1981, p. 125, emphasis mine.

52. Ibid., p. 127, emphasis mine.

53. Roland Barthes, *The Pleasure of the Text*, trans. A. Miller (New York: Hill and Wang, 1975), p. 47, emphasis in original.

54. Fredric Jameson, "Pleasure: a Political Issue," in *The Ideologies of Theory: Essays 1971–1986*, vol. 2, *Syntax of History* (Minneapolis: University of Minnesota Press, 1988).

55. Frederick Dolan, *Allegories of America: Narratives-Metaphysics-Politics* (Ithaca, N.Y.: Cornell University Press, 1994), p. 92.

7. Denying Imperial Decline at the End of the Cold War

All references in this chapter are to *Reader's Digest* except where noted otherwise.

1. Tom Engelhardt, *The End of Victory Culture: Cold War America and the Disillusioning of a Generation* (New York: Basic Books, 1995).

2. Francis Fukuyama, "The End of History," *National Interest* supplement, Summer 1989.

3. Geoffrey Bennington, "Postal Politics and the Institution of the Nation," in *Nation and Narration*, ed. Homi K. Bhabha. (New York: Routledge, 1990), p. 121.

4. James DerDerian, *Anti-Diplomacy: Spies, Terror, Speed, and War* (Oxford: Basil Blackwell, 1992), p. 66.

5. Frederick Dolan, *Allegories of America: Narratives-Metaphysics-Politics* (Ithaca, N.Y.: Cornell University Press, 1994), p. 80.

6. There are, however, a number of definitions of its end, some earlier, others not accepting the end of the Cold War until the dissolution of the Communist Party and the USSR itself. Thus there is an overlap in the years analyzed in this and the previous chapter. Some articles after 1985 were structured very clearly around a U.S.-USSR geopolitical binary while others are more appropriate to post–Cold War modes of representation. Nevertheless, 1985 does represent a point after which *Reader's Digest* began to challenge its demonization of the Soviet Union in a way that had not been seen in the magazine since before World War II.

7. See, for example, R. Evans and R. Novak, "Gorbachev: The Man with a Nice Smile and Iron Teeth," Oct. 1987, pp. 70–75.

8. F. Barnes, "Can Gorbachev Last?" May 1988, p. 89.

9. See William Pietz, "The 'Post-Colonialism' of Cold War Discourse," *Social text* 19/20 (Fall 1988): 55–75.

10. After the fall of communism, Russia and other post-Soviet states continued to be represented as difficult to change. Drawing upon a different trope of the discourse of change, some articles discussed the continued decline of the CIS as a result of their communist heritage. Exceptions were figures who represented economic enterprise or democracy. Yeltsin, for example, was presented by *Reader's Digest* as a

popular leader struggling for democracy; one article compared him with John F. Kennedy (L. Elliott and D. Satter, "Three Days That Shook the World," Jan. 1992, pp. 60–203). In the one article concerned with the rise of Vladimir Zhirinovsky, the *Digest* writer reported that the Russian nationalist wanted to reestablish a Russian empire and see the downfall of the United States (R. Chelminski, "The Man Who Would Rule Russia," Dec. 1994, pp. 139–44); needless to say, the article suggested that Zhirinovsky was secretly planted and supported by the remains of the KGB.

11. Richard Nixon quoted in Barnes, "Gorbachev," p. 89.

12. K. Adelman, "Arms Control: Games Soviets Play," March 1989, p. 69.

13. Interview with the president, Jan. 1990, p. 54.

14. A. Rosenthal, "Gorbachev's Hidden Agenda," March 1988, pp. 71–72.

15. "Countdown to the 21st Century: Freedom on the March," Jan. 1990, pp. 34–45.

16. Ibid., p.45.

17. John McClure, *Late Imperial Romance* (London: Verso, 1994).

18. The exemplary deconstruction of the reason of neorealism can be found in Richard Ashley, "The Geopolitics of Geopolitical Space: Towards a Critical Social Theory of International Politics," *Alternatives* 14 (1987): 403–34.

19. McClure, *Romance*, p. 3.

20. But again see Ashley, "Geopolitics."

21. See David Campbell, *Writing Security: United States Foreign Policy and the Politics of Identity* (Minneapolis: University of Minnesota Press, 1992); James Der-Derian, *Anti-Diplomacy*; Michael Billig, *Banal Nationalism* (London: Sage, 1995).

22. P. Martin, "The Mad, Mad Romania of Nicolea Ceausescu," Jan. 1986, pp. 118–22; quotations from pages 112 and 118.

23. Carl Pletsch, "The Three Worlds; or, The Division of Social Science Labor, circa 1950–1975," *Comparative Studies in Society and History* 23 (1981): 565–90.

24. R. K. Bennett, "Defenseless Against Missile Terror," Oct. 1990, pp. 112–16.

25. Ibid., p. 112.

26. Ibid., p. 114.

27. Quoted in J. Carlin, "FBI to Get More Power to Tackle Terrorism," *Independent,* April 25, 1995, p. 9.

28. N. Adams, "The Terrorists Among Us," Dec. 1993, pp. 76–77.

29. B. Netanyahu, "Terrorism: How the West Can Win," July 1986, p. 111. It is probably worth noting that when this article was published, its author was Israel's ambassador to the United Nations.

30. Ibid., pp. 110–11.

31. C. Glass, "Kidnapped in Beirut," April 1993. This is in stark contrast to "good muslims": In Robert Kaplan's "Why the Afghans Fight," (May 1989, pp. 128–32), we are told that the author's translator prayed five times a day and exhibited no tension when the author said he is Jewish: "In Afghanistan—the Islamic Faith has not been poisoned by Middle East Politics" (p. 129).

32. The classic work on Western representation of the rest of the world is Edward Said's *Orientalism* (New York: Vintage, 1978).

33. N. Adams, "Iran's Mastermind of World Terrorism," Sept. 1990. p. 62.

34. Netanyahu, "Terrorism."

35. Adams, "Iran's Mastermind," pp. 59–65. See also N. Adams, "The World's Most Hunted Man," Oct. 1986, pp. 156–60: "His specialty is killing innocent people. And now Americans are his target."

36. DerDerian, *Anti-Diplomacy*, p. 115, emphasis in original.

37. H. Hurt, "They Dared Cocaine—and Lost," May 1988, pp. 81–87.

38. W. Bennett, "Should Drugs be Legalized?" March 1990, pp. 90–94.

39. N. Adams, "Profiteers of Terror: The European Connection," Aug. 1986, p. 55.

40. M. McConnell, "Crack Invades the Countryside," Feb. 1989, pp. 73–78.

41. Ibid., p. 73.

42. Abe Brown, community organizer, quoted in E. Methvin, "Tampa's Winning War on Drugs," July 1991, p. 57.

43. DerDerian, *Anti-Diplomacy*, p. 107.

44. Ibid., p. 110.

45. N. Adams, "Cocaine King: a Study in Evil," Dec. 1988, pp. 227–72; quotation from p. 228.

46. Ibid., p. 230.

47. Condensation, "Why We're Losing the War on Drugs," Oct. 1989, pp. 83–88; quotation from p. 88.

48. See, for example, K. House, "Are We Underestimating America's Future?" May 1989, pp. 185–92.

49. G. Gilder, "A New Breed of Innovators," Aug. 1989, pp. 126–28.

50. C. Reese, "Our People Get It Done," Aug. 1989, p. 130.

51. J. Shear, "Don't Envy the Japanese," May 1991, pp. 43–46.

52. Ibid., p. 44.

53. E. Methvin, "Our New Defense Weapon—Competition," Sept. 1986, pp. 99–103.

54. F. Barnes, "The Japan That Won't Play Fair," Aug. 1990; quotations from pp. 34, 35, 36.

55. Armand Mattelart, *Mapping World Communication: War, Progress, Culture* (Minneapolis: University of Minnesota Press, 1994), p. 220.

56. A. Rosenthal, "Don't Remilitarize Japan," Feb. 1991, p. 59.

57. Campbell, *Writing Security*, p. 196.

58. D. Lynch, "The Real Risk of AIDS," May 1993, pp. 207–10.

59. T. Sowell, "Who Says It's Hopeless?" June 1994, p. 180.

60. C. Brandt, "Let Our Police Take on the Drug Dealers," Jan. 1990, p. 78.

61. J. Blyskal, "You *Can* Fight City Hall," Jan. 1989, pp. 103–7. There are significant parallels here with right-wing arguments surrounding the Oklahoma bombing in 1995, when citizens fought city hall in a more violent manner than apparently the *Digest* expected.

62. E. Methvin, "Crusader for Peru's Have-Nots," Jan. 1989, pp. 137–40.

63. Ibid., p. 140.

64. T. Armbrister, "Why Are They Always Trying to Take Our Freedom Away?" Oct. 1986, pp. 124–28.

65. R. Evans and R. Novak, "Congress Is Crippling the CIA," Nov. 1986, pp. 99–103; W. Brookes, "Don't Raise Taxes," Oct. 1987, pp. 163–66; D. Reed "Do South Africa Sanctions Make Sense?" Feb. 1989, pp. 51–56.

66. G. Cartwright, "Freed to Kill Again," Dec. 1992, pp. 134–40; M. Irby, "Why Free Criminals to Kill?" June 1991, pp. 57–62.

67. Once again, the *Digest*'s political rhetoric resonates with the voice of right-wing militias.

68. C. Sykes, "No More Victims Please," Feb. 1993, p. 22.

69. J. Reed, "It's Not My Fault!" Aug. 1994, p. 114.

70. Ibid., p. 114.

71. J. Epstein, "Today's Professional Victims," April 1991, p. 122, emphasis mine. Despite the *Digest*'s claim to have reach into more subgroups than any other popular magazine (Edward Thompson, editor in chief 1976 to 1984, personal communication, 1991), this article is evidently addressing an audience that excludes "radical feminists, ethnic minorities, homosexuals and other activists."

72. C. Murray, "Tomorrow's Underclass," March 1994, p. 52.

73. S. Jacoby, "When Rights Run Wild," Aug. 1992, p. 129.

74. Dolan, *Allegories*, chapter 1.

75. P. Noonan, "Why Are We So Unhappy When We Have It So Good?" Jan. 1993, pp. 35–36.

76. J. Coudert, "Who Says Experts Are Always Right?" Jan. 1988, pp. 141–42. See also P. Lynch with J. Rothchild, "The Power of Common Knowledge," Aug. 1989, pp. 85–90, and I. Kristol, "Whatever Happened to Common Sense?" Feb. 1990, pp. 19–20.

77. Kristol, "Common Sense," pp. 19–20.

78. P. Hamill, "Can America's Black Underclass Be Saved?" June 1988, pp. 105–10; quote from p. 110.

79. H. Hurt, "Portrait of a Patriot," July 1989, p. 66.

80. P. Hamill, "It's Not My Fault," Oct. 1991, pp. 11–12.

81. P. Michelmore, "From Outcast to Supercop," Nov. 1992, p. 179.

82. W. Bennett, "What *Really* Ails America?" April 1994, pp. 197–202.

83. Editorial review, "The Closing of the American Mind," Oct. 1987, pp. 81–87.

84. For example: "Let's Hear It [the Constitution] in English," Sept. 1994; "The Supreme Court Is Wrong about Religion," Dec. 1994; "Thought Police on Campus," May 1991.

85. M. Novak, "All Things Are Not Relative," Nov. 1994, p. 78.

86. Bennett, "What *Really* Ails America?" p. 201.

87. Novak, "All Things," p. 79.

88. M. Greenfield, "Why Nothing Is 'Wrong' Anymore," Nov. 1986, pp. 224–28.

89. C. Krauthammer, "Don't Blame 'Society,'" Aug. 1989, pp. 54–55; quotations from p. 55.

90. Ibid., p. 55.

91. R. K. Bennett, "The Closing of the American Mind," Oct. 1987, pp. 81–84.

92. G. Bauer, "What We Must Teach Our Children about Freedom," May 1987, pp. 102–4.

93. E. D. Hirsch, "Cultural Literacy: What Every American Needs to Know," Dec. 1987, pp. 79–83.

94. Ibid., p. 80, emphasis in original.

95. B. Stein, "Cultural Literacy," Dec. 1987, p. 81.

96. Hirsch, "Cultural Literacy," p. 83.

97. P. Summerside, "Education Money Can't Buy," July 1990, p. 81.

98. Sykes, "No More Victims," pp. 22–24.

99. Gearóid Ó Tuathail and Timothy Luke, "Present at the (Dis)Integration: Deterritorialization and Reterritorialization in the New Wor(l)d Order" *Annals, Association of American Geographers* 84, no. 3 (1994): 382.

100. Whitman quoted in Carlin, "A Gentlewoman's Challenge to Newt's Republican Revolution" *Independent on Sunday,* April 9, 1995, p. 9.

101. Campbell, *Writing Security*, p. 195.

102. Ibid.

103. Fukuyama, "End of History," p. 16.

104. Richard Peet, "Reading Fukuyama: Politics at the End of History," *Political Geography* 12 no. 1: 64.

105. Obviously, *Reader's Digest* is famous for its advice to individual readers and has included a heavy dose of articles on the "American" character in almost every issue since first publication. I would argue, however, that there is a greater emphasis—and urgency—to this character definition in the years since the end of the Cold War than at any other period.

106. Rosenthal, "Gorbachev's Hidden Agenda," p. 72.

Conclusion

1. Henry Cantril, *The Invasion from Mars: A Study in the Psychology of Panic* (1940; reprint, New York: Harper Torchbooks, 1966), pp. 3, 47, vi–vii.

2. Michael Billig, *Banal Nationalism* (London: Sage, 1995).

3. Sacvan Bercovitch, *The American Jeremiad* (Madison: University of Wisconsin Press, 1978), p. 176.

4. Ibid., p. xi.

5. Gertjam Dijkink, *National Identity and Geopolitical Visions: Maps of Pride and Pain* (London: Routledge, 1996), p. 67.

6. David Campbell, *Writing Security: United States Foreign Policy and the Politics of Identity.* (Minneapolis: University of Minnesota Press, 1992), p. 196.

7. For examples of analyses that go further along this line of reasoning, see Mary Kaldor, *The Imaginary War: Understanding the East-West Conflict* (Oxford: Blackwell, 1990), and Noam Chomsky, *Necessary Illusions: Thought Control in Democratic Societies* (Boston: South End, 1989).

8. Kaldor, *Imaginary War*, p. 105.

9. Ibid., p. 107.

10. Indeed, some commentators have attributed conservative anxiety at the close of the Cold War to nothing more than the deleterious effects on the U.S. economy that would result from deinvestment in military spending.

11. J. Barron, "The Spy Who Knew Too Much," *Reader's Digest*, June 1983, p. 214.

12. James Chalmers, "Plain Truth," in *Tracts of the American Revolution*, ed. M. Jensen (Indianapolis: Bobbs-Merrill, 1978), p. 450.

13. Albert O. Hirschman, *The Rhetoric of Reaction: Perversity, Futility, Jeopardy* (Cambridge, Mass.: Harvard University Press, 1991).

14. On the importance of romance, see John McClure, *Late Imperial Romance* (London: Verso, 1994).

15. T. Sowell, "Who Says It's Hopeless?" *Reader's Digest*, June 1994, p. 179.

Index

Acheson, Lila Bell. *See* Wallace, Lila Bell Acheson

Adams, John, 79

advertising, 20–21

aesthetics: of perversity, 101; of terrorists, 145

Afghanistan, Soviet invasion of, 122

Afghan jihad, 126

Agnew, John, 33

AIDS, 150

Althusser, Louis, 33, 49

American Dream, 9, 77–78, 80, 81, 154–55

American flag, 15, 18–19

American identity, ix–xvi, 28–29, 137–62, 165–73

American jeremiad, 166–67

Anderson, Benedict, 34, 49, 165

arms negotiations, 114

"art of condensing," 9, 11, 20

Ashley, Richard, 30

authority, 45–47

Barnes, Fred, 148

Barthes, Roland, 42, 66, 90, 135

Baudrillard, Jean, 25–26

Bennett, R. K., 142–43

Bennington, Geoffrey, 27

Bercovitch, Sacvan, 166–67

Bhabha, Homi K., 8

Billig, Michael, 50, 165–66

Bolsheviks, 58–72

boredom: and communism, 116–17; at the end of the Cold War, 161–62

boundaries, 28, 160–62, 168, 173

Boyer, Paul, 39

Brezhnev, Leonid, 117

bureaucracy. *See* government, big

Campbell, David, 28, 35, 149, 161, 168, 173

cannibalism, 104

capitalism, 64, 68, 93

capitalists, 80

Carter, Jimmy, 122–23

Ceaușescu, Nicolae, 141

Chalmers, James, 170

CIA, 21, 137

Clinton, Bill, 144, 160

Cold War, ix–xii, 29, 39, 168, 170–72; end of, 137–62, 198n.6; first, 83–106; second, 122–36

Collins, Jane, 47

colonialism, 189n.11

Committee of the Present Danger, 122

common sense, xiii, xvi, 12–13, 14, 41–43, 156, 158–59, 162, 179n.40

communism, 57–72, 86–87, 87–90, 97–98, 111, 138–39; and poverty, 95; and religion, 126–27. *See also* socialism; Soviet Union

communists: Chinese, 92, 130; and global domination, 93–95, 115; identity, 72, 87–90; ontological, 87; and seduction, 135; and sex, 102–3

203

Joanne P. Sharp is lecturer in the Department of Geography at the University of Glasgow. Her interests lie in cultural and political geography and feminist geography. She is a coeditor of *Space, Gender, Knowledge*, of *A Feminist Glossary of Human Geography*, and of *Entanglements of Power*.